STRESS

Concept, Meaning and Management

About the Editor

Dr. Mujibul Hasan Siddiqui, M.A (Economics), B.Ed., M.Ed., M.Phil. (Education), Ph.D.(Education), PGDHE, PGDDE, MADE, CCCA, CCPALA is working as Associate Professor in the Department of Education, Aligarh Muslim University, Aligarh-202002, Uttar Pradesh, India. He has also worked as Acting Chairperson in the Department of Education, Aligarh Muslim University, Aligarh. He has authored and edited several books, encyclopaedias in the area of education, research and innovative teaching, published more than fifty research papers, reviewed eighty national and international research papers. He has attended several national and international seminars, workshops, conferences in India. He is a member of Scientific Advisory Committee of International Conferences, USA IISTE Journal of Education and Practice, IISTE International Institute of Science Technology and Education, Accelerating Global Knowledge, Creation and Sharing IISTE USA P.O. Box 5934, New York, NY 10016 USA and Institute of Knowledge, Sri Lanka and India. He is a member of editorial board of several national and international journals of research. He is the foreign examiner of Ph.D. research scholars and M.Ed. Students and evaluated Ph.D. theses and Dissertations in Faculty of Education of the University of South Africa (UNISA) and University of Zululand, South Africa. He has received several academic and research excellence awards in India like Life Time Education Achievement Award, Bharat Gaurav Ratan Award, Best Educationist Award, Bharat Shiksha Ratan Award, Eminent Educationist Award, Rashtriya Vidya Saraswati Puraskar. He has visited Lootah Groups of Companies as Educational Adviser Dubai, UAE. Member in the International Pannel of the Board of Research Advisers North Carolina, U.S.A. Vice-President of Commonwealth Association for Educational Administration and Management, Uttar Pradesh. He also worked as acting Chairperson in the Department of Education, Aligarh Muslim University, Aligarh. He was invited by the Lootah Groups of Company as Educational Advisers in Dubai United Arab Emirate to make the observation of Company, dated 27-29 April, 2006.

Hopefully, this will serve the purpose of one and all concerned.

STRESS

Concept, Meaning and Management

Edited by
Mujibul Hasan Siddiqui

CONCEPT PUBLISHING COMPANY PVT. LTD.
NEW DELHI-110059

ISBN-13: 978-93-88937-81-8

First Published 2021

Published and Printed by

Concept Since 1974

Concept Publishing Company Pvt. Ltd.
A/15-16, Commercial Block, Mohan Garden,
New Delhi-110059 (INDIA)
T: 91 11 25351460, 91 11 25351794
E: publishing@conceptpub.com *W*: www.conceptpub.com

Cataloging in Publication Data--Courtesy: D.K. Agencies (P) Ltd. <docinfo@dkagencies.com>

Stress : concept, meaning and management / edited by Mujibul Hasan Siddiqui.
pages cm
Contributed articles.
Includes bibliographical references and Index.
ISBN 9789388937818

1. Stress (Psychology)—India. 2. Stress (Psychology) 3. Stress management—India. 4. Stress management. I. Siddiqui, Mujibul Hasan, editor.

LCC BF575.S75S77 2021 | DDC 155.9042 23

Preface

Primarily stress is a feeling of emotional or physical tension. It can come from any event or thought that makes one feel frustrated, angry, or nervous. Stress is one's body's reaction to a challenge or demand. Stress is a type of psychological pain. Small amounts of stress may be desired, beneficial, and even healthy. Positive psychological stress can lead to motivation and challenge instead of anxiety. The effects of experiencing eustress, which is positive stress, *versus* distress, defined as negative stress, are significant. While colloquially lumped together, the various types of stress should be treated as separate concepts. Note that stress also plays a factor in motivation, adaptation, and reaction to the environment. Excessive amounts of stress, however, may lead to physical harm. Thus, stress can increase the risk of strokes, heart attacks, ulcers, and mental illnesses such as depression and OCD etc.

Remarkably everyone of us experience stress in varying forms and degrees everyday. Evidently in small doses, stress can actually be beneficial to us. It is only when the stress becomes too great, affecting our physical or mental functioning, that it becomes a problem. Coming to causes, big stressors include money troubles, job issues, relationship conflicts, and major life changes, such as the loss of a loved one. Whereas smaller stressors, such as long daily commutes and rushed mornings, can also add up over time.

Everyone reacts to stress differently. Each of us has a different level of pressure and anxiety that we can handle without a bad outcome. Only one can assess one's level of tolerance to stressful situations. The best treatment for stress is to prevent getting into situations that are likely to overwhelm your ability to cope. This is not always possible because the stressors may often come from outside sources that are beyond your control.

This book is a collection of empirical research articles, penned by different buddings as well as seasoned scholars from India and abroad. Initially organized in four main themes—Stress: concept and meaning; Types of stress; Stress management; and Stress in human life, there are twenty one chapters encompassing vital information on all aspects of stress and its coping mechanism.

Hopefully this will serve the purpose of one and all concerned.

I express my gratitude to all the chapter contributors for their timely submission of papers to make these academic exercises a success. At the same time, I am deeply beholden to my teachers, seniors, colleagues, friends and students for their guidance, cooperation, moral support and assistance. Last but not the least, I am thankful to Shri Ashok Mittal and Nitin Mittal of Concept Publishing Company Pvt. Ltd., Delhi for bringing out this volume in elegant way.

Editor

Contents

Contributors

Dr. Afa Dul Mujiaba, Lecturer, Department of Education, Govt. Degree College, Kalakote (J&K).

Dr. Anjum Ahmad, Research Scholar.

Professor Akbar Husain, Ex-Head, Department of Psychology & Dean Faculty of Social Sciences, Aligarh Muslim University, Aligarh.

Aktar Ali, Research Scholar, Department of Education, Aligarh Muslim University, Aligarh. **Email:** *aktaralig@gmail.com*

Dr. Anshu Lochab, Associate Professor, Rukmini Devi Institute of Advanced Studies, Guru Gobind Singh Indraprastha University, Delhi. **Email:** *anshulochab@gmail.com*

Barkat Hussain Para, Research Scholar, Dept. of Education, AMU, Aligarh.

Chiamaka R. Nwaoru, Psychology Lecturer at Abia State Polytechnic, Aba, Nigeria. **Email:** *chiamakanwaoru@gmail.com*

Dada Ab Rouf Bhat, Research Scholar, Department of Commerce. **Email:** *d.a.roufbhat@gmail.com*

Eisha Rahman, Research Scholar, Department of Psychology, Aligarh Muslim University, Aligarh (U.P.).

Komy Biswas, Research Scholar, Department of Education, Aligarh Muslim University. **Email:** *omybiswas630@gmail.com*

Kounsar Jabeen, Research Scholar, Department of Education, Aligarh Muslim University, Aligarh.

Dr. M. P. Tripathi, Associate Professor, Teacher Education, R.R.P.G. College, Amethi.

Maliha Batool, Research Scholar, Department of Economics, University of Jammu. **Email:** *malihamughal1991@gmail.com*

Marami Goswami, Associate Professor, Department of Education, Guwahati College, **Email:** *marami525@gmail.com*

MD Rajesh Ali, Research Scholar, Department of Education, Aligarh Muslim University, Aligarh (U.P.).
Email: *rajeshali.alig@gmail.com*

Mudassir Hamid, Research scholar, Department of Education, Aligarh Muslim University, Aligarh.

Dr. Mujibul Hasan Siddiqui, Associate Professor, Department of Education, Aligarh Muslim University, Aligarh. **Email:** *mhsiddiqui50@gmail.com*

Dr. Poonam Chauhan, Supervisor, Department of Education, Aligarh Muslim University, Aligarh.

Qudsiya Jan, Junior Research Fellow, Department of Education, Kashmir University.

Dr. Rasna Shehrawat, Assistant Professer, Department of Education, Amity University, Noida (U.P.)

Dr. Shabana A. Memon, Faculty, Bharati Vidyapeeth Deemed University Institute of Management, Kadamwadi, Kolhapur, Maharashtra, India.
Email: *memon.shabana@gmail.com*

Shaila Bi, Research Scholar, Department of Education, Aligarh Muslim University, Aligarh.

Dr. Sunil Kumar, Assistant Professor, Rukmini Devi Institute of Advanced Studies, Guru Gobind Singh Indraprastha University, Delhi.
Email: *sunil.kumar@rdias.ac.in*

Prof. Sunita Godiyal, Department of Education, Hemvati Nandan Bahuguna Garhwal University, S.R.T. Campus, Badshahithaul, Tehri Garhwal, Uttarakhand.

Wahid Ahmad Dar, Kashmir University.

Zayon O. Nzegbulam, Ph.D. Scholar, Department of Defence and Strategic Studies, Punjabi University, Patiala.

STRESS : CONCEPT AND MEANING

1
Understanding Stress in New Light

Akbar Husain and *Eisha Rahman*

Introduction

A word 'stress' is used more often in social, family, and organizational sectors than any other. Indeed, many of us use words such as strain, distress, hassles, and tension as synonymous expressions of stress. However, these narrow expressions of stress lead to the understanding that all human sectors are struggling for its management and it is nothing but a cause of worry. If we attach stress with negativity it becomes distress and if we attach it with positivity it becomes 'eustress'. Therefore, stress in itself holds both strings and it is only the matter of perception which makes it positive or negative. This notion segregate stress from being mere synonymous of these expressions and represent a more holistic aspect in its domain.

In a highly competitive and stress-ridden world, curry, hurry, and worry are major killers. Today, young adults are being afflicted by the stress-related disorders. It is spreading among individuals, family, organizations, and environment and is affecting their health. It develops a number of physical and psychological disorders among people. However, some people consider stressful experiences as a source of motivation and are therefore less prone to these disorders. It is estimated that three out of four visits to the doctor are stress related. Above all, stress impacts the way we think, feel and behave, leading to negative psychological states.

Presently, people's lifestyles have experienced some drastic changes, as a result of the evolving nature of physical and socio-cultural environment of the society and the advent of numerous information technologies. It is believed that automated technology has reduced our workload but, in fact, it has increased our mental workload and reduced person to person interaction resulting in higher stress levels. Machines are replacing humans in office and even at home for our basic needs, for example, shopping on internet, using ATM for banking, driving a car with cruise control and using vending machines for foods, tea and beverages. Thus, technology has captured all facets of our life and is therefore becoming one of the potential sources of stress in the form of mental load, lack of situational awareness, degradation of manual skill, insecurity about job, apprehension of not performing up to mark, strong competition at workplace, etc.

Stress refers to any environmental, organizational or internal demands, which require the individual to readjust the usual behaviour pattern. The degree of stress depends on the perception of individuals and the type of event or situation. Stimuli or situations that can result in the experience of stress are called stressors. Stressors in itself possess no threat, however it is liable to individual perception and their ability to cope with it, for becoming eustress or distress. Thus, we can rhetorically say that stress is like correlation as it has both magnitude and direction.

Positive Side of Stress

McGonigal (2013) describes in her book, The Upside of Stress, is the shift in mindset that allows one to have a healthier, even beneficial relationship with stress. She discovered that perceiving stress through a negative lens can actually be harmful to health. But when we view stress as a helpful tool and motivator, and learn how to harness it to our advantage, our health is less likely to be negatively affected. In fact, stress may actually be good for us, if we learn to embrace it and use it properly.

Stress can serve as a great motivator for reaching goals or accomplishing simple tasks. Whether it is a new job promotion, meeting a deadline, or completing a task, a little stress can push one to take actions. If we perceive stress in positive terms i.e. 'eustress' which is essential for personal growth we can reframe stressors to add meaning to our life and impart positive purpose to stress. When stress is perceived positively it contributes to motivation, building of resilience and boosting of cognitive performances. Pairing stress with a purpose allows us to broaden our perspective as to why it exists and the kind of benefits it provides.

A 2013 study from the University of California, Berkeley, found that acute stress can generate new nerve cells in the brain, improving cognitive and mental performance. We can thus conclude that a certain amount of stress can promote optimal levels of focus; improved memory and enhanced learning of new tasks. The determinant affects of stress is therefore susceptible to our perception rather than being a mystery to unveil trauma. However, excessive amount of anything is poisonous, and so is the case with stress. Therefore, we must timely combat stress with all the resources available and avoid being overwhelmed by it.

This chapter aims at merging various theoretical perspectives and sources of stress to provide a new and more comprehensive approach to its understanding.

Stress as a Stimulus

The notion of stress as a stimulus refers to any environmental stimulation, internal or external as an independent variable taxing the well-being of an individual. Stress as a stimulus also put forward the idea that there are so many life circumstances which act as stimuli and lead us to experience stress, such as loss of loved one, death of spouse, divorce, an accident, migrating to a new city, natural calamities, entering into a new institution (e.g. old age home, hostel) etc. The stress experienced by an individual out of that stimulation depends on its threshold.

The most common definition of stress adopted by psychologists has been, that it is a stimulus. Stress stimuli are most commonly thought of as an event impinging on the person. Stimulus definitions include conditions arising within the person, for example, drive stimuli such as hunger, or sex, which are based on tissue conditions and stimuli arising from neurological characteristics, as in White's (1959) "effectance drive."

Miller (1953) defines stress as "any vigorous, extreme, or unusual stimulation which being a threat, cause some significant change in behaviour ..." Basowitz, Perssky, Korchin, and Grinker (1955) defines it as "stimuli more likely to produce disturbances." Lazarus and Cohen (1977) speak of three types of stressors: major changes, often cataclysmic, and affecting large number of persons; major changes affecting one or a few persons; and daily hassles.

Stress as Transaction

Transaction is basically a process of continuous reciprocal way of interaction between person and the environment, both affecting and being affected by each other. The transactional paradigm of stress states that explanation of stress as a stimulus and as a response is incomplete because the mediating factor that is cognition actively works in between stress perceived as a stimulus and the response given. This is the reason behind the same stressor eliciting different pattern of strain among different people.

Thus event that we experience as provoking stress also depends upon the cognition that is how we evaluate the event. Sarafino (2006) in his book *Health Psychology* mentioned that "transaction in stress generally involves an assessment process…" (p. 63). Lazarus (1999) termed this transaction as cognitive appraisal. So we can say that appraisal is the cognitive evaluation of stressful event where we evaluate two things broadly: (a) whether the demands of an event is threatening the well-being (i.e. physical and psychological), and (b) whether we have coping resources to fulfil the demands of the event.

Stress as a Response

Among the theories pertinent to explain stress as a response, the theory of Hanse Selye in his book *The Stress of Life* published in 1956 is most prominent in the field. In that he gave physiological perspective of stress. Selye (1956) defines stress as a non-specific response of the body to noxious stimuli. In the same response paradigm of stress he gave a chain of reflex actions known as GAS—Generalized Adaptive Syndrome. The three responses to stress provided by him are purely physiological in nature, namely, alarm stage, resistant stage and stage of exhaustion.

Thus, the notion of stress as a response largely explains the physiological reaction to stress where there is marked absence of cognition over stress. Stress as a response also emphasis on three things: (a) change is a universal phenomenon and therefore experienced by all, (b) changes are stressful because they continuously pinch the coping mechanism of an individual, and (c) the response given to those changed life circumstances depend on how successfully an individual mobilize his coping mechanism to get supremacy over stress.

Kushnir (1986) defines stress as an adaptive response that is a consequence of any external action, situation or event that places special physical and or psychological demands upon a person. Williams and Huber (1986) define stress as "a psychological and physical reaction to prolonged internal and/or environmental conditions in which an individual's adaptive capabilities are overextended." They argued that stress is an adaptive response to a conscious or unconscious threat.

Responses to stress can either be psychological or physiological in nature. A stimulus is a stressor which produces a stressful behavioural or physiological response, and this response is stressful if it is produced by a demand, harm, threat, or load. Feeling of nervousness, hot flashes, chills, worry are some common psychological responses. The physiological responses to stress include hypertension, rapid palpitation, muscle twitchiness etc. Sarafino (2006) mentioned that "the psychological and physiological responses to stressor are called *strain*" (p. 62).

Sources of Stress

The sources of stress may range from environmental, to social, to spiritual and these are as follows:

Environment as a Source of Stress

We all want to have a stress free life but, what if the environments where we dwell become a continuous source of perceived stress? Environment as a source of stress is not only limited to different kinds of environment pollution such as pollution in water, air and noise but have reached far beyond that. The category of perceived environmental stressor includes:

- Overcrowding
- Inadequate health services in the local area
- Crime peculiar to specific area
- Racial/caste discrimination
- Travel and traffic jams
- Natural disaster
- Residential environment

Above are all the physical stressors which impinge psychological impact. The point behind raising this issue is that these environmental stressors are working more prominently in urban and semi-urban areas affecting the well-being of the whole community. Among the entire factors, major contributory factor to environmental stress is overcrowding or we can say population density at a particular territory. Heimstra and McFarling (1974) define population density as "the number of people or other types of animals occupying a given unit of space. Space in this case may refer to a room, a building, a city, or any other definable unit" (p. 154). The term density involves so many types that could add up to become stressors such as social density, spatial density, inside density and outside density. Thus, when the density of people cross the optimal number of people who could live comfortably in a limited area it becomes overcrowding. According to Heimstra and McFarling (1974) "when density increases and people are forced to live closer and closer to one another, at some point a person will feel overcrowded and will perceive the situation as involving some degree of threat and, consequently, will experience stress" (p. 155).

Psychological studies of individual differences suggest that some people perceive environmental stressor as stressor while some do not. The difference lies in channelizing the emotion felt as a result of environmental stressors. For example, problem of traffic jam is very common in metros but we find that some people just listen music while others continuously honk and thereby disturb their own well-being as well as of others. So the difference lies in the emotional coping mechanism of an individual. To eradicate environmental stressors, community level programme is needed to be run but how far these programmes will be efficacious in our country is another topic of investigation. Maloney and Ward (1973) while discussing their research in this area mention that "most people say they are willing to do a great deal to help curb pollution problems and are fairly emotional about it, but, in fact, they actually do fairly little and know even less" (p. 585). Thus both community-environmental awareness as well as active participation to correct the macrocosm is needed.

Social Factors as the Cause of Stress

Social factors represent human life as an existence. Today, social factors are creating stress in our life in terms of inharmonious relationship with family members and others, that in turn is affecting our existence. Social factors include: the locale of residence, migration from rural to urban areas, divorce, tension, discrimination, group conflicts, unemployment, inflation, scarcity, poverty, aggression, violence and terrorism. These factors affect individuals, families, and communities which in turn become the challenge of existence.

Spiritual Distress

"A man's concern, even his despair, over the worthwhileness of life is a *spiritual distress* but by no means a mental disease" (Frankl, p. 163). Spiritual distress is a disturbance in a person's belief system. *Spiritual Distress* is defined as "a disruption in the life principle that pervades a person's entire being and that integrates and transcends one's biological and psychological nature."

Spiritual distress can be a devastating experience. If it occurs during the course of an illness, a time when there is increased likelihood that it can affect the patient's course, outcome, and quality of life, then the outcome is majorly negative and destructive. Spiritual distress can prevent growth, healing, and recognition of one's own potential for change and coping at a time when such entities are immensely helpful. Mostly spiritual distress or spiritual pain is defined as a loss of sense of wholeness. There is a feeling that things are not right and that life has lost meaning, hope, and purpose. There may also be a feeling of loss of identity, since the person may no longer have his/her usual role or independence. In addition, a sense of disconnectedness may occur where relationships with family, friends, and the world may seem to lose its usual character. Thus, the person may experience a sense of floating where nothing makes sense for him and his life stops seeming as worthwhile.

Conclusion

Stress is a relativistic phenomenon. The phenomenon of stress discussed above flow from the previous studies. This is an important chapter from the perspective of the conceptualization of stress. The problem of stress has become a prime concern of psychologists, psychiatrists, and medical researchers. We suggest that 'stress and well-being' should be a top priority research area in future because stress is alarmingly increasing in modern technology period, causing a heavy human life loss.

Sri Sri Ravi Shankar says: "As it is almost impossible to reduce the workload and increase the time, the only option we are left is to increase the energy level within us. When we have enough energy and enthusiasm, we are able to handle any challenge." This inner source of energy can be developed by the practice of *yoga* and meditation.

No matter how much time we spend to manage or avoid it altogether the burden of stress is ever dominant. But if we focus on the ways to use stress to our advantage we can free ourselves from the unnecessary worry of curbing it.

References

Basowitz, H.; Perssky, H.; Korchin, S.J. and Grinker, R.R. (1955). *Anxiety and Stress.* New York: McGraw-Hill.

Frankl, V.E. (1976). *Man's Search for Meaning*. New York: Washington Square Press.

Kushnir, T.C. (1986). "Stress and social facilitation: The effect of the presence of an instructor on students' behaviour", *Journal of Advancing Nursing, 11.*

Lovallo, W.R. (1997). *Stress and Health: Biological and Psychological Interactions*. Thousand Oaks, CA: Sage.

Selye, H. (1983). *The Stress of Life*. New York: McGraw-Hill.

Sarafino, E.P. (2006). *Health Psychology: Biopsychosocial Interactions* (5th ed.). USA: Wiley.

Lazarus, R.S. and Chen, J.B. (1977). "Environmental Stress", In I. Altman and J.F. Wohlwill (Eds.), *Human Behaviour and the Environment: Current Theory and Research,* New York: Plenum.

Lazarus, R.S. (1999). *Stress and Emotion: A New Synthesis*. New York: Springer.

Heimstra, N.W. and McFarling, L.H. (1974). *Environmental Psychology*, California: Wadsworth Publishing Company.

Maloney, M.P. and Ward, M.P. (1973). "Ecology: Let's hear from the people", *American Psychologist, 28*, 583-586.

McGonigal, K. (2013). *The Upside of Stress: Why Stress is Good for You, and How to Get Good at It*, New York: Penguin Group.

Miller, J.G. (1953). The development of experimental stress—sensitive tests for predicting performance in military tasks. *PRB Technical Report 1079*, Washington DC: Psychological Research Associates.

White, R.W. (1959). "Motivation reconsidered: The concept of competence", *Psychological Review, 66,* 297-333.

Williams, J.C., and Huber, G.P. (1986). *Human Behaviour in Organizations.* Cincinnati, OH: South-Western Publishing.

2
Concept of Stress

Mujibul Hasan Siddiqui and *Mudassir Hamid*

Stress is derived from the Latin word *Stringere*, meaning to draw tight, and was used in the 17th century to describe hardships or affliction. During the late 18th century stress denoted "force, pressure, strain or strong effort", referring primarily to an individual or to an individual's organs or mental powers (Hinkle, 1973).

Worry caused by a difficult situation, or something that causes this condition,

Psychological stress refers to the emotional and physiological reactions experienced when an individual confronts a situation in which the demands go beyond their coping resources. Examples of stressful situations are marital problems, death of a loved one, abuse, health problems, and financial crises.

Definitions of Stress

Stress has a different meaning for different people under different situations. Some of the important definitions of stress are as under:

Hans Selye: "Stress is the non-specific response of the body to any demand." In Behavioural Science Stress is regarded as the "perception of threat, with resulting anxiety, discomfort, emotional tension and difficulty in adjustment".

In psychology, **stress** is a feeling of strain and pressure. Stress is a type of psychological pain. Small amounts of stress may be desired, beneficial, and even healthy. Positive stress helps improve athletic performance. It also plays a factor in motivation, adaptation, and reaction to the environment. Excessive amounts of stress, may lead to bodily harm. Stress can increase the risk of strokes, heart attacks, ulcers, and mental illnesses such as depression.

Stress can be external and related to the environment, but may also be caused by internal perceptions that cause an individual to experience anxiety or other negative emotions surrounding a situation, such as pressure, discomfort, etc., which they then deem stressful.

Causes of Stress

Financial Problems

According to the American Psychological Association (APA), money is the top cause of stress in the United States. In a 2015 survey, the APA reported that 72 per cent of Americans stressed about money at least some of the time during the previous month. The majority of the study participants reported money being a significant source of stress, with 77 per cent feeling considerable anxiety about finances.

Signs of financial stress may include:

1. Worrying and feeling anxious about money.
2. Arguing with loved ones about money.
3. Feeling guilty about spending money on non-essentials.
4. Being afraid to open mail or answer the phone.

Financial stress can take months or years to dig out from. In the long-term, stress related to finances results in distress, which may bring up blood pressure and cause headaches, upset stomach, chest pain, insomnia, and a general feeling of sickness. Financial stress has also been linked to a number of health problems, including depression, anxiety, skin problems, diabetes, and arthritis.

Work

According to the Centre for Disease Control and Prevention (CDC), Americans now spend 8 per cent more time at work compared to 20 years ago, and about 13 per cent of people work a second job. At least 40 per cent report their jobs are stressful, and 26 per cent report they often feel burned out by their work.

Any number of things can contribute to job stress including too much work, job insecurity, dissatisfaction with a job or career, and conflicts with a boss and/or co-workers. Whether you are worrying about a specific project or feeling unfairly treated, putting your job ahead of everything else can affect many aspects of your life, including personal relationships and mental and physical health.

Factors outside of the job itself also have a role in work stress, including a person's psychological make-up, general health and personal life. And the amount of emotional support they have outside of work.

The signs of work-related stress can be physical and psychological, including:

1. Fatigue.
2. Headache.
3. Muscle tension and pain.
4. Stomach problems.
5. Heart palpitations.
6. Anxiety.
7. Depression.
8. Mood swings.
9. Difficulty concentrating or making decisions.

Fatigue

Fatigue is defined as too much tiredness developing from mental or physical exertion or illness. Fatigue is physical or mental exhaustion that can be caused by stress, medication, overwork, or mental and physical illness or disease.

Physically, fatigue is characterized by a profound lack of energy, feelings of muscle weakness, and slowed movements or central nervous system reactions. Fatigue can also cause serious mental tiredness. Continued fatigue could result in a lack of mental clarity (or feeling of mental "fuzziness"), increasing the level of difficulty in concentration. Heavy physical fatigue causes memory loss.

Causes and Symptoms of Fatigue

There are several causes of fatigue as under:

1. Inadequate rest.
2. Improper diet.

3. Work and home stressors.
4. Poor physical conditioning.
5. Cronic medical conditions.
6. Diseases process in the body.
7. Low blood pressure.
8. Diabetes.
9. Iron deficiency anaemia.
10. Narcolepsy.
11. Cancer.
12. Acute viral and bacterial infections.
13. Mental disorder such as depression.

Headache

"Headache is the symptom of pain anywhere in the region of the head or neck. It can occur as a migraine, tension-type headache, or cluster headache". [Robert A. Baron and Misra, Girishwar] Frequent headaches can affect relationships and employment. There is also an increased risk of depression in those with severe headaches.

Headaches can occur as a result of many conditions whether serious or not. There are a number of different classification systems for headaches. The most well-recognized is that of the International Headache Society. Causes of headaches may include dehydration, fatigue, sleep deprivation, stress, the effects of medications, the effects of recreational drugs, viral infections, loud noises, common colds, head injury, rapid ingestion of a very cold food or beverage, and dental or sinus issues.

Treatment of a headache depends on the underlying cause, but commonly involves pain medication. A headache is one of the most commonly experience of all physical discomforts.

Causes of Headache

There are three types of headache as under:

1. Primary headache such as migraine caused by nausea and vomiting, sensitivity to light and sound, smell and touch affected vision, such as an aura, numbness of the face or extremities (hands and feet).

2. Secondary Headache caused by infection, head injury, vascular disorder, brain bleed or tumours.

Muscle Pain

The most common causes of muscle pain are tension, stress, overuse and minor injuries. Pain throughout our whole body is called systemic muscle pain. It is due to an infection, an illness or a side effect of a medication.

Causes of Muscle Pain

There are many causes of muscle pain as under:

1. Muscle cramps.
2. Myalgia.
3. Back muscle pain.
4. Generalised musculoskeletal pain.
5. Vague muscle aches.
6. Hand cramps.

Heart Palpitations

A heart palpitation is the sensation that your heart has skipped a beat or added an extra beat. It may feel like your heart is racing, pounding, or fluttering. You may become overly aware of your heartbeat. This sensation can also be felt in the neck, throat, or chest. It is also possible that your heart rhythm can change during the palpitations.

Most heart palpitations are harmless and resolve on their own without treatment. But in rare cases, heart palpitations can indicate a serious condition.

Causes of Heart Palpitations

Heart palpitations are used to happen due to strenuous exercise, caffeine, nicotine from tobacco products such as cigarettes and cigars, stress, anxiety, fear, panic, dehydration, hormonal changes, including pregnancy, electrolyte abnormalities, low blood sugar, anaemia, overactive thyroid, or hyperthyroidism, low levels of oxygen or carbon dioxide in the blood, blood loss, shock, a fever, over-the-counter

(OTC) medications, including cold and cough medications, herbal supplements, and nutritional supplements, prescription medications, including beta-blockers, asthma inhalers, and decongestants, illegal drugs, such as amphetamines and cocaine, heart disease, arrhythmia, or an irregular heart rhythm, abnormal heart valves, smoking etc.

Immediate Medical Attention

We should also take medical attention if we have palpitations that occur with other symptoms such as: dizziness, weakness, light-headedness, fainting, a loss of consciousness, confusion, difficulty in breathing, excessive sweating, pain, pressure, or tightening in our chest, pain in our arms, neck, chest, jaw, or upper back and a resting pulse rate of more than 100 beats per minute.

Anxiety

The American Psychological Association (APA) states that anxiety is "an emotion characterized by feelings of tension, worried thoughts and physical changes like increased blood pressure."

Anxiety happens due to work, money, family life, health, and other crucial issues that require a person's attention without necessarily desiring the 'fight-or-flight' reaction.

Anxiety disorders affect daily function of people of our society. An anxious feeling out of proportion to the original trigger or stressor is termed as anxiety disorder.

Symptoms of Anxiety

The symptoms of Generalized Anxiety Disorder (GAD) often include the factors such as restlessness, and a feeling of being "on-edge", uncontrollable feelings of worry, increased irritability, concentration difficulties, sleep difficulties, such as problems in falling or staying asleep.

Types of Anxiety

There are several types of anxiety disorder such as under:

Generalized Anxiety Disorder (GAD)

This disorder involves excessive, long-lasting anxiety and worries about non-specific life events, objects, and situations. It is also termed as a chronic anxiety disorder.

Panic Disorder: It is sudden attacks of intense terror and apprehension characterizes panic disorder and includes shaking, confusion, dizziness, nausea, and breathing difficulties.

Specific Phobia: This is an irrational fear and avoidance of a particular object or situation. Phobias occur due to a specific cause.

Agoraphobia: This is a fear and avoidance of places, events, or situations from which it may be difficult to escape or in which help would not be available if a person becomes trapped. A person with agoraphobia may have a fear of leaving home or using elevators and public transport.

Selective Mutism: This is a form of anxiety that some children experience, in which they are not able to speak in certain places or contexts, such as school, even though they may have excellent verbal communication skills around familiar people. It may be an extreme form of social phobia.

Social Anxiety Disorder or Social Phobia: This is a fear of negative judgment from others in social situations or of public embarrassment. Social anxiety disorder includes a range of feelings, such as stage fright, a fear of intimacy, and anxiety around humiliation and rejection. This disorder could cause persons to avoid public situations and human contact to the point that everyday living is rendered extremely difficult.

Separation Anxiety Disorder: High levels of anxiety after separation from a person or place that provides feelings of security or safety characterize separation anxiety disorder. Separation might sometimes result in panic symptoms.

Causes of Anxiety

The following are main causes of anxiety:

1. Environmental stressors, such as difficulties at work, relationship problems, or family issues.
2. Genetics, as people who have family members with an anxiety disorder are more likely to experience one themselves.

3. Medical factors, such as the symptoms of a different disease, the effects of a medication, or the stress of an intensive surgery or prolonged recovery.
4. Brain chemistry, as psychologists define many anxiety disorders as misalignments of hormones and electrical signals in the brain.
5. Withdrawal from an illicit substance, the effects of which might intensify the impact of other possible causes.

Treatment

Treatments will consist of a combination of psychotherapy, behavioural therapy, and medication.

Self-treatment

In some cases, a person can treat an anxiety disorder at home without clinical supervision.

There are several exercises and actions to help a person cope with anxiety disorders as follows:

- **Stress Management:** Learning to manage and organize any upcoming pressures and deadlines, make a list of difficult tasks more manageable, and commit to complete in desired time on priority basis.
- **Relaxation Techniques:** These techniques involve meditation, deep breathing exercises, long baths, resting in the dark, and *yoga*.
- **Exercises to Replace Negative Thoughts with Positive Ones:** Making a list of the negative thoughts that results anxiety, and another list next to it containing positive, believable thoughts to replace them.
- **Support Network:** Talking with familiar people who are supportive and helpful, such as a family member or friend.
- **Exercise:** Physical efforts could improve self-image and release chemicals in the brain that provides positive feelings.

Counselling

Counselling plays significant role in reducing level of anxiety. One of the most important ways of treating anxiety is psychological counselling. Cognitive Behavioural Therapy (CBT), psychotherapy, or combinations of therapies are very useful for the people who have high level of anxiety.

Depression

Depression is a mood or emotional state that is indicated by feelings of low self-worth or guilt and a reduced ability to enjoy life.

A person who is depressed usually has feelings of sadness, hopelessness, or pessimism; lowered self-esteem and heightened self-depreciation; a decrease or loss of ability to take pleasure in ordinary activities; reduced energy and vitality; slowness of thought or action; loss of appetite; and disturbed sleep or insomnia.

Causes of Depression

Depression may be caused by various factors which include:

1. Life event such as loss of job.
2. Family history.
3. Personality—a tendency worry a lot, low self-esteem, sensitive to personal criticism or self-critical or negative.
4. Serious medical illness.
5. Drug and Alcohol Use.
6. Changes in the brain.

Types of Depression

In fact, there are three types of depression which include:

1. **Bipolar Disorder**: Alternating states of depression and mania (abnormal elevation of mood) or hypomania (distinct, though not necessarily abnormal, elevation of mood).
2. **Major Depressive Disorder**: An effect on appetite, sleep, work, or the ability to enjoy life. It may occur at any age, ones or multiple times in the life of human beings.
3. **Persistent Depressive Disorder:** Persistent depressive disorder consists of symptoms that last two or more years, sometimes showed by episodes of major depression.

4. **Postpartum Depression**: It develops in women in the period of following childbirth. At this stage symptoms of postpartum depression involves anxiety, a lack of interest in caring for the infant and child, feelings of sadness, hopelessness or inadequacy.
   It is longer-lasting depression and more severe than the "baby blues." After childbirth, women have mood swings, feelings of sadness, and crying spells.
5. **Psychotic Depression**: Psychotic depression occurs when a severe depressive illness includes some form of psychosis. The psychosis can be hallucinations such as hearing a voice telling us that we are not good or worthless and delusions such as intense feelings of worthlessness, failure, or having committed a sin or some other break with reality or paranoia.
6. **Seasonal Affective Disorder:** Seasonal affective disorder involves depressive symptoms in autumn and winter which are alleviated with increased exposure to natural light in spring and summer.

Some people may feel overwhelmed and struggle to cope, which can impact their behaviour as well. Job stress may prompt individuals to have:

1. Increased sick days.
2. Drops in work performance.
3. Problems with personal relationships.
4. Diminished creativity and initiative.
5. Lower levels of patience and increased levels of frustration.
6. Disinterest.
7. Isolation.

Personal Relationships

There are people in all of our lives that cause us stress. It could be a family member, an intimate partner, friend, or co-worker. Toxic people lurk in all parts of our lives and the stress we experience from these relationships can affect physical and mental health.

There are numerous causes of stress in romantic relationships and when couples are constantly under pressure, the relationship could be on the risk of failure.

Common relationship stressors include:

1. Being too busy to spend time with each other and share responsibilities.
2. Intimacy and sex are become rare due to busyness, health problems, and a number of other reasons.
3. You and your partner are not communicating.
4. You and/or partner are consuming too much alcohol and/or using drugs.
5. You or your partner are thinking about divorce.
6. There is abuse or control in the relationship.

The signs of stress related to personal relationships are similar to normal symptoms of general stress and may include physical health and sleep problems, depression, and anxiety. You may also find yourself avoiding or having conflict with the individual, or becoming easily irritated by their presence.

Sometimes, personal relationship stress can also be related to our relationships with people on social media platforms, such as Facebook. For example, social media tends to naturally encourage comparing yourself to others, which can lead to the stress of feeling inadequate. It also makes bullying easier.

Daily Life and Busyness

Day-to-day stressors are our daily inconveniences. They include things like misplacing keys, running late, and forgetting to bring an important item with you when leaving the house. Usually, these are just minor setbacks, but if they become frequent, they become a source of anxiety affecting physical and/or psychological health.

The stress of being too busy is getting more and more common. These days, people are busier than ever and that adds a lot of stress to their lives. In some cases, busyness is due to necessity, such as having to work a second job. Other times, it is due to guilt and not wanting to disappoint others. People may not say "no" and end up having little time for themselves, or they overlook their own basic needs, such as eating right and exercising due to lack of time.

References

1. Robert A. Baron, Misra, Girishwar (1999). *Psychology* Indian sub-continent.
2. Hussain, Akbar, Illyas Khan Mohd. (2006). *Recent trends in human stress management*, Global Vision Publishing House, New Delhi.
3. www.stress.in
4. www.stresswikipedia.com
5. Cox, T. (1978). *Stress*, London/New York: Macmillan; 2nd ed. (1985).
6. Grinker, R. (1953). *Psychosomatic Concepts*, New York.
7. Hinkle, L.E (1973). The Concept of Stress in the Biological Social Sciences. *Stress medicine and Man.*
8. https://medical-dictionary.thefreedictionary.com/fatigue
   https://en.wikipedia.org/wiki/Headache
   https://www.mayoclinic.org/symptoms/muscle-pain/basics/causes/sym-20050866
   https://www.nhsinform.scot/illnesses-and-conditions/stomach-liver-and-gastrointestinal-tract/stomach-ache-and-abdominal-pain
   https://www.healthline.com/health/heart-palpitations#when-to-seek-help
   https://www.medicalnewstoday.com/articles/323454.php
   https://www.britannica.com/science/depression-psychology
   https://www.britannica.com/science/depression-psychology

3
Concept of Stress and Various Components of Environmental Stress in Nigeria

Zayon O. Nzegbulam and *Chiamaka R. Nwaoru*

Introduction

The environment provides all life support systems, including air, water and land, as well as other materials that make life worth living. In this sense, in its simple term, the environment may be defined as the natural world of land, sea, air, plants and animals, including the humans who depend on them for sustenance and survival; in fact, it is the sum total of all conditions that surround man at any point on the earth's surface. In this work, however, we look at and see the environment as the sum total of all the circumstances, including people, events, natural and man-made phenomena that influence the attitudes and general life of the individuals co-existing and subsisting in a particular place or area. It seems to be from this standpoint that Efobi (1994) has defined the environment as "the total set of circumstances that surround an individual or a community, these circumstances are made up of physical conditions such as air, water, climate and landforms; and also the social and cultural aspects such as ethics, economics, aesthetics and such circumstances which affect the behaviour of individuals or a community of individuals".

Thus, the environment encompasses constantly interacting sets of physical (natural and man-made) elements and non-physical, living and non-living (e.g. social, cultural, religious, political, economic) systems, which determine the characteristic features, growth and sustainability of both the component elements of the environment and the environment itself (Muoghalu, 2004).

Going by the above understanding of what constitutes environment, Environment Related Stressor (ERS) refers to any form of community and societal relationships that cause stress to the individuals that inhabit within such a community or society. For some decades the term stress has enjoyed increasing popularity, this is because nobody is immune to stress. In our everyday life we are caught up in a situation or situations that cause or trigger stress. Thus, whether young, old, rich, poor, professionals and laymen, we are all prone to a particular form of stress in one way or the other. Stress has become part and parcel of life in human societies and existence. The frustrations, disappointments and pressures of daily life constitute the genesis of stress. While some of such stressful situations can be tolerable and even help to develop coping and positive adjustment mechanisms after overcoming them, others could become so overwhelming to the extent of exceeding both our adjustment and coping mechanisms. It is usually the latter aspects of stress that concern us the most whenever we discuss stress as a problem.

Conceptual Framework of Stress

Stress is a term used to express the feelings of worries and tense situations because of life difficulties. Stress could either be mental or physical, but the two types of stress usually go together as mental stress can easily lead to physical stress and *vice versa.* In fact, stress is the body's natural defence against threatening life situations and danger. It flushes the body with hormones and prepares our systems to evade or confront danger. This is known as the "fight-or-flight" mechanism. In medical parlance, stress is interpreted as the body's response to a situation or an environment that is unwelcome, unpleasant, unwarranted, unconquerable and unplanned (Satsangi, 2014). Scientific researches carried out on stress have established that when one is experiencing stress, the brain releases high levels of two specific hormones known as adrenaline and cortisol through the hypothalamus located at the base of the brain. This set of chemical compounds pumped directly into the blood stream releases emergency energy which put the person on the state of alertness to deal with the stressor situation. As Satsangi (*ibid*) opines, "stress refers to a state of imbalance within an organism that is elicited by an actual or perceived disparity between environmental demands and the organism's capacity to cope with these demands, and is manifested through a variety of psychological, emotional and behavioural responses".

When we are faced with any stressful challenge, part of our response is physical. The body activates resources to protect us by preparing us either to stay and fight or to get away as fast as possible from the unpleasant or unwanted situation. The body produces larger quantities of the chemicals called cortisol, adrenaline, and noradrenaline. These trigger out an increased heart rate, heightened muscle preparedness, sweating and alertness. All these factors improve the ability to respond to a hazardous or challenging situation. The environmental factors that trigger off this reaction are called "stressors". Stress slows down other normal body functions, such as the digestive and immune systems. All resources can then be concentrated on rapid breathing, blood flow, alertness, and muscle use. Thus, during stress, the body changes in the following ways:

- blood pressure and pulse rate rise.
- breathing is faster.
- the digestive system slows down.
- immune activity decreases.
- the muscles become tense.
- a heightened state of alertness prevents sleep (Nabi *et al.*, 2013, June 26).

How we react to a difficult situation will affect how stress affects us and our health. Persons who feel they do not have enough resources to cope will be more likely to have a stronger reaction, and one that can trigger health problems. Thus, stressors affect individuals in different ways.

Scholars have conceptualised stress in different ways. Halgin and Whitbourne (2003) explained stress as an unpleasant emotional reaction a person has when he or she perceives an event to be threatening. These scholars are of the view that this emotional reaction may include heightened physiological arousal due to increased reactivity of the sympathetic nervous system. In their own view, Agwu and Tiemo (2012) have noted that "stress reaction is seen as an individual's response to a given stress; which can be behavioural, perceptual, physiological, emotional and cognitive, or signs and symptoms of illness or disorders such as headaches, alcohol abuse, obesity, cardiovascular disease and hypertension.

Thus, stressor is the event itself, which is also called a stressful life event. In the context of this work however, we refer to stress as a condition or situation within the environment that makes people anxious, feel depressed, angry, hostile and frustrated. Therefore, we see environmental stress as that which occurs when external pressures exceed coping mechanisms the individual was already used to. It is one of the contributing factors to numerous emotional and mental health disorders, as well as physical illnesses when it overwhelms an individual's coping capacity.

Some people may experience stress from lack of finances, work-related stress, stress due to chronic illness, and stress from death of a loved one, stress arising from difficulty of paying children's school fees, family issues and etcetera. All these external pressures could take a toll on a person and affect overall health and well-being of the individual. In some cases, it leads to mental instability and therefore needs to be recognized and managed on time. Different people have different manifestations of stress; some may have physical symptoms, while others may have mental or behavioural symptoms. Physical symptoms of stress include insomnia, loss of sexual drive or decrease in sexual performance, prolonged fatigue, chronic headaches and body pains and heart palpitations. Mental symptoms may include depressed state, confusion, decreased memory, etc. Emotional and behavioural symptoms include eating disorders, excessive smoking and alcohol intake, restlessness, excessive crying, etc. (Iyizoba, 2017). Most of such symptoms are nothing but coping mechanisms being adopted by the affected individual to deal with the stressful situations. Certainly, such so-called measures are negative by themselves and are capable of triggering further stress.

Types of Stress

The American Psychological Association (APA) identified three major types of stress from which all other forms of stress are derived. They include the following:

1. **Acute Stress**: This type of stress is the most common and frequent one and as the name implies, it is usually brief. It is believed by Psychologists to be as a result of negative, reactive thinking concerning events or situations that have recently occurred or about to happen. However, the stress

fizzles out or subsides when the thought-induced stress is removed or reduced.

2. **Episodic Stress**: This type of stress is usually experienced by individuals who frequently have episodes of acute stress. Persons who suffer from episodic stress have an excessive competitive drive, aggressiveness, impatience, abrupt, and a sense of time urgency, with some deep-seated feeling of insecurity over job performance or coping with some basic living conditions.
3. **Chronic Stress:** Chronic stress usually sets in when an individual feels hopeless, does not seem to see possible solution to the cause of stress, and gives up hope on seeking practical solutions. Such adverse socio-economic conditions as long term poverty, repeated abuse in any form, unemployment, dysfunctional family, poor work environment, substance abuse, or an unhappy, loveless marriage, can lead to significant chronic stress.

Some chronic stresses stem from traumatic, early childhood experiences that become internalized and remain forever present and painful. Some experiences profoundly affect personality. A view of the world, or a belief system, may be created that causes unending stress for the individual (e.g., the world is a very insecure and unsafe place, creating a belief system that makes you think you are perfect while you are really not). When personality or deep-seated convictions and beliefs must be reformulated, recovery requires active self-examination, often with professional help (Bauma, 1990).

The worst aspect of chronic stress is that people get used to it and attempt to live with it as if it does not matter. People are immediately aware of acute stress because it is new; they ignore chronic stress because it is old, familiar, and sometimes, almost as part of living.

"Chronic stress kills through suicide, violence, heart attack, stroke and, perhaps, even cancer. People wear down to a final, fatal breakdown, sometimes without being conscious of what is happening to them. Because physical and mental resources are depleted through long-term attrition, the symptoms of chronic stress are difficult to treat and may require extended medical as well as behavioural treatment and stress management" (Anderson & Anderson, 2003).

Nigerian Environmental Situations and the Stressors Therein

In Nigeria, the environmental stressors are more of man-made than natural and appear to be acute, chronic and pervasive, and capable of inducing and triggering off the three major types of stress as mentioned above. The unchecked rapid perversity with which the human induced socio-economic environmental stressors are increasing in the country should be a source of great and justifiable concern to all, including the governments at all levels that wield the big ace of political and economic authority and power, and civil organisations and good spirited individuals that matter both within and outside the Nigerian state.

It is from the above standpoint that this book chapter attempts to x-ray some components of the environmentally induced stress situations and their implications in Nigeria. These virtual man-made stressor conditions range from bad governance/mismanagement of available resources, to outright systemic failure, leading to: Non-payment of salaries, hyperinflation, Kwashiorkor power supply system, poor road networks and maintenance, insecurity even with increasing number of uniformed gun-wielding security personnel on highways. All the above mentioned environmental man-made stressors are both direct and indirect fall-outs of bad governance and mismanagement leading to misappropriation of public funds, embezzlement and other sundry forms of official corruption, resulting to various forms of the stressful conditions to most Nigerians as discussed hereunder.

Stress Associated with Non-payment of Salaries

Stress is a common phenomenon for every living human which can be necessitated by physiological and psychological factors. Our everyday life and activities are surrounded by stressors of various type and level. However, at workplaces, stress is one of the conditions that every worker must experience at different times and levels. Such workplace stresses are nothing but psychological and emotional responses that can happen when there is a conflict between job demand on the employee and the control mechanism adopted by the worker in meeting such demands. As Alexandros-Stamatios, Matilyn and Cary (2003) state, "Stress is created where the employee lacks information regarding his authorities, tasks to be performed, duties and powers.

They further argue that "factors intrinsic to the job" means extra workload, variety of tasks and rates of pay. The combination of high effort and low reward at work has been found to be a risk factor for cardiovascular health, sickness, absenteeism, as well as self-reported symptoms (Tsutsumi & Kawakami, 2004).

As Elstad and Vabo (2008) also observe, work-related stress can severely impact workers' general achievement levels in a negative way in respect of both efficiency and accuracy. For example, besides the impact on workers' health and well-being, a poor psychosocial work environment usually contribute to work-related stress conditions that could lead to increased absenteeism and presenteeism, as well as reduced motivation, satisfaction and commitment, along with a greater rate of staff turnover and intention to quit (Elstad & Vabo, 2008).

The motive of every worker is to receive rewards at the end of every work done. This reward can be distributed to employees in three different ways: **money, which is adequate salary, esteem (respect and support and security which the Job offers, promotions and status consistency)**. Money is an extrinsic reward and it can be used to influence employees' behaviours (Darmon, 2004). Extrinsic rewards can include salary, fringe benefits, and so on (Kreitner, 2005). Organizations that reward their members in accordance with performance (paying of salaries as the basic and other benefits) typically experience fewer problems than organizations that do not (Muczyk, *et al.*, 2004).

Thus, as it is obvious from the above, salaries and bonuses, as extrinsic rewards, are not just used as good tools to motivate workers for better performance, but the entire socio-economic life-wire of the worker and his/her family are dependent on them, for survival.

In Nigeria however, payments of salaries to workers at different states (administrative divisions) have been so politicised that the issue has become one of the major workplace environmentally induced stress to an average Nigerian worker and the families they need to support and cater for. Workers of many organisations, companies, ministries and government parastatal are owed salary arrears ranging from 6, 7, 8, 9, 10 months, sometimes for one year or more. This has been having profound effect on not only the individual workers and their families, but also on the entire economy of the country as a whole in the sense that majority of the nation's workforce is deprived of the financial capacity to patronize the goods and services produced by business investors and traders. A situation where a worker is not paid at the end of the month, it is obvious that even those around him and those directly depending on him will suffer. So many Nigerian workers are psychologically and emotionally distressed as they are unable to take care of themselves and their dependents when it comes to the basic necessities of life such as payment of house bills, food and healthcare. Many workers can hardly afford their children's school fees and pay for their books; all these bring nothing but emotional and psychological stresses and have led to frustration, depression, poverty-induced mental destitution and even to the death of many. Moreover, many unemployed weak-minded dependent youths of some of these workers have taken to different forms of criminal activities in the name of survival, thereby compounding the ugly security situation in the country. In Nigeria of our time, no day passes without reported cases of armed robbery, kidnapping for ransom, oil-pipeline vandalisation and other different types of petty crimes. All the above mentioned situations have added some multiplier effects to the stresses Nigerians pass through as a result of virtual systemic failure.

Stress Asscciated with Poor Electricity Supply

Power supply is an indispensable driving force of all socio-economic, industrial and business activities of any country to greater pedestals. Ekpo (2013) states that the positive multiplier effect of constant power supplies cannot be overemphasized. The benefits of energy to commercial, transportation, industrial and household activities can hardly be overstressed. Hence, an impressive performance of Gross Domestic Product (GDP) of any nation today is driven by the effective generation and supply of energy. As a key component of national development, energy (electricity) is the major source of advancement and improvement in the standard of living of the people by stimulating other sectors like health, education, agriculture, commerce, transportation, industries and other developmental strides of the country. At individual level, increase in energy consumption is likely to be one of the most important causes of improvement in welfare of the people. At national level, in this era of digital economy, it is not possible to envisage development without the use of modern energy generation and effective supply system (Worlde Rufael, 2006).

In Nigeria, the present poor power generation and ineffective supply system, and lack of it at all in some areas of the country, have been so frustrating and distressing that it has stagnated Nigeria's economic development as so many small/medium scale industries and even larger ones have been forced to close down or relocate to neighbouring countries where power supplies are relatively stable; even individuals are not finding the situation easy as they come home everyday only to stay in darkness, thus adding to their frustration and stress.

The essence of electricity in a nation is so pertinent that when an individual lives in an area where there is poor, lack of or unstable power supply, it makes life epileptic and distressing to live in today's global computer age. The unsteady and lack of energy supply have profited the generator companies as everybody struggles to get one in order to have access to personal power supply. As power generating sets are owned by most Nigerians, the noise and air pollution they generate increase the level of stress and distressful health challenges faced by Nigerians.

It is also pertinent to note that even when there is hardly power supply in some areas of the country, the exorbitant estimated bills that the individuals, organizations, and industries are forced to pay at the end of each month by the Electricity companies are so breath-taking to the extent that some businesses have been driven out of existence. So many have opted for the pre-paid meter system of billing thinking that it would serve as a better option, they have only found out that the so-called pre-paid meter cards run so fast, even when the power supply is so epileptic to serve any useful purpose. In fact, the status of power supply in the country has further compounded the stresses average Nigerians and their businesses are constrained to face each day of their existence.

Stress Associated with Poor Road Network

The problem of bad roads in Nigeria has become a dreadful nightmare. In many parts of the country, motorists are in constant distress as their vehicles are never in good shape. This situation has left many with no choice than leaving their private car and its convenience to opt for public commercial transportation, with all the attendant dangers, as the drivers of such commercial vehicles hardly have value for the lives of the passengers they always carry, and even as such vehicles are poorly maintained by their owners. Unmaintained, poor road-networks have always led to sudden breakdown of vehicles on highways, leading to fatal accidents and loss of lives. In most cases, journeys that ought to take less than two hours could end up taking a whole day due to poor road network.

Worse still, armed robbery, kidnapping and other hideous criminal activities perpetrated on our highways are made a lot easier at those portions of the roads where the criminals are sure that their victims would be tracked down easily due to the poor conditions of the road. Furthermore, there is also the problem of erosion impacting on the road network. Whole sections of our roads are being washed away by erosion and poorly planned or non-existent drainage system. In addition, there are many bridges without any warning signs and even handrails. Vehicles have been known to plunge into the rivers with grave consequences. As Afolabi (2009) observes, accidents cause significant losses to present and future productive manpower of our country, as well as, in many cases, profound social problems, deaths or serious injuries. Sometimes, this results in loss of breadwinners, pushing the affected families into poverty, and jeopardizing the educational upbringing of their children. Other victims that might not have died are known to carry relics of handicaps such as loss of limbs, blindness, or even bound to wheel-chairs for life (Emenike and Ogbole, 2008). Such victims and their families are left with nothing but psychological, emotional and cognitive stress. Unfortunately, those who are not directly affected may certainly not comprehend the extent of traumas the victims and their families have to live with throughout their existence.

Thus, in a country with hardly any functional railway system, risky air services and poorly maintained road networks, the citizens' endurance capacities are obviously stretched to breaking point, thus leading to complicated combination of acute episodic and chronic stress syndromes.

Stress Associated with Inadequate or Lack of Security

The precarious security situation in Nigeria has shown very clearly that Nigeria's perception of security threat is more from within than from any external aggressors. In fact, it was only in recent years when the threat of Boko Haram jihadist elements in the north-east of the country started allying themselves with Al Qaeda and later ISIS that Nigeria began to perceive serious threats beyond its territorial boundaries. Ordinarily, the primordial paradigm of security, which centres on gun-wielding soldiers and intimidating weaponry to scare the citizenry seems to still pervade the mentality of our political and military leadership as far as national defence and security of the country is concerned. This could go a long way to suggest how the military operations against the Islamist insurgent jihadists were casually executed at the early stages of the insurgency. Any wonder then also that in Nigeria today, gun-wielding soldiers, policemen and other paramilitary forces are found at short distances mounting road-blocks and check-points around the country, yet security and safety of the citizens and their property are yet hardly guaranteed.

Today, average Nigerian citizens are perennially inundated with both acute, episodic and chronic stress syndromes arising from not only the presence of gun-wielding security personnel on highways and reckless security vehicle convoys conveying the leaders and politicians, but also daily stress suffered by commuters plying the poorly maintained bad road network across the country. Besides those living close or have anything to do with the north-east zone of the country who live in perpetual fear of the Boko Haram insurgency and the military operations going on there, and the menacing security to lives and property by the killer herdsmen in some parts of the country, generally, Nigerians suffer from perennial **Stress associated with Road Blocks and Check-points mounted by security personnel, the police and the military** in particular.

Fundamentally, the Nigeria Police is one of the most formidable para-military forces statutorily vested with the responsibilities of protecting the people and maintaining internal security, law and order within the Nigerian state, while the complex task of keeping Nigeria one, and of protecting the nation from external aggression and attacks undoubtedly rests primarily on the Nigerian armed forces, which include the army, navy and the air force. In Nigeria, the functions of the military, is contained in the Federal Constitution (1999: 105) thus:

The protection of the country against all forms of internal and external danger/threat or attack is a primary responsibility of government performed through the armed forces in collaboration with the civilian population. Subversion of government policy from within or without, religious intolerance and fanaticism, ethnic antagonism and class struggles, unemployment, hunger, actual/perceived inequality and social injustice, etc., are the major sources of internal threats to security, while the grave forms of external threats are aggression or actual attack on our territorial integrity, both of which represent an assault on our very survival as a people.

However, in Nigeria today, security forces, notably the police and the army seem to have deviated from these their fundamental mandate of being the protector of their civilian compatriots. The realities on our highways today speak volume of the intimidation and extortions helpless Nigerians routinely face on daily basis as they struggle to go about their legitimate businesses. Road-blocks and check-points mounted on highways supposedly meant to checkmate the activities of miscreants and other criminal elements are unfortunately misused by these armed security personnel to extort money from already impoverished motorists, especially commercial vehicle operators and other naive commuters. These unlawful acts by the security personnel have permeated deep into the psyche of the Nigerian populace that they have come to see it as a sort of fate accomplice in the society they call their own. Everyday, we encounter police corruption and they take various forms: extortion, intimidation, bribery, and etcetera. Sometimes this has been blamed on the poor remuneration packages of the police outfit (*The Guardian*, 2015). But what about the military which ought to be an embodiment of discipline in all ramification and conduct? This research therefore sees greed and systemic depravity as the major cause of these ugly and unpatriotic behaviours by the security personnel in a country where everyone is struggling to live beyond his means as if no one is in control of anything. The public perception of police has created mystical impression suggesting that whenever one has any encounter with a Nigerian police officer, all he wants is money.

Thus, because of the ever presence of these armed security personnel on our highways and the impunity with which they operate, the general public in Nigeria have become so naïve that they have virtually lost their civility and senses to insist on their basic civil rights as they continue to suffer molestations and harassment from the same law enforcement agents who supposed to protect and defend them from criminal elements (NOPRIN, 2007). Seeing that the economy of the country is so bad and for the fact that most of these commuters (bus drivers, tricyclists, bike riders and lorry drivers) are only struggling to eke a living through their commercial transport services, it create emotional and physical stress on them when they are delayed unnecessarily just for the purpose of extorting money from them without any known offence or crime they have committed. Most of the time, even when all vehicle particulars are up-to-date, the police would want to delay the poor commercial transporters and even private owned vehicles until they are ready to offer some money (bribe). More often than not, these transport operators part with such moneys in tears and silent curses.

Shamefully still, the security personnel at such road-blocks or check-points, some of which are even unauthorized, produces change from their pocket when a driver insists not having a smaller currency denomination to part with. Such scenario has also created a distorted view on the part of some naïve commuters that drivers who do not want to comply with the police are those who want to stress the passengers they carry by delaying them unnecessarily on the highways. Thus, it has become a common sight on our highways to see lines of drums filed with sand for the purpose of road-blocks to prevent vehicles from moving freely, thereby causing unnecessary traffic hold-ups on our road ways and leading to untold mental and physical stress on Nigerians.

Besides all that have been discussed above, systemic corruption, mismanagement of resources, policy summersaults/inconsistency, political and ethnic rancor, then the most threatening one, i.e. religious intolerance and inept leadership, have all contributed in no small degrees in laying siege on the psyche of average Nigerians, resulting in absolute sense of insecurity and their stress syndromes. As Chukuma and Jubrin (2006) aptly observe, electoral fraud has become an impediment to Nigeria's search for internal security, the country having had a long history of electoral rigging and fraud that have been frustrating the wishes of the people to choose those who exercise political power; precisely because of this history, elections in the country have often been associated with political tension, and indeed, violence and crises.

As Azeez (2005) and Babawale (2007) also noted, "the concept of good governance and accountability are still a mirage and lacking in the agenda of our political leaders, be it at the local government, state government or central level and these also are affecting the private sector of the economy".

How Can We Cope With or Manage Stress?

In fact, coping with or managing stress could be a lot easier if we were able to easily identify the sources and also have control over our environmental stressors in particular. However, no matter how we may try, we cannot easily or fully control the sources of stress in our environs since we are all bonded together in the environment we find ourselves even against our will. Every society or country has its own environmental sources of stress, which could be natural or man-made. The coping or management measures adopted by each society and individuals within the same society do vary according to the nature of such stressing situations and the capacity of the government agencies and the individuals themselves.

The American Psychological Association generally recommends the following ways of managing stress by individuals in the sense that the major victims of any stressful situations, be they man-made or natural, are usually the individuals themselves. These measures include:

- Taking a break from the stressor, which is suggestive of temporarily leaving the scene of stress for some relief to take care of oneself before returning with more energy to face the reality.
- Taking regular exercise, for its known benefits of refreshing and relaxing the mind and the body.
- Smiling and laughing out, which enables the individual to ease off some tension and pent-up emotions.
- Getting social support, which suggests sharing built-up tensions and emotions with trusted friends in order to free oneself from unwanted, negative thoughts and tendencies.
- Taking time out for meditation, in order to release emotions that may have been causing the body physical stress.

However, taking cognizance of the sources of stress which Nigerians are constrained to contain with in their own peculiar socio-cultural, socio-economic, political and security environments, the possible ways to deal with the stress average Nigerians face on routine basis in their daily lives can only come by removing the sources of the stress as have been discussed above. Otherwise, applying the APA recommended stress management measures in Nigerian own situation would only amount to dealing with the symptoms of the stress and not with the sources of the stress themselves. It is for the above reason that these researchers are of the view that the attention of relevant authorities to the threatening situations is needed, and also solicit the assistance and collaborative efforts of government, non-governmental organizations, relevant international agencies, humane spirited leaders and individuals, in order to obviate the causes of these stressful conditions in the country which are so overwhelming and beyond the coping capacities of the individuals.

Conclusions

In determining components of stress and its effects on Nigeria and Nigerians, this study revealed that non-payment of Salaries has impact on employee's health and it is the source of psychological, emotional and physical stresses being experienced by majority of workers in Nigeria, including their families and the country in general. Lack of power supply was also identified as a component of stress, as this has led to many people patronising generator companies and road side fuel dealers (black marketers) with their attendant hazards and associated adverse economic implications. Because of trying to make-ends-meet, so many of these road-side and black-market fuel dealers have been patronizing oil pipe-line vandalizers whose activities have always caused petroleum pipe-line explosions that claim innocent lives and loss of properties, thus leaving many families bereaved with virtual perpetual psychological and emotional distress, causing such families both episodic and chronic stresses. Lack of security, good roads and illegal road-blocks by the military and other security agents were also stated, as all of these have always caused a lot of tensions in the minds and psyche of the citizenry, causing many to flee the state, leaving their businesses for even smaller neighbouring countries like Ghana and Togo, where they believe there is comparative safety, thereby affecting the economy of the country adversely. Bad roads have led to so many accidents leaving family members devastated. Besides, a journey that ought to take a maximum of 30 minutes may end up taking almost three hours just because of bad roads and road-blocks used for extortion.

The President of the country, Governors of various states in Nigeria and all agencies of government owe it as both statutory and moral duty to account for their role in what is going on and happening to Nigeria and Nigerians.

The Nigerian government, albeit, the National Assembly should enact appropriate laws that must serve as deterrent to the security personnel who violate the purpose for which any road-blocks or check-points are mounted wherever and whenever necessary at all in the country. Moreover, the Central Government and the National

Assembly should enact a law to make non-payment of salaries or wages by organisations, be they government or private owned an act of economic sabotage. Not just because of its traumatic effect on the workers and their families, but also for the adverse impacts it has on the entire business environment of the country, its trade and economy. This is so because the businesses and trades of any community or country depend on the salaries and wages paid to its workers for survival and when the workers are denied of their purchasing power, which is their wages, many businesses are forced to close down and trades stagnate and the governments of such a country or community begin to run deficit in tax and revenue collection to function effectively.

Furthermore, these researchers are of the view that it is rather high time Nigerian authorities should consider reviewing their perception of what constitutes national security and make a paradigm shift from looking at security as mere acquisition of military hardware and weaponry, to that of looking at it from the perspective of making adequate provisions for the socio-economic well-being of the people and guaranteeing the safety and security of their future in order to dissuade them from criminal tendencies against fellow citizens and the Nigerian state.

In fact, Nigeria must not be allowed to implode from within since the veritable source of insecurity and stresses to Nigerians are in Nigeria itself. The international community and relevant international organisations should not abandon poor Nigerians to their helpless fate in the hands of their inept, corrupt political leaders, as that might amount to conspiracy to create another Syria, Libya, Afghanistan or even Yemen. Even while they try to mind their business interests in the country, they must also not turn their eyes the other way when their Nigerian business environments are inimical to the citizens and general inhabitants of the country.

When these are done, we hope that Nigeria and Nigerians, and indeed, Nigeria's neighbours, will have relative peace and less stress as no country is absolutely stress-proof.

References

Afolabi, J.O. (2017). "Topical Issues on Road Safety in Nigeria", *The International Journal*, 2017; Volume 17, Issue 42, April 2017.

Agwu, M.O. and Tiemo, J.A. (2012). "Problems and Prospects of Stress Management in the Nigeria Liquefied Natural Gas Construction Project", Bonny: *Journal of Emerging Trends in Economics and Management Sciences (JETEMS) 3*(3): 266-271.

Alexandros-Stamatios G.A.; Matilyn J.D. and Cary, L.C. (2003). "Occupational stress, job satisfaction and health state in male and female junior hospital doctors in Greece", *Journal of Managerial Psychology, 18*(6): 592-621.

Anderson, N.B. and Anderson, P.E. (2003). *Emotional Longevity: What Really Determines How Long You Live*, New York: Viking.

Azeez, C.T. (2005). *The Real World of Democracy*. Lagos: Methodology Publishers.

Babawale, T. (2007). *Good Governance, Democracy and Democratic Best Practices,* CBAAC Occasional Monographs.

Baum, A. and Polsusnzy, D. (1999). "Health Psychology: Mapping Biobehavioural Contributions to Health and Illness", *Annual Review of Psychology*, Vol. 50, pp. 137-163.

Chukwuma, C.S. (2006). *Can Nigerian be the China of Africa?* Lagos: Adegozo Ltd.

Darmon, R.Y. (2004). *The Measurement of Sales Force Motivation Revisited*, ESSEC Business School.

Ekpo, H.E. (2013). *Promoting Inclusive Growth in Nigeria: Issues of Policies Reform, People Expectation and Private Sector Responses*, Public Lecture delivered on 13th June, 2013 at University of Lagos, Akoka, Lagos.

Elstad, J. and Vabo, M. (2008). "Job stress, sickness absence and sickness presentism in Nordic elderly care", *Scandinavian Journal of Public Health, 36*(5): 467-474.

Emenike, G.C., and Ogbole, A. (2008). "Accidents and the Road Transport Industry in Nigeria", *Journal of the International Centre for Constructive Research (ICCR)*.

Halgin, R.P., and Whitbourne, S.K. (2003). *Abnormal Psychology*. USA: McGraw-Hill.

Ibrahim, A.A. (2015). Police Corruption and the State: Prevalence and Consequences, *Global Journal of Arts, Humanities and Social Sciences*, 3(3): 19-29, March 2015. Published by European Centre for Research Training and Development UK (www.eajournals.org).

Jibrin, I. (2006). *Legislation and the Electoral Process: The term agenda and the future of Nigerian democracy*, Lagos, Panof Press.

Kadir, K.O. (2006). "Planning Sustainable Cities in Nigeria", *Research Journal of Social Science, 1*(1): 40-50.

Kreitner (2005). *Organisational Behaviour*, 2nd ed., Irwin, Boston, MA.

Imobigbe, T.A. (1990). "Doctrines for and threat to internal security", In A.E. Ekallo and Vogh M.A. (Eds.) *Nigerian Defence Policy: Issues and Problems*, Lagos: Malthouse Press Ltd.

Iyizoba, N. (2017). Managing stress in world's most successful country: Retrieved from *The Guardian Newspaper*, 14 September 2017 from http://t.guardian/ Features/managing stress in world's most stressful country.

Muoghalu, L.N. (2004). "Environmental Problems and their Effects on Human Life: From Awareness to Action", In H.C. Mba *et al.* (eds.), *Management of Environmental Problems and Hazards in Nigeria,* Hants: Ashgate Publishing Ltd.

Muczyk, J.P. (2004). The Strategic Role of Compensation, *Human Resource Planning*, *11*(3), 225–39.

Nabi, H.; Kivimäki, M.; Batty, G.D.; Shipley, M.; Britton, A.; Brunner, E.J.; Vahtera, J. and Singh-Manoux, A. (2013, 26 June). Increased risk of coronary heart disease among individuals reporting adverse impact of stress on their health: the Whitehall II prospective cohort study, *European Heart Journal*, 34(34), 2697-2705; also visit: https://academic.oup.com/eurheartj/article/34/ 34/2697/617400/Increased-risk-of-coronary-heart-disease-among-individuals-reporting-adverse-impact-of-stress-on-their-health (Accessed 22/ 10/018).

NOPRIN. (2007). *Criminal Force?: An Interim Report on the Nigeria Police Force, Network on Police Reform in Nigeria,* NOPRIN: Lagos.

Satsangi, Alok (2014). *The DBS: Handbook of Disaster Management*, Patiala: Madaan Book House.

Tenibiaje, D.J. (2011) *Counselling Psychology,* Ibadan: Esthom Graphic Prints.

Tsutsumi, A. and Kawakami, N. (2004). A review of empirical studies on the model of effort-reward imbalance at work: Reducing occupational stress by implementing a new theory. *Social Science and Medicine*, 59, 2335-2359.

Wolde, R.Y. (2005). "Energy Demand and Economic Growth: African Experience", *Journal of Policy Modeling.* Vol. 27, 891–903. *Journal homepage*: www.elsevier.com.

4
Stress: Its Meaning, Definition and Types

M.P. Tripathi

Introduction

Of late, the use of term "Stress" in our daily life has increased. We generally talk about stress but it isn't clear 'what stress really is'? We are well aware with some terms like stress, conflict, tension, depression and pressure which are used synonymously for stress but these are quite different. People consider stress as something that happens to harm or encourage them. The term stress is being generally used to describe a variety of negative feelings and reactions that accompany threatening or challenging situations, however, all stresses are not negative. Stress can be both, a positive and a negative. Stress is said to be positive when situation offers an opportunity to one to gain something. Eustress is the term used to describe positive stress. It is negative (Distress) when stress is associated with harm. This chapter explains the concept of stress, meaning of stress, types of stress and the techniques of its management.

Basic Concept of Stress

Stress is often described as a feeling of being overloaded, tensed, worried and interference with our abilities but sometimes it helps us to motivate to get a task finished, or perform well. Stress is our body's response to certain situations. It is subjective, so something that is stressful for you may not be stressful for others. Stressful events are called stressors. The physical or psychological demands from the environment that cause stress are called stressors. There are many types of stressors but all of these are not unpleasant. Stress is the spice of life and the absence of stress makes life monotonous. Stress is what happens to our bodies, psyches and our behaviours in response to an event. When something happens to us, we as a reflex action start evaluating the situation. Stress is the body's natural defense against real or imagined danger. It flushes the body with hormones to prepare systems to confront danger. This is known as the **"fight-or-flight or freeze" response.**

Meaning of Stress

The term Stress is derived from the Latin word STRINGERE meaning to draw tight (Arnold, 2005). Stress is body's biological response mechanisms. To understand the meaning of stress, it is useful to state what does not constitute stress:

- Stress is not simply anxiety or nervous tension.
- Stress need not always be damaging.
- Stress is not always due to overwork but may also result from having too little to do.
- Stress cannot be avoided.
- Our body has limited capacity to respond to stressors.

Stress is a stimulus, environmental events (stressors) and/or a threat which affect the body in complex ways. Stress is a bodily reaction to stressors. Stress is also an interaction between environmental events (stressors) and bodily reactions to stressors.

Stresses can be external (from the environment, psychological, or social situations) or internal (illness, or from a medical procedure). Stress can initiate the "fight or flight" response, a complex reaction of neurological and endocrinological systems.

Stress has generally been viewed as a set of neurological and physiological reactions that serves an adaptive function (Franken, 1994).

Stress is an adaptive response to an external situation that results in **physical**, psychological and/or behavioural deviations for organizational participants (Fred Luthans, 1998).

Ivancevich and Matteson have defined stress as, "An adaptive response, medicated by individual characteristics and/or psychological processes, that is a consequence of any external action, situation, or event that place special physical and/or psychological demands upon a person."

Stress is the "psychological, physiological and behavioural response by an individual when they perceive a lack of equilibrium between the demands placed upon them and their ability to meet those demands, which, over a period of time, leads to ill-health" (Palmer, 1989).

According to Selye, an important aspect of stress is that a wide variety of dissimilar situations are capable of producing the stress such as fatigue, effort, pain, fear, and success.

One of the most comprehensive models of stress is the Bio-psychosocial Model of Stress (Bernard & Krupat, 1994). According to the Biopsychosocial Model of Stress, stress involves three components: an external component, an internal component, and the interaction between the external and internal components. The external component of the Biopsychosocial Model of stress involves environmental events. The internal component of stress involves a set of neurological and physiological reactions to stress. The Bio-psychosocial Model of Stress is the interaction between the external and internal components, involving the individual's cognitive processes.

According to the Transaction Theory of Stress, the cognitive appraisal of stress is a two-part process which involves a primary appraisal and a secondary appraisal. Primary appraisal involves the determination of an event as stressful. Secondary appraisal occurs after assessment of the event as a challenge. During secondary appraisal, the individual evaluates one's coping resources and options. Dienstbier (1989) offers a reformulation of the Transaction theory, which focuses on the emotional consequences of appraising an event as a stressor or as a challenge. In a medical or biological context stress is a physical, mental, or emotional factor that causes mental tension.

The Signs of Stress

When we face a stressful event, our bodies respond by activating the nervous system and releasing hormones such as adrenalin and cortical. These hormones cause physical changes in the body which help us to react quickly to get through the stressful situation. This is sometimes called the 'fight or flight' response. The hormones increase our body pains, heart rate, sleeplessness, breathing, perspiration, anxiety, anger, depression, fatigue, blood pressure, dilation of pupils, muscle tension, lack of concentration and lack of confidence. These physical changes help us try to meet out the challenges of the stressful situation. These physical changes may cause other physical or psychological symptoms if the stress is ongoing and the physical changes don't settle down.

Types of Stress

According to American Psychological Association (APA), there are three types of stress—Acute Stress, Episodic Acute Stress, and Chronic Stress. These three types of stress have their own characteristics, symptoms and treatment approaches.

1. Acute stress

Acute stress is the most common type of stress. It is our body's immediate reaction to a new challenge, event or demand and it triggers our fight-or-flight response. Acute stress is not always negative. Isolated episodes of acute stress should not have any lingering health effects. In fact, they might actually be healthy for you, as these stressful situations give your body and brain practice in developing the best response to future stressful situations. Acute stress such as stress as the victim of a crime or life-threatening situation can lead to mental health problems, such as post-traumatic stress disorder or acute stress disorder. Acute stress causes signs and symptoms in the body, brain and emotions, but does not cause the significant amount of damage as Episodic Stress and Chronic stress.

Effects of Acute Stress

Acute stress exists for **short-term** in anyone's life.

It is highly manageable. However, repeated acute stress can become very harmful for our physical and mental health. The most common signs and symptoms of acute stress are:

- Transient Emotional Distress—some combination of anger or irritability or anxiety.
- Transient Muscular Distress—tension, body pain, and other muscular tensions.
- Transient stomach — bowel problems, heartburn, acidity, diarrhea, constipation.

- Transient hyper arousal—high blood pressure, rapid heartbeats, rapid pulse rate, sweaty palms, dizziness, cold hands or feet, shortness of breath, and sleep problems.

2. Episodic Acute Stress

When acute stress happens frequently, it is called episodic acute stress. People who always seem to be having a crisis tend to have episodic acute stress. They are often short-tempered, irritable, and anxious. People who are pessimistic or who tend to see the negative side of everything also tend to have episodic acute stress. It is difficult for people with this type of stress to change their lifestyle, as stress becomes as a part of their life. Episodic acute stress leads to more pronounced health issues such as, high blood pressure and heart disease, and Irritable Bowel Syndrome (IBS). There are two personality types that frequently present with Episodic Acute Stress: (1) "Type A" personality and (2) The "Worrier".

- **"Type A" personality:** Type A personality has an excessive competitive drive, aggressiveness, impatience and a sense of time urgency. These personality traits create frequent episodes of acute stress. Friedman and Rosenman, found 'Type A' personalities to be significantly likely to develop coronary heart disease.
- **The "Worrier":** The Worrier presents with negative thoughts causing episodic acute stress on physical and mental health. "Worry warts" have core beliefs that the world is a dangerous, unrewarding place where something awful is always about to happen. These negative thinkers also tend to be over-aroused and tensed.

Effects of Episodic Acute Stress

The most common signs and symptoms are similar to acute stress, but due to the extended frequent overarousal or extended hyper-arousal there is ongoing damage and suffering. The most common signs and symptoms of **episodic** acute stress are:

- *Emotional distress:* Anger or irritability, anxiety and depression, short-tempered, impatient, tensed.

- *Cognitive distress:* Compromised concentration and mental fatigue.
- *Interpersonal relationships:* Interpersonal relationships deteriorate. The family, society and workplace become very stressful places for them.
- *Muscular distress:* Tension, bodypains and pulled muscles.
- *Physiological Imbalance:* Irritable Bowel Syndrome (IBS), heartburn, acidity, constipation, high blood pressure, rapid heartbeat, sweaty palms, dizziness, cold hands or feet and shortness of breath.
- *Immune System Disorder:* Frequent colds/flu, allergies, asthma, and other immune system illnesses.

3. Chronic Stress

If acute stress is not resolved and lasts for long time, it becomes chronic stress. This stress is constant and does not go away. When an individual lives with chronic stress, his/her behavioural actions and emotional reactions become ingrained. There is change in the hardwiring of the neurobiology of the brain and body. Thereby making them constantly prone to the hazardous stress effects on the body, mind and cognition. Chronic stress is the most harmful type of stress. If chronic stress is left untreated over a long period of time, it can significantly and often irreversibly damage our physical health and mental health.

Effects of Chronic Stress

People with chronic stress have the list of signs and symptoms previously mentioned, but the signs and symptoms are chronic, intense and can result in a physical and mental breakdown that can lead to suicide, violent actions, homicide, psychosis, heart attacks, and strokes. Chronic stress is grinding stress. It wears people away day by day. Chronic stress destroys lives, bodies, and minds. It is the stress of poverty, dysfunctional families, violence, abuse, trauma, ethnic rivalry, war etc.

Management of Stress

Stress management is "the set of techniques and programmes intended to help people deal more effectively with stress in their lives by analysing the specific stressors and taking positive actions to minimize their effects." (Gale Encyclopedia of Medicine).

In the words of William James:

> "The greatest weapon against stress is our ability to choose one thought over another".

Epictetus, the Greek Philosopher, said:

> "Men are disturbed not by things but by the views they take of them".

It is impossible to completely get rid of stress. The goal of stress management is to identify stressors, which are the things that cause the most of the problems. Stress management can be complicated because each of these three types of stress can present as single, repeated, complicated, or chronic. Therefore, they require different levels of treatment interventions, management, and psychological treatment modalities according to the stressors like the nature of the person's environment, lifestyle, developmental history, coping resources and personality. Learning to handle stress in healthy ways is very important. **Stress management** is a wide spectrum of techniques and psychotherapies aimed at controlling a person's level of **stress**, especially chronic **stress**, usually for the purpose of improving everyday functioning.

Recovery from stress requires active self-examination with professional psychological and/or medical help. Psychological treatment is very effective. How we react to a difficult situation will affect. How stress affects our life and our physical and mental health. Being aware of how one reacts to stressors and seeking professional help can help to reduce the effects of stress, and to manage it effectively. If you continue to feel stress, anxious, overwhelmed, panic, worried, then consult with a clinical psychologist who can help you learn how to manage stress effectively. The psychologist can help you identify situations, thoughts, and behaviours that contribute to your stress and anxiety. Treatment will involve developing an action plan to get you healthy.

People with Chronic Stress require extended medical and/or psychological treatment. Chronic stress can be detrimental to one's health, as it can contribute to several serious diseases or health risks, such as heart disease, cancer, lung disease, accidents, suicide etc. People wear down to a fatal breakdown. The chronic stress is difficult to treat. The worst variable of chronic stress is that some people habituate to it. They almost forget it is there. In some ways, one could say it is an adaptation in the form of an ultimate psychological defense mechanism. Individuals with chronic stress frequently ignore the signs and symptoms of the stress because it is old, familiar, and also because often they feel helpless and hopeless. With no hope, the individual gives up searching for solutions/treatment.

The experts recommend the following approaches to manage stress:

I. Action-orientated Approaches

- **Be assertive:** Assert your feelings, opinions, or beliefs instead of becoming angry, defensive or passive, Eat healthy and well-balanced meals, Keep a positive attitude.
- **Reduce the Disturbances:** eat healthy food, Regular exercise and relaxation, take care of yourself.
- **Manage your time:** getting plenty of sleep.

II. Creating Boundaries

Identify Warning Signs, **Emotion-oriented Approaches**

- **Affirmations and Imagery Cognitive Restructuring:** connect socially, as it is easy to isolate yourself after a stressful event, share your thoughts and feelings with others when opportunities arise, take a break from whatever is causing you stress.
- **ABC Technique:** The ABC technique was created by psychologist Dr. Albert Ellis and was later adapted by **Martin Seligman**. The letters ABC stand for: A—Adversity, or the stressful event. B—Beliefs, or the way that you respond to the event. Then C—Consequences.

III. Acceptance-oriented Approaches

- **Diet and Exercise:** Regular meal times, waking and bedtimes.

- Meditation and Physical Relaxation.
- **Build resilience:** Don't rely on alcohol, drugs, find support by talking to other people to get your problems off.

Conclusion

Stress is a part of life and not all stress is bad. Stress is what gives us our fight-or-flight mechanism and has helped us survive for so long. But too much stress is unhealthy. There are many types of stress, from minor incidents that last a little while, to chronic or long-term stress that is ongoing. Stress affects everyone differently but it can lead to a variety of health issues. Managing stress is important to maintaining a healthy and fulfilling life.

References

Abascal, J.R. (2012). *Stress Mastery: The Art of Coping Gracefully*, New Delhi: Jain Book Depot.

Agrawal, Rita (2001). *Stress in Life and Work*, New Delhi: Response Books.

Goel, Aruna (2005). *Stress Management and Education*, New Delhi: Jain Book Depot.

Greenberg, J.S. (2009). *Comprehensive Stress Management*, New Delhi: Jain Book Depot.

Mathur, P. (1999). *Stress in Police in India: Recognition, Diagnosis and Coping Strategies*, New Delhi: Gyan Publishing House.

Saxena, N.S. (1987). *Law and Order in India*, New Delhi: Abhinav Publications.

TYPES OF STRESS

5
Behavioural Stress

Anshu Lochab and *Sunil Kumar*

Human behaviour is complex in nature. The balance of life is governed by our internal milieu constant in this ever changing environment. Though various situations tend to arise different forms of stress responses, there are also individual differences in stress responses attached to the same situation. The more skilled an individual becomes at averting stress before it being a cause of dysfunction, the better would be chances of staying healthy, balanced and happy in life.

Introduction

The prevalence of ancient concept in any culture has an impact on the development of knowledge, especially in the field of psychology. If we go by the ancient Indian literature, two most studied scriptures are: the two Epics *Ramayana* and *Mahabharata*, principal Puranas, major Upanishads, Jataka stories, Jaina stories, and Ocean of stories (Bruhath-Katha-Saritsagara). However, in the last few decades, there has been a large-scale borrowing of eastern concepts in the practice of mental health, which has completely altered the definitions of the concept.

Selye (1956) used the term "stress" to represent the effects of anything that seriously threatens homeostasis. The actual or perceived threat to an organism is referred to as the "stressor" and the response to the stressor is called the "stress response." According to Cropanzano, Howes, Grandey and Toth (1997), stress is a mental feeling when job duties are beyond person's capabilities. These mental feelings create anxiety and tension which are symptoms of stress (p. 164). Although genetic inheritance is responsible for determining individual differences in response to the stimulus. The evolution has provided human beings effective homeostatic mechanisms (e.g., baroreceptor reflex), which is helpful in dealing with short-term stressors. Acute stress response does not cause much harm to a healthy individual. And thus, do not impose a health burden. Contrary to that, in case of an unhealthy individual the effects of the response may lead to health damage. Aggressive effects of chronic stressors are visible in humans, as their high capacity for symbolic thought may cause persistent stress responses to a wide range of adverse living and working conditions. The chapter focuses on behavioural stress, its causes and remedial steps to control the same.

Entities Involved: Individual and Stressors

As per "General Adoption Syndrome", individuals show resistance against stressful conditions. Certain individuals can be tolerant against stress while the others can't. When an individual encounters a stressful environment, general adoption syndrome starts working. At stage one, it is known as "warning". Under such circumstances, an individual feels stress without any reason and find himself in a state of dilemma. If the stressor is strong, the individual is unable to handle it. He will use his both physical and mental power to resist the negative effects of the stress. At stage two, individual starts to resist the effects of the stress factor. Resistance is maximum at this stage. Many a times the stressors die-down at this level only. However, if an individual fails to do so then he enters the third stage of syndrome called exhaustion. Under this stage a person loses all his hope and is not able to encounter the stress. Visible changes in behaviour are dominant at this stage of stress.

Sources of Stress

In 1999, Pestonjee, proposed three important sectors of life from which stress originated:

- job and the organization,
- social sector, and
- intra-psychic sector.

The job and organisation is referred to as an individual's work environment. The social sector reflects the social and cultural frame of one's life. The intra-psychic sector involves intimate things and personal deeds of an individual's life. Physiological responses to stress are automatic and normally we do not have any control over them. Stress bearing capacity varies from one person to another. There are three types of stress which are prevalent, namely, behavioural, emotional and cognitive aspects.

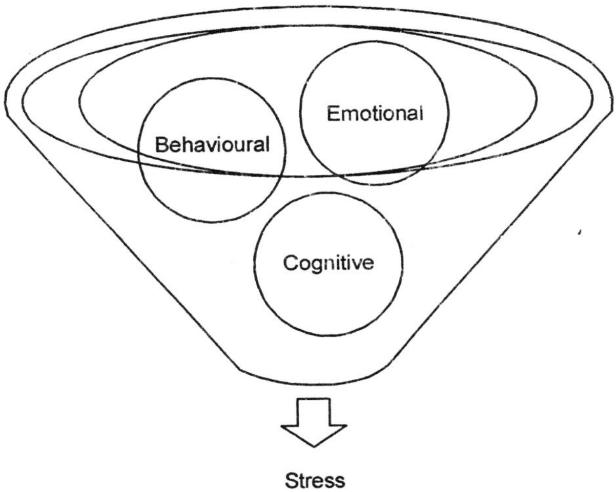

1. **Behavioural Stress:** To activate and intensify biologically significant behaviour, including; eating, aggression and sexual behaviour, mild stress levels are enough to create an impact, followed by moderate stress level, in which an individual's performance is improved. Protection seeking support towards others and better learning attitudes are reflected at this stage. Under acute stress level defensive reactions, suppressed behaviour and immobility.
2. **Emotional Aspects:** The stress responses are related with emotional front of an individual. The stressors under this condition are manageable. In acute state, the stressors are negative and leads to anger, anxiety, discouragement and depression.
3. **Cognitive Stress:** The stressor has been interpreted as threatening to one's well-being or self-esteem, a variety of

intellectual functions get adversely affected. Stress situation at this time interferes with the flexible thinking, attention, the ability to problem solving, the ability of judgment and decision-making, creativity, etc.

Behavioural Stress: Coping up the Complex!

Keeping in view the above mentioned stress aspects, it is being evident that behavioural stress is critical to handle. An individual's life is always governed by social strata. And it is important to note that psychosocial, as well as behavioural forces do not exist within a vacuum; that is, lifestyle behaviours, exposure to stressful life events, the experience of chronic stress and the level of psychological resources are rooted in the socio-structural context of people's lives. With changing health patterns mental, behavioural and substance use disorders are coming to the fore in health care delivery systems. These disorders contribute for significant morbidity, disability and even mortality amongst those affected. Due to the prevailing stigma, these disorders often are hidden by the society and consequently persons with mental disorders lead a poor quality of life. Social determinants of health are categorized here into three broad groups: social structural, behavioural, and psychosocial.

In medical sciences, the term used for behavioural stress is cognitive-behavioural stress (CBS). Normally in psychology we call it behavioural stress. A situation in which an individual faces chronic depression, threaten to undermine even the most resilient coping strategies and overwhelm the most abundant interpersonal resources.

Features of Stressful Environment

Fig. 5.1 concludes the key features of the stress process highlighted from the previous studies conducted. The key indicator of potential stressors includes workplace roles, relationships, and environment. Along with, the responses mediated by organisational, personal and social resources. Behavioural stress is always negative in nature and has a strong impact on the individuals, organisations, co-workers, families and social groups as a whole. Positive interpersonal relations within organisation have a strong positive impact on individual's job satisfaction and organisational commitment.

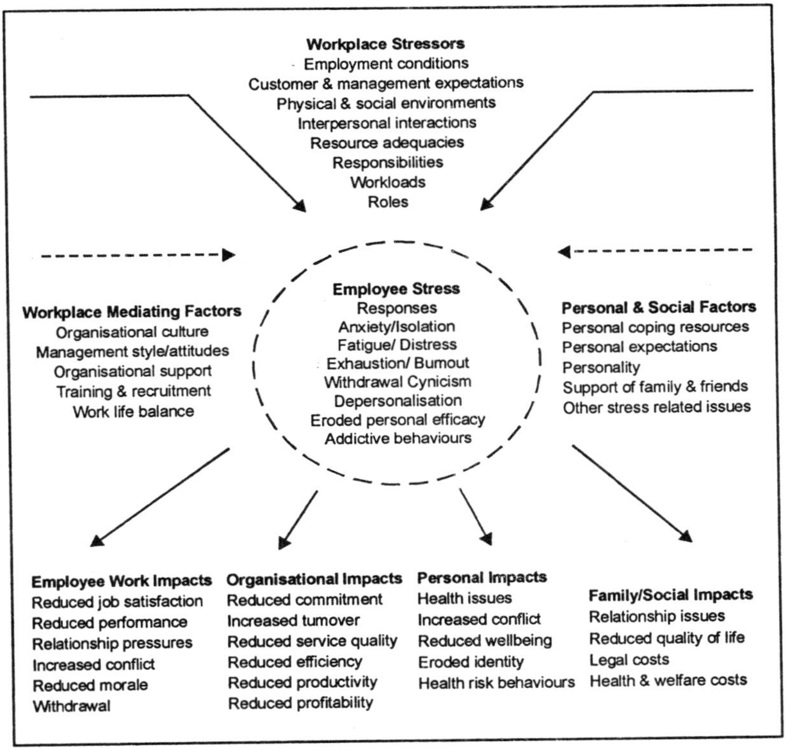

Fig. 5.1: Features of Stressful Environment.

Source: Tiyce, M.; Hing, N.; Cairncross, G. and Breen, H. (2013). "Employee stress and stressors in gambling and hospitality workplaces", *Journal of Human Resources in Hospitality and Tourism*, 12(2): 126-154.

Symptoms and Stress Management Remedies

The common symptoms of behavioural stress include:

- Change in appetite patterns, either not eating or heavy eating.
- Bad mood, mood swings, procrastinating work, avoiding responsibilities.
- Indulged in alcohol, drugs, or cigarettes.
- Demonstrating nervous behaviours, nail biting, fidgeting, and pacing.
- Precede anxiety disorders as well.

With the intervention of psychosocial such as cognitive-behavioural stress management (CBSM) techniques, the quality of life can be improvised to a greater extent. It has been rightly concluded that sooner you spot stress it is easier to manage. It is always advisable to be vigilant with the stress symptoms. There are many ways in which stress is reflected and behavioural stress is most evident of all. It is imperative to be vigilant of the symptoms.

The behavioural symptoms are easy to identify. Few of the common behavioural patterns are mentioned below:

1. **Insomnia:** The most common tell-tale sign of behavioural stress is insomnia. It is difficult for people to sleep and rest completely. They are always in a state of anxiety or lost behaviour. Driven by fear of having forgotten something, negative thought provoking attitude. Along with, energy deficiency during morning hours i.e., not having enough energy to complete the daily chores. Eventually leading to more stressful environment entire day. This tendency of lesser sleep will ultimately be converted into a vicious cycle.
   Remedies: Henceforth, sound sleep is the key component for peaceful mind and sound body. Try not to ignore this symptom and get enough sleep. Proper sleep is the fundamental to avoid behavioural stress.
2. **Absenteeism:** Individuals start skipping important work. They tend to avoid difficult situation or facing people. Absenteeism is quite evident in their behaviour either at workplace or at informal gathering. This doesn't helps an individual rather worsens the situation.
   Remedies: Visit a doctor, seek help from your colleagues in work.
3. **Addictive behaviour:** At times people take easy route to curb a problem into alcohol. Without giving heed to long term consequences, people indulge themselves in alcohol, intake of drugs etc. Individuals find it as the way to get away from any stressful situation but they tend to forget the long term adverse effects. One need to check whether he/she is using that substance to escape your problems and if so, take corrective action. Substance abuse is actually one of the more common behavioural symptoms of stress.
   Remedies: Don't consider addictives as stress releaser.

4. **Suicidal Tendencies:** Stress can damage an individual's confidence and self-respect. The sufferer starts feeling helpless and worthless. Under such conditions, an individual may reflect the symptoms of acute stress but such individuals always feels preoccupied in their thoughts.
   Remedies: Share your problem before it is too late.
5. **Unhealthy eating styles:** Unhealthy eating habits leads to high intake of diet rich in salt, sugar, fat and acids which in turn convert a healthy person into an obese, having high blood pressure and heart related ailments. There are another category of individuals who do not eat at all under such circumstances. They develop suppressed appetite and negative association with food. And this condition is in fact most severe one, as food provides us energy to carry out our daily routine.
   Remedies: Healthy eating habits are often considered as solution to such situations.

Concluding Remarks

Behavioural stress is a very miserable state of an individual's life. In order to understand both life and evolution, stress is the nodal point. Individuals face threats to change knowing the fact that change is the law of nature. It is recommended to prepare oneself for the future task without taking stress. Try to adopt a healthy lifestyle including effective sleep and good eating habits. An individual cannot live in isolation, discussing one's problems or dilemmas with people in vicinity may reduce the consequences of acute stress level. Consult Psychiatrists well in time. Try to live a good life, free yourself from all kinds of burden.

References

Cannon, W.B. (1929). *Bodily Changes in Pain, Hunger, Fear and Rage*. 2nd ed. New York: Appleton.

Chung, Y.W. (2018). "Workplace ostracism and workplace behaviours: A moderated mediation model of perceived stress and psychological empowerment", *Anxiety, Stress and Coping*, *31*(3): 304-317.

Colligan, T.W. and Higgins, E.M. (2006). "Workplace stress: Etiology and consequences", *Journal of Workplace Behavioural Health*, *21*(2): 89-97.

Cropanzano, R.; Howes, J.; Grandy, A. and Toth, P. (1997). "The Relationship of Organizational Politics and Support to Organizational behaviours, Attitudes and Stress", *Journal of Organizational Behaviour*, 159-180.

Jahanian, R.; Tabatabaei, S.M. and Behdad, B. (2012). "Stress management in the workplace", *International Journal of Academic Research in Economics and Management Sciences*, *1* (6), 1.

Moorhead, G. and Griffin, R.W. (1995). *Organizational Behaviour: Managing People and Organization*. Boston: Houghton Mifflin Company.

Schneiderman N.; Antoni M.H.; Saab P.G. and Ironson G. (2001). "Health psychology: Psychosocial and biobehavioural aspects of chronic disease management", *Annu. Rev. Psychol*, 52:555–580.

Schneiderman, N. (1983). "Pathophysiology in animals", In: Dembroski, T.M.; Schmidt, T.H. and Blümhen, G. (Eds.) *Biobehavioural Bases of Coronary Heart Disease*, Basel: Karger, pp. 304-364.

Selye, H. (1956). *The Stress of Life*, New York: McGraw-Hill.

Tiyce, M.; Hing, N.; Cairncross, G. and Breen, H. (2013). "Employee stress and stressors in gambling and hospitality workplaces", *Journal of Human Resources in Hospitality and Tourism*, *12*(2): 126-154.

6
Acute Stress

Mujibul Hasan Siddiqui and *Aktar Ali*

Introduction

Stress is as old as human being but now-a-days it has forced us to think about its gravity because the present century has become the century of stress due to various reasons. The fast paced lifestyle demands of the people make them under pressure. This pressure ultimately leads the vast majority of people to stress. This stress causes various problems in human being such as anxiety, depression, tension etc. Different people take the meaning of this word in their own ways such as management consultants take it in terms of organizational challenges; psychologists use this word in terms of behaviour and doctors talk about this word in terms of mechanism. Each and every individual has to face it throughout his/her life. One of the special characteristics of life is stress. Various reasons are there which are responsible for the widen presence of stress in human being such as multiple interactions of human with surrounding issues and the complexity of human social personal and ecological environment. In psychological point of view, stress is nothing but a feeling of mental pressure and tension. Stress might be desired and useful when the level of stress is low. Stress might be positive if it facilitates performance. Stress may help in motivation and adjustment to environment when it is positive. Stress having high intensity causes various physiological, social and psychological impacts. Severity of stress is also responsible for different, emotional problems such as negative feelings, mental pressure, anxiety and sadness. Usually we experience threat that may be physical or psychological which is perceived immediately. This kind of threat is responsible for stress. It is not necessary that these threats would be having high intensity that may such as new assignment at workplace.

Among the various types of stress, acute stress is important one which is not so damaging. Sometimes it may be serious as for example frequent occurrence of acute stress may lead to chronic stress. Stress is a psychological matter which occurs from the reaction to a disturbing change or threat in the environment. Various psychological and physiological changes occur due to stress. These changes sometimes lead to other problems or severe diseases such as post-traumatic disorder, acute stress disorder etc. Stress is a state or condition that leads to physical or mental disturbance of an individual. In other words, we can say that stress is a kind of mechanism which helps all animals to survive in the world.

Meaning of Acute Stress

There are various types of stress. Acute stress is the most common one. Acute stress is a kind of stress which an individual can experience due to demands and pressures of the near past and future. Generally, acute stress lasts no longer, if it lasts longer than one month, it may lead to other severe problems. There is a short term stress which can cause headache, upset and other symptoms. An important characteristic of acute stress is that it arrives quickly and also does not last longer.

Symptoms of Acute Stress

The symptoms of acute stress can be recognized by most of the people. The most common symptoms are as follows:

- Negative thoughts, sadness and low mood etc. which are called negative mood symptoms of acute stress.
- Insomnia or other sleep disturbance, difficulty in concentrating, irritability, aggression, mental health disorder, anxiety and depression, these symptoms are called arousal symptoms.
- Excessive worrying, fatigue, restlessness, persisting feeling of hopelessness, crying unexpectedly, loss of interest in activities, thought of suicide etc.
- Blood pressure, problems of breath, rapid heartbeat, dizziness, back pain, jaw pain etc.

- Acid stomach, constipation, heartburn, gut, bowel and stomach problems.
- Tension, headache, diarrhoea, chest pain, and cold hand and feet.

All the above mentioned symptoms might be developed within a few minutes or hours. Sometimes these symptoms may persist more than one or two weeks.

Causes of Acute Stress

People can develop acute stress excessive tension and pressures near past and future or from one or more traumatic events. Significant physical, emotional, or psychological harm are caused due to traumatic events. There are various causes of acute stress which are as follows:

The Death of a Loved One

Death of the loved one is one of the important causes of acute stress. At the time of death of closest one an individual can experience emotional shock, sadness, loneliness, anxiety and tension. At this time, he/she needs mental support otherwise acute stress might be developed and finally it may lead to other severe physiological and psychological problems.

Serious Injury

This is another cause of acute stress. If a person experiences serious injury, he may develop fears, anxiety, and tension about his future and all these things help in developing acute stress within a person.

Overload of Work

Overload of work or pressure of work is also responsible for acute stress. When a person feels extra pressure or any work that is imposed upon him without considering his capacity and interest, he may experience acute stress. Sometimes, overworking also leads to acute stress.

Natural Disaster

There are various natural disasters such as earthquake, floods, forest fire, cyclone etc. At the time of natural disaster people become anxious and nervous about their food and shelter and also about their future that finally leads to acute stress. These natural calamities create too much stress and anxiety for those who are directly or indirectly affected. At this time people may feel fear and anxiety about future, disorientation, difficulty in making decision, irritability, anger, sadness, powerless and difficulty in sleeping. All these things are responsible for acute stress directly or indirectly.

Motor Vehicle Accidents

Although road conditions, driver education and vehicle safety have been improved, millions of people are facing the problems of road accidents and getting injured. Many of these people experience acute stress after facing accident. Acute stress resulting from motor vehicle accidents may have persisting disabling effects also.

Remedial Measures

Delegation of Work

Delegation of work to some individuals or subordinates plays a very important role in reducing stress, tension and anxiety to make the individuals free from stress and anxiety. There should not be any kind of rigidity, a person should have. For example a manager should not work all the work himself; he can delegate to a subordinate.

Relaxation

Relaxation is the another way to make the individuals free from stress and anxiety. There should not be any kind of rigidity; a person should have freedom to what he wants to do according to his capacity and interest.

Meditation

Meditation is an effective way of coping with stress. An individual will get physical and mental well-being if he engages himself in regular meditation and ultimately this kind of meditation helps in disconnecting an individual from stress and anxiety. Meditation also helps in sound sleep that refreshes body and mind and finally helps in avoiding stress.

Regular Exercise

There is another way to cope with stress and anxiety that is regular exercise, we should engage in moderate exercise regularly that will help in enhancing immune system and reducing the risk of developing stress.

Healthy Diet

Healthy diet also plays an important role in coping with stress. To enhance the ability to cope with stress we should take healthy diet that means balanced diet that will make our immune system strong.

Sound Sleep

Without uninterrupted and sound sleep an individual cannot be stress free. Seven to eight hours uninterrupted sound sleep helps in refreshing our body and mind. It is rightly said that healthy mind lies in healthy body that means if we are mentally and physically strong, that will make us free from stress and anxiety.

Express Yourself

There are various ways to express yourself e.g., writing, painting, passing time with friends and family, and watching movies etc. We should look for humour and comics in stressful situation that also helps us to be free from stress.

There are other many ways to deal with acute stress which are as follows:

If anyone experiences acute stress he should talk with his family members and spend his leisure time with them and his friends. Sharing feelings and experiences with closest ones helps in reducing acute stress and one can get some suggestion from them how to come out from the stressful situation, he should avoid aloofness.

When a person is in stressful situation he should get help from reliable people and from whom he can get valuable advice and financial support when he is in need.

Acute stress is nothing, more or less most of the people experience acute stress in their lives, if the symptoms of acute stress lasts longer than one month, he should consult with professional counsellor otherwise it may lead to acute stress disorder or other severe mental and physical problems.

There are various creative activities which help a person to come out of the stressful situation such as drawing, painting, singing and writing article in journal and newspaper. These creative activities help to express one's feelings, experiences and memories.

Everybody should have sense of humour that plays a very important role in reducing stress. Only a trifle word can make someone free from tension in a stressful situation, only a person can do this who is having sense of humour.

A person who is experiencing acute stress should ensure that whether he/she is taking balanced diet or nutritious foods, doing exercise everyday etc. Because these help in reducing acute stress and he should avoid alcohol totally if he wants be free from acute stress.

On the basis of above discussion we can draw a conclusion that every person experiences stress in his/her life and it is also important because it not only creates problem in our lives and leads to various diseases sometimes it is also healthy and fruitful. It also motivates us, we can put a example here that students should have stress at the time of examination otherwise they will not study sincerely or they will take it lightly if they are stress free regarding their exams. Lastly, we can say that stress in somewhat is required in our lives but when it exceeds its limits it becomes unhealthy and it is suggestive that we should keep in our mind various remedial measures and strategies mentioned above of managing stress so that we can cope with stress.

References

American Psychiatric Association. *Diagnostic and Statistical Manual of Mental Disorders,* Fifth Edition. Arlington, VA: American Psychiatric Association; 2013. 280-6.

American Psychological Association. (2011). Stress: The different kinds of stress.

Amir Mohammad Shahsavarani, Esfandiar Azad Marz Abadi, Maryam Hakimi Kalkhoran (2015), "Stress: Facts and Theories through Literature Review", *International Journal of Medical Reviews*, Volume 2, Issue 2.

Australian Psychological Society (2012). Understanding and Managing Stress, www.Psychology.org.au

Bisson JI, Deahl MP (1994). Psychological debriefing and prevention of post-traumatic stress. More research is needed. *Br. J. Psychiatry*. Dec. 165(6):717-20. [Medline].

Dismukes, K.R.; Goldsmith, T.E. and Kochan, J.A. (2015). *Effects of Acute Stress on Aircrew Performance: Literature Review and Analysis of Operational Aspects*, NASA/TM 201-5 218930

file:///C:/Users/user/Downloads/StressManagementChapter-Broman-FulksKelso.pdf

http://www.dartmouth.edu/~ajordan/papers/Litz,%20Hundert,%20&%20Jordan %20-%20ASD%20entry.pdf

http://www.douglas.qc.ca/info/stress-causes-and-consequences

https://ada.com/conditions/acute-stress-disorder/

https://en.wikipedia.org/wiki/Acute_stress_reaction#Causes

https://medical-dictionary.thefreedictionary.com/acute+stress+disorder

https://stress.lovetoknow.com/Define_Acute_Stress

https://www.apa.org/helpcenter/stress-kinds

https://www.apa.org/topics/health-disparities/stress.pdf

https://www.atsdr.cdc.gov/emes/surviving_stress/documents/TrainingWorkbook stress-editp1.pdf

https://www.disorders.org/anxiety/acute-stress-disorder/

https://www.medicalnewstoday.com/articles/324354.php

https://www.mhanational.org/coping-disaster

https://www.slideshare.net/hemanthcrpatna/stress-management-in-bpo

https://www.verywellmind.com/all-about-acute-stress-3145064

LeBlanc, V.R (2009). The Effects of Acute Stress on Performance: Implications for Health Professions Education, *Academic Medicine*, 84, 10.

McGnagle, K.A. and Kessler, R.C. (1990). "Chronic Stress, Acute Stress and Depressive Symptoms", *American Journal of Community Psychology*, 18, 5.

United Nations—Department of Peace Keeping Operations (1995)—United Nations Stress Management Booklet.

World Health Organization (2013). *Guidelines for the Management of Conditions Specially Related to Stress.*

7
Chronic Stress

Shaila Bi and *Poonam Chauhan*

The modern world, which is said to be a world of success, is also a world of tension or stress. Whether it is a family or an organizationţ economic, social, or politicalţ we can see stress everywhere. The human is inevitably subjected to numerous stressful situations right from the time of birth to the last day of life.

Source: http://bit.ly/33omgZx

In our everyday lives, stress is a regular part but remember not all stress is negative. Many people see stress as something that is happening to them, an occurrence such as trauma or loss of job. Some believe that stress may affect our mind, body, and behaviour in reaction to an incident (example—worry, heart beating fast, and hypertension). The critical factor is our ideas and thoughts about the circumstances in which we are in. We automatically evaluate the situation mentally if something happening to us. Stress can arise from anything that makes you feel annoyed, upset, or worried. Everyone has a different view of circumstances and different coping abilities. Therefore, no two individuals will react to a given situation exactly like the same way as others did. In addition, not all situations known as "stressful" are negative.

Stress is when your body responds to certain threats or situations of any kind. If you feel danger — whether it is real or imagined — the defense system of the body kicks into high gear in a rapid and automatic process which is known as the "fight-or-flight" reaction or the "stress reaction." The response to stress is the way your body protects you. It helps you remain concentrated, energetic, and alert when working properly. Stress can be helpful to act quickly in emergencies, for example, by giving one more power to protect oneself and pressing the brakes to avoid a car accident.

Stress is subjective in nature because when something is stressful to you might not be stressful to someone else. For example, cooking can be a lot of stress to some but pleasant to others. We may think that circumstances are "stressful" because we do not feel ready to deal with them. In small amounts; stress can be good, it can motivate you and help you become more productive. But, it can be harmful to have too much stress.

Stress: Concept and Definitions

The root of the concept of stress predates ancient times. It is derived from the Latin word "Stringere." Stress was widely used in the seventeenth century to mean suffering, struggle, hardship, or illness. This was used in the eighteenth and nineteenth centuries, referring to an object or individual, to indicate pressure, force, strain, or strong effort. Stress can be called as pressure or it is the pressure that creates tension. It always gives an unpleasant feeling. Cannon (1929) was the first who used the word "stress." He suggested both the physiological and psychological aspects of this stress.

In life sciences, Hans Selye (1936) was the first who presented the idea of stress. "Stress like relatively, is a scientific concept which has suffered from the mixed blessing of being too well known and too little understood" (Selye, 1956). Mason (1975) defines stress as a state wherein expected functioning gets disrupted. Morse and Furst (1979) defined, "Stress is a mental or emotional, disruptive or disquieting influence of distress." This definition and the idea of most people is that stress is a negative or destructive outcome. "Stress is considered a reaction to a situation that requires the individual to adapt to a change physically or psychologically" (Chatterjee, 1992).

The term 'stress' is defined differently by Selye (1979) as referred to "(a) stimulus (external forces acting on the organism), (b) response (changes in physiological and psychological functions), (c) interaction (between an external force and the resistance opposed to it as in biology), and (d) more comprehensive combinations of the above factors (i.e. stimulus, response and interactional outcomes)".

The most common and popular definition of stress is "physical, mental, or emotional pressure or tension." Psychologists define stress as the body's reaction to a change that requires a physical, emotional, or mental adjustment or response. In other words, you feel unable to deal with the demands that are being made on you, and this causes you to respond negatively.

All Stress is Bad?

Stress is not all bad. Indeed, some stress increases your senses and help you to act quickly for avoiding an accident, or meeting an unexpected deadlines, and keeping your mind clear in high pressured situations. This is the response of "fight-or-flight" that your body triggers in times of compulsion. However, stress is supposed to be temporary. After the situation has passed, your body should go back to its natural state. Your heart rate should be steady, your muscles will relax, and you should return to normal breathing.

Modern life's pressures and demands can put your body in a heightened state for a long time, making it hard to work your heart and close your blood vessels longer than your body can handle. These physiological demands can take your body toll over time.

Chronic Stress

As already stated, Chronic stress is the form of stress that is most dangerous. When chronic stress is not treated for a long time, it can drastically damage your physical well-being and also weaken your mental well-being. The opposite of acute stress is chronic stress; it is not interesting and enjoyable, but it is harmful and unhealthy. When acute stress is not addressed, it becomes chronic stress which tends to increase or lasts for long periods. This stress is continuous and is not going away. Long-term exposure to stressors, such as unemployment, unhappy marriage, long-term poverty, broken families, political issues, chronic diseases, and relationship disputes triggers this type of stress. Some chronic stresses can be caused by aversive experiences in childhood or traumatic experiences in later life, and that have developed a belief system that causes the stress sufferer to see the world as a threatening and dangerous place. Usually, the person with chronic stress considers that there is no end to their miserable condition and gives up searching for solutions.

The physical behaviours and emotional reactions become rooted when a person lives under the chronic stress. The hard wiring of the brain and body's neurobiology is changing. There, we are continually susceptible to the dangerous effects of stress on the mental mind + body + cognitive irrespective of the circumstances. People with chronic stress have a number of signs and symptoms listed above, but the signs and symptoms are never-ending and it may contribute to a physical and mental deterioration that can lead to murder, heart attacks, psychosis, suicide, strokes, and acts of violence.

Chronic stress is the stress of grinding. Day after day, year after year, it wears people away. Chronic stress is damaging minds, bodies, and lives. Through long-term attrition, it causes havoc. It is the stress of trauma, poverty, families with dysfunction, despised job, violence, ethnic rivalry, abuse, and war. Chronic stress can result in suicide, violence, heart attacks, stroke, and cancer. These stressful situations appear to be endless, and the accumulated stress resulting from exposure to them may be life-threatening and may even lead a person to resort to violent actions, self-harm, and suicide. Serious diseases such as heart attack, stroke, cancer, and psychological issues like post-traumatic disorder and clinical depression may be caused by chronic stress.

Like acute stress, which is new and often has an immediate solution, chronic stress can go unnoticed, because individuals have become get used to it. It can become part of the personality of an individual, making them constantly prone to stress effects irrespective of the situations they face.

Stress is a biological response to challenging situations. It causes hormones to be released by the body, like adrenaline and cortisol. These stress released hormones help to prepare the body for action example, by increased breathing and heart rates. When this happens, a doctor may describe a person in a condition of increased excitement or alertness. Several factors may cause a response to stress, includes psychological pressure and hazardous situations like examinations, sports events, and work deadlines. Usually, the stress's physical effects do not last long. Some people find themselves in an almost constant state of increased alertness. That's all called chronic stress.

Causes

In our modern lifestyle, this type of chronic stress response occurs too frequently. From a high-pressure job to loneliness to crowded traffic, everything can hold the body in a state of perceived danger and chronic stress. Besides, an excessive amount of stress may result in a severe emotional burden. Although individuals may overcome or resolve the small incidents of stress by entering into the natural defenses of their body to adjust to changing circumstances, prolonged chronic stress, which is continuous, and persist for a long time, may affect our body physically and psychologically.

Like the stressors of daily life, when chronic stress is neglected for a long time or managed poorly, it can lead to a serious traumatic event. Chronic stress disrupts almost all systems of your body. There are serious effects of chronic stress; especially it can weaken your immune system, increase the risk of stroke and heart attack, disrupt your reproductive or digestive system, and accelerate your aging process. Researches indicate that stress could lead to serious diseases, such as anxiety, obesity, depression, and heart disease. Several research studies have even indicated that improper handling of chronic stress, like over-eating of "comfort" foods, has lead to an increased risk of obesity problems. People who suffer from anxiety and depression are twice as likely to die with heart disease other than the people who are not suffering from these conditions. Yet, despite its association with disease, APA's Stress in America study disclosed that 33 per cent of Americans never talk to their health care supplier about their ways of managing the stress.

We all respond differently to our stressful circumstances. Everyone has their own way of reacting to a difficult situation. Situation which is stressful to you may not be stressful to the other person. Even a little thing can lead to stress. Simply talking about something or other small things may cause stress to some people.

Commonly major events in life that can cause stress are:

- **A bad work-life balance:** Stress can be caused by unmanaged employment. Feeling dissatisfied with how much time you spend at work and neglecting other aspects of life because of your job can increase your susceptibility to stress. Increased stress levels can lead to burn-out or more severe mental health issues if not addressed early.
- **Family problems:** All, who live in families, experience stress due to household tasks and responsibilities. Hill (1949) suggested the ABC-X model to study the process of family stress. A family is a state of extreme disorganization that faces a state of crisis.
- **Financial difficulties:** Money plays an important role in life. The problem of lacking money puts enormous pressure on us. According to the American Psychological Association (APA), 72 per cent of adults reported feeling stress about money at least sometimes and nearly 22 per cent say they have extreme stress about their finances.
- **Death:** The death of a loved one is the most traumatic and stressful event in life and it may contribute to a severe emotional crisis. You undergo bereavement after the death of someone you love, which means "being robbed of life." The circumstances of death affect your emotions, particularly when it's unexpected or accidental. Your emotions are also affected by the relationship you have with the person who died.
- **Poverty:** Poverty is a chronic stressor that can lead to mental and physical problems. Studies from low and middle income countries showed a correlation between measures of poor health and socio-economic status (SES) such as employment, food insecurity, shelter, social class, and financial stress.
- **Migration:** Migrants are people who come to live for work in a foreign country. They are often exposed to a specific risk of problems related to mental health, primarily related to vulnerability to stressful or painful situations, including urban violence, racial discrimination, forced removal and separation from their families, harassment by law

enforcement officers, incarceration or reclusion, and/or expulsion.

- **Illness:** A long term of illness can lead to chronic stress. A chronic illness may never go away and can disrupt your life and your family life. It can also affect your ability to do work.
- **Relationship stress:** During moments when we feel stressed, relationships are a great support. Nevertheless, people around you, whether you are a wife, child, mother, colleague or friend, may increase your level of stress from time to time. Challenging relationships, unhappy marriage and larger family crises like death, affair or illness, etc. are the factors that probably affect the way how you behave, think, and feel. Therefore, these factors may affect your stress levels. Even if a relationship is no longer good, a break-up or divorce can be extremely painful as it reflects the failure not only of the partnership, but also of the hopes and promises that you have made to each other.
- **Pregnancy:** During pregnancy, feeling stressed is normal. But you may be frustrated with too much pressure. Stress can cause sleeping problems, nausea, loss of appetite and overeating. Some stress-related hormones may play a role in pregnancy-related complications. Severe and constant chronic stress can influence the immune system, which helps in protecting you from infection. This could increase the risk of uterine disease. This type of infection can result in premature birth.
- **Cataclysmic stress:** These factors or major life events tend to occur suddenly and affect many people simultaneously (e.g. plane crashes, derailment, accident, etc.) are called cataclysmic factors or stressors. Such kind of stressors are trapped by Holmes and Rahe (1967).
- **Overcrowded, Excessive Noise and Pollution:** High traffic roads are a very important source of these. Research has shown that older adults living in areas with high-traffic relation pollution are more likely to suffer from Alzheimer's disease than people living in cleaner locations.

The pressure of chronic stress on the human body lasts for a longer time, which can cause several symptoms and increases the risk of certain illnesses. Some situations affect some people in an entirely different way than others. Some of the experiences of the past may affect how people respond. But, many times there is no particular cause. Problems of mental health such as anxiety, depression, or frustration make some people feel more stressed as compared to others.

After a traumatic event like an accident or some kind of violence, people experience ongoing stress. This is referred to as post-traumatic stress disorder (PTSD). People who are working in stressful employment, such as the emergency services and armed forces, they will have a medical screening session after a significant event and should be supervised for PTSD.

Signs and Symptoms

Stress is the most dangerous thing that it can easily get on you, and you are getting used to this. In the beginning, it feels familiar and even ordinary. But it affects your whole body when it does not get into notice. Various physical or psychological signs may render it more difficult to function regularly. So, it is important to know the various signs and symptoms of chronic stress. The severity of symptoms will vary greatly from person to person.

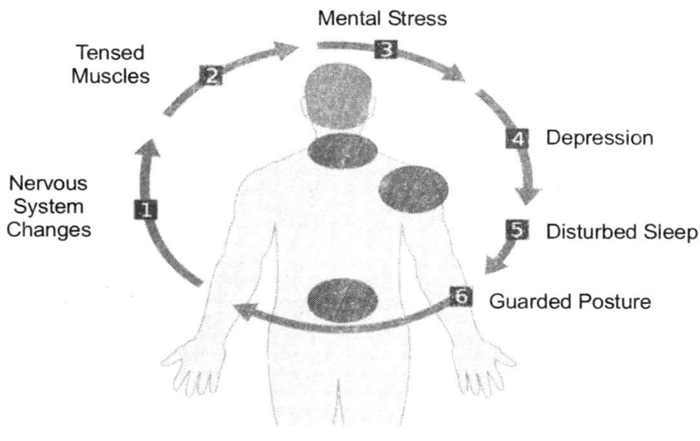

Fig.: Chronic Pain Management.

Source: http://bit.ly/2Iq6xkq

Physical symptoms of stress can include:

- headache.
- diaphoresis.
- diabetes.
- back pain and chest pain.
- erectile dysfunction and libido loss.
- spasms of the muscles and cramps.
- ulcers.
- fainting.
- dry mouth.
- high blood pressure.
- difficulty in breathing.
- diseases related to heart.
- diarrhea or constipation.
- aches in the muscles.
- twitching.
- frequent urination.
- needles and pins.
- lower immunity against diseases.
- frequent cold or flu.
- difficulty in sleeping/insomnia.
- stomach aches.
- fertility problems.
- low sex desire.
- irregular menstrual periods.

Research suggested that stressors faced by parents, such as economic problems or running a single parent family, may contribute to obesity in their kids.

Emotional symptoms of stress can include:

- moodiness or anger.
- anxiety.
- a sense of insecurity.
- burnout.
- low self-esteem.
- depression.
- withdrawing from friends.
- forgetfulness.

- nail biting.
- sadness.
- irritability, which can be extreme.
- restlessness.

Behavioural symptoms of stress can include:

- sudden anger outbursts.
- food cravings or eat too little or too much food.
- increased use of drugs, alcohol or smoking.
- social withdrawal.
- crying frequently.
- neglecting or delaying duties and responsibilities.
- issues in the relationships.
- hygiene and appearance deterioration.
- avoiding eye contact.
- childishness.
- changes in appetite.

Cognitive symptoms of stress can include:

- tension.
- difficulty in concentration/contemplation.
- confusion.
- memory problems.
- seeing only the negative.
- avoidance.
- narrowed perception.
- frequent feelings of fatigue.
- disorganized thoughts.
- constant worrying.
- difficulty in decision making.

Diagnosis

Normally, a doctor can diagnose stress by asking question to their patients about their life events and symptoms. It is a complicated diagnosis. It can rely on a lot of variables. Questionnaire, biochemical measurements, and physiological methods will be used, but they may not be either objective or successful. A comprehensive, stress oriented, and face to face interview is the most direct method of diagnosing stress and its impact on a person.

Treatment

When an individual never finds a way out from a difficult condition, over almost a long period he experiences stress over unrelenting demands and pressures. The person would give up looking for answers without any hope. Following a balanced diet plan that makes you healthy. Your health is largely based on your thoughts, body, mind, feelings and emotions, and environment.

Treatment involves self-help and certain medicines in situations where stress is caused by an inherent state. When the self-help technique is not helping you in reducing the stress, it is very important to consult with the doctor for the help of advice. Aromatherapy, reflexology, and Cognitive Behavioural Therapy (CBT) are the therapies that the doctor may suggest, and that can help to induce relaxation. One of the CBT defined goals is to help an individual to cope with chronic stress. A therapist works in structured sessions to allow an individual to change their habits, ideas, and emotions about stressors. CBT can also assist an individual develop tools to handle stress reactions and coping processes. A doctor also suggests medications to help treat certain signs of chronic stress.

Medicines

Generally, the doctors will not prescribe medicines to cope with the stress, if the person has an inherent illness, like depression or any form of anxiety. The doctor will treat a mental illness in that situation and the stress. Sometimes, doctors may prescribe an antidepressant to treat this illness. But there is a danger for using these medicines because these only help in hiding the stress rather than to cope or deal with it. Adverse effects may also be associated with antidepressants. Doctors can prescribe sedatives for people with sleeping difficulties.

Before stress hits, developing some strategies to cope with stress can help a person handle new circumstances and maintain physical and mental health. There is a need for medical assistance when you are experiencing a vast amount of stress.

How Chronic Stress Affects Your Body?

Cardiovascular and Respiratory Systems

Stress hormones affect the cardiovascular and respiratory system. You breathe rapidly during the stress response in an attempt to deliver oxygen rich blood to your body quickly. A person without respiratory disease, stress is generally not the problem and the body can manage the work of breathing properly. But the people who have already breathing problems such as emphysema and asthma, stress can make breathing more difficult. During the stress, the heart pumps at a faster rate. Stress hormones allow your blood vessels to contract and deliver more oxygen to your muscles so that you have enough energy to function. Yet, it also increases the blood pressure.

Prolonged or frequent experience of chronic stress will make your heart can work too hard for too long. So the risk of having a heart attack and stroke can be high when the blood pressure increases.

Central Nervous and Endocrine Systems

Our central nervous system is responsible for the reaction of "fight or flight." During the time of stress, the hypothalamus a series of nuclei that link the brain and endocrine system, asking your adrenal glands to increase the production of adrenaline and cortisol hormones. Such hormones restore your heart-beat and carry blood to the areas that most need it in an emergency, like your heart, lungs, and other vital organs. The hypothalamus must instruct all the system to return to normal when the perceived stress is gone. When the nervous system is not going to return to normal or if the stressor does not go down than the response will begin.

Often, chronic stress is a factor that changes in behaviour like eat too much or too little, drug, and addiction to alcohol and isolation from society.

Musculoskeletal System

When you are stressed, your muscles are tensed to be protected from injury. Once you relax, they begin to release again, but if you're under constant stress your muscles may not have the opportunity to relax. Tighten muscle are responsible for body aches, pain in shoulder and

and back, and headaches. This can begin a harmful process over time when you stop doing exercise and turn to control your pain through medication. Stress-reducing exercises have been shown to improve mood and everyday activity for those who have chronic pain conditions.

Digestive System

During stress, the liver produces excessive blood sugar (glucose) to give you an energy boost. With the increase in excess glucose, the body may not be able to cope with when you are under chronic stress. Hence, there is a risk of increasing type 2 diabetes. The digestive system may also be disrupted by fast breathing, increased heart rate, and hormone surge. Because of a rise in stomach acid, heartburn and acid reflux are more likely to occur. Stress does not cause ulcers (a bacterium also named as *H. pylori* does), but it can increase your risk to them and triggers the action of current ulcers.

Stress can make it easier to feel pain, bloating, nausea, and other abdominal irritation. Vomiting can occur when stress is serious enough. It can also influence how quickly food moves through your body which can be resulting in either diarrhea or constipation.

Immune System

Stress activates the immune system, which can be a benefit for emergency cases. Such activation can be helpful in their diseases and cure wounds. Yet stress hormones will weaken your immune system over time and decrease the response of your body to foreign invaders. Individuals suffering from chronic stress, or any other illnesses, are more susceptible to viral diseases such as common cold or flu. Stress may also increase the time you need to heal from disease and injury.

Reproductive System

Stress for both mind and body is very exhausting. If you are under intense stress, it is not unusual to lose your desire. Although short term stress can trigger men to release more male hormone testosterone, this impact is not lasting. But if the stress is going on an extended period, it can affect the production of testosterone leading to a decrease in sex drive and libido and may even be caused by impotence and erectile dysfunction. Chronic stress can have a negative impact on the development and maturation of sperm creating problems for couples who are trying to conceive. It can also increase the risk of being infected male reproductive organs such as the testes, prostate and urethra.

For women and adolescent girls, stress can influence the cycle of menstruation in a number of ways. For example, a high-stress rate can lead to absent or irregular, more painful, heavier periods, and change in duration of cycle. Chronic stress may have a major impact on the reproductive plans of a female. It may adversely affect the ability of a woman to conceive, her childbirth's well-being, and her postpartum adjustment. Depression is the main symptom of complications in pregnancy. Chronic stress may also magnify menopause physical symptoms.

How to Manage Your Stress?

Chronic stress may seem overwhelming, and an individual may feel unable to regain control over his lives. There are several strategies that can help to reduce the stress level and improve overall well-being.

There are some methods for preventing or managing the stress which includes:

Understand the signs and symptoms: An individual may be so worried about the issue that causes stress and that they do not realize how they impact on their body.

The first stage to take intervention is to notice signs. These signs and symptoms of stress may vary from individual to individual, but if an individual recognizes their stress signals then they can handle them better. People who have experienced long hours of job stress may require "take a step back." It might be the time to check their work practices or discussing with the manager about reducing the burden.

Exercise: Physical activity improves the output of endorphins in the body, which are chemical substances that enhance the mood and decrease stress. Exercise may include jogging, walking, working out, running, cycling, or practicing sports. Research studies show that exercise may improve the physical and mental condition of a person.

Nutrition: In moments of stress, a good and healthy balanced diet with lots of vegetables and fruits are helping in maintaining the immune system of our body. A poor diet is going to result in ill health and extra stress.

Reduce consumption of drugs, caffeine, and alcohol: The consumption of these substances is not going to help out from the stress but it makes the situation more badly. So, the intake of all these things is supposed to be reduced or cut out.

Talking: Talking about your ideas and concerns with family, friends, peers, and your boss will assist you "let off steam." You might be comforted to discover that you are "not the only one." Talking to others helps out in finding that there is an easy solution that you are never heard of.

Prioritizing: Take some time to organize the list to see that what is important to you. Then concentrate on what you have done or finished for the day instead of what you still need to complete.

Time: Take out sometime for yourself everyday. Take time to organize and relax your life, or pursuing your own desires and interests.

Relaxing and Breathing: *Yoga*, massage, and meditation may help you in reducing stress. The techniques of relaxing and breathing are very helpful in slowing down the body system and make you feel relaxed. Breathing is also a key component of meditation.

Look for your destressor: Generally, most of the individuals have something to help them relax, like reading a book, listening to songs, spend some quality time with your friends or a pet, and go for a walk. Some individuals are helped by joining a choir or a gym.

Detection of causes: Stress causes cannot always be stopped. So, we should take notes of specific causes that trigger stress and help an individual to develop some strategies for dealing and coping with the stress.

Trying mindfulness: It is mind and body techniques that help us to respond differently to experiences. This means that paying attention to our thoughts and feelings without judging them is a way which increases our sense; so that we can handle a difficult situation and make a decision wisely. Individual who practices meditation uses the techniques of breathing and thinking for creating an awareness of their environment and body. Studies indicates that mindfulness plays a positive role in reducing the effects of stress, depression, and anxiety and also helps in improving the quality and quantity of sleep of those individual who have a problem of insomnia.

According to a 2009 American Psychological Association (APA) study, people recommended by their health specialist to create changes in their lifestyle specially connected with activities or stress disorders

—such as eating good foods, quitting smoking, having more sleep, or decreasing overall stress—were the least probable to report achievement in creating lifestyle adjustments. For increasing overall health there is a need for improving our lifestyle and making better decisions about their behaviour.

The following suggestions are forwarded by APA for dealing with chronic stress:

Setting the limit: Note down all the commitments and activities that make you feel stressed. Recognize those activities that you think you have to do completely to survive and reduce anything that is not essential. For work-related projects, address with your manager a list of your duties and get your feedback on objectives and how best way to address the projects at hand. For social or non-work related commitments, such as voluntary and community activities, consider contacting the individual to whom you have made these commitments and let them realize that you are unable to meet such responsibilities at this time. You may also ask for help in accomplishing these tasks. Do not accept furthermore commitments until you think that your stress is under control. It is important to reduce chronic stress by setting the limit on non-essential commitment.

Establish your support system: People develop a network of social support with friends and/or family with whom they can share anything. When you are having a tough time, they can provide you emotional support and guidance. Sharing your problem with close one always makes you feel lighter.

Even if you don't feel stressed today, being part of a group will avoid the production of stress and provide support and practical help if difficult times arrive. Maybe your friends and relatives may experience similar challenges that you have faced later and you have useful ideas and experience from this. However, support from friends and families can help you get going and continue to take care of yourself. Social networking sites like, Facebook, WhatsApp, Email, Telegram, Skype, etc. can also make you feel relaxed, but it cannot replace the face to face communication. These sites can be very helpful to keep you stay in touch with your family and friends who are far away from you.

Make a commitment related to health: It is important to do things that can help you to improve your health will give you the strength and energy to overcome the obstacles that you are facing. A small step such as reducing the intake of caffeine can have a positive impact on health. Various studies indicate that people reported feeling comfortable, sleep well, less nervous, less heartburn and feel more strength and less muscle aches when they do not use caffeine. Likewise, a brisk walk or any other aerobic activity can improve the level of your concentration and energy and reduce the anxiety level. Regular aerobic exercise can help in reducing the level of body stress hormones and increases endorphins production i.e. the brain chemicals and the body's natural pain killer and it elevates the mood. For better health, take some positive steps that will allow you to better deal with your stress.

Improve your quality of sleep: People with chronic stress frequently suffer from a less amount of sleep and, in some cases insomnia caused by stress. There is a strong connection between the insomnia and chronic stress. According to the APA's Stress in America study 2009, almost 40 per cent of all the adults say that they awake at night because of the stress. Experts advise you to go to sleep at a regular time each night, aiming for at least 7-8 hours of sleep, and removing disturbances from the bedroom, such as television or computers. Before you go to bed start cooling down for an hour or two, and engage in relaxing practices like reading an interesting book, listening to music, taking a warm bath, and performing some relaxation techniques such as meditation. Avoid eating a heavy meal, caffeine, alcohol, and intense physical activity just before you go to sleep.

Seek a positive viewpoint: Positive values, thoughts, and feeling in human kind must be the preclude to the stress-free life. Thinking more positively at the circumstances ignoring negative feelings and viewing challenges as opportunities are both the crucial ways of stay positive and help in reducing the stress. How you look at the difficult circumstances or the situations that are stressful to you will make your life more manageable. There is a way to work out for every difficult circumstance; keeping problems in mind and doing what you can do to move forward in life.

Search for more help: When you keep feeling stressed, feel hopeless, or find it difficult to get through the daily routine work, ask for advice from a licensed mental health specialist like a psychiatrist or psychologist. With stress management techniques, a psychiatric or a doctor can often provide aid to the people. They are qualified and trained to help you with developing strategies to manage stress effectively and also help in changing the lifestyle for improving overall health.

Most of the Americans who experience long term stress do not make a change in their lifestyles for reducing the level of stress and eventually they lead to health problems. For reducing chronic stress and improving overall health, we should improve our lifestyle and change in behaviour. An important key in managing stress is to understand and change the habits that cause chronic stress, yet it is very difficult to change your behaviour.

For improving emotional health and reduce the level of stress, we should take a small step like take a walk everyday, it can be very helpful. It is a very small step for being active but a powerful improvement that helps you in managing the stress. Physical activity enhances the production of your body of nostalgic endorphins, a type of brain neurotransmitter, and it helps to relieve moderate forms of anxiety and depression. Therefore, improving both the quality and quantity of sleep and eat a balanced and healthy diet may be helpful. Remember that if a high level of stress lasts for a long period, or the various psychological problems of stress continues to interfere in your daily life habits, it is important to consult a licensed mental health specialist like a psychiatrist. Researches show that chronic stress can be treated with effective measures, like changes in behaviour and lifestyle, rehabilitation, and treatment in certain cases. Psychiatrist can help in overcoming the barrier that stop you from living a healthy life, successfully reduce stress, and help you to understand the behaviour and conditions that result in your consistent high stress level.

Conclusion

Chronic stress is a long-term and continuous form of stress that is typically caused when a person faces continuous problems in his life. In this case, it can negatively affect a person's physical or mental health if it goes untreated. The everyday stresses of family and work or any traumatic circumstances can trigger stress. It can lead to self-harm, suicide, heart attack, and violent actions. Long-term chronic stress results in stress-related harmful diseases and decreased quality of life. To control or manage chronic stress, we just need to know what it is, what it can do, and how it affects the whole body. When you recognize the chronic stress in your life, it is important to use stress managing ways for improving your well-being.

References

Cannon, W.B. (1929). *Bodily Changes in Pain, Hunger, Fear and Rage*. New York: Appleton and Company.

Chatterjee, A. (1992). "Commitment, cognitive appraisal and occupational stress." *Productivity*, 3.

Felman, A. (2017). "Why stress happens and how to manage it." *Medical News Today*. Retrieved from: https://www.medicalnewstoday.com/articles/145855.php.

Freshwater, Shawna. (2018). 3 Types of stress and health hazards. *Empathysites*. Retrieved from: https://spacioustherapy.com/3-types-stress-health-hazards/

How to manage and reduce stress. *Mental Health Foundation*. Retrieved from: https://www.mentalhealth.org.uk/publications/how-manage-and-reduce-stress

Husain, A., and Ali, J. (2001). "Identifying stress sources, stress effects and coping behaviour among hockey players." In A. Husain (Eds.). *Stress Research and Stress Management*, 84-106.

Jahan, A., and Bhardwaj, B. (2001). "Assessing source of stress among school teachers." In A. Husain (Eds.). *Stress Research and Stress Management*, 107-131.

Know your stress to manage your stress. (2014). *Life at Its Best*. Retrieved from: http://www.ppccfl.com/know-your-stress-to-manage-your-stress/

Kandola, A. (2018). "What are the health effects of chronic stress?" *Medical News Today*. Retrieved from: https://www.medicalnewstoday.com/articles/323324.php

Mason, J.W. (1975). "Historical view of stress field." *Journal of Human Stress*, 6-12.

Morse, D.R., and Furst, M.L. (1979). *Stress for Success — A holistic approach to stress and its management*. New York: Van Nostrand Reinholt Company.

Selye, H. (1936). "A syndrome produced by diverse nocnous agents." *Nature*, 138, 32.

Selye, H. (1956). *The Stress of Life*. New York: McGraw Hill.

Selye, H. (1979). "The stress concept today." In I.L. Kutash *et al*. (Eds.). *Handbook on Stress and Anxiety*, San Francisco: Jossey Bars.

Stress Effects. *The American Institute of Stress*. Retrieved from: https://www.stress.org/stress-effects

Stress and Stress Management. (2010). *Klinic Community Health Centre*. Retrieved from: https://hydesmith.com/de-stress/files/StressMgt.pdf

Sincere, S.M. (2012). Three Different Kinds of Stress. *Explorable*. Retrieved from: https://explorable.com/three-different-kinds-of-stress

Stress effects on the body. *American Psychological Association*. Retrieved from: https://www.apa.org/helpcenter/stress-body

Understanding chronic stress. *American Psychological Association*. Retrieved from: https://www.apa.org/helpcenter/understanding-chronic-stress

What's your stress type? (2016). *Healthline*. Retrieved from: https://www.healthline.com/health/whats-your-stress-type

8
Episodic Acute Stress

Komy Biswas

Meaning of Stress

Stress is a type of negative feeling people having when they are struggling to manage with challenges they face everyday in their workplaces, environment, relationships, and other situations. Moreover, stress is realizing when a person responding to any type of demand and threat whether it is real or imagined. Anxiety, fearful, feeling anxious, nervous, overwhelmed, stressed-out or panic etc. are often using interchangeably with the word stress. Not all stress is bad. Stress is that gives us our fight-or-flight mechanism and help us survive for so long. However, so much stress is not good for health. There are so many types of stress; some are short-term stress that lasts is little and some are long-term stress that is going on. Stress affects everyone in a different way but it can lead to severe health issues. Stress management is important for a fulfilling and healthy life. Each person has stress in his or her life and it is a normal part of life. A person feels stress when he has too much to do but he cannot organize the work. Under stressful situation, the body automatically increases metabolism, heart rate, blood pressure, respiration and blood flow to the muscles of the body. However, when the body instantaneously reacting to stressful situations without making any significant adjustments to counter the effects, a person feeling stress that can be threatening for his health and well-being. Stress is the body's natural defense against real or imagined danger. The human body is an intelligent operating system, but the body is unable to determine the difference between imagined non-life threating stressors and life threatening external threat. The body produces significantly huge quantities of the chemicals cortiçal, adrenaline, and noradrenalin. The Neurobiology of stress is a complex operating mechanism.

Stress has an effect on both mental and physical health and behaviour of a person. Body responds to any stress by producing hormones and chemicals to help stand up against the challenge. The heart rate increases; the brain works faster and has a sudden burst of energy. However, so much stress can have harmful effects on the human body as well as in the mind. It is not possible to eliminate bad stress completely from life, but it can be reduced from life. Stress is also a body's response towards some certain situations. It is subjective, so something that is stressful for a person is not necessarily stressful for another person.

There are many types of stress exists but all of them are not bad. Stress can help to act quickly in an emergency. This is the "fight-or-flight" response that your body activates in the times of coloration. However, stress is lasting for only a limited period. When the situation has passed the heart rate becoming slow, muscles becoming relax, and breathing becoming return to normal when the body returning to a natural state.

Changes in the Body

Stress dysfunction the normal system of the body like slow down the digestive and immune system of the body. Then all the resources of the body totally concentrating on blood flow, muscle use and rapid breathing. So the body changes during stress in such a way that the muscles become tense, immune activity decreases and pulse rate rises, the digestive system slows down, blood pressure, breathing becomes faster and a heightened state of alertness prevents sleep of a human. Our reaction to a tough situation will influence our health and it decides how stress affects us.

Some experiences like having a baby, going on a trip, moving to a nicer house or being promoted that are generally considered as positive experience can also lead to a stressful situation because such experiences involve a new responsibility, a major change, an extra effort and a need for adaptation. The people steps into an unknown situation that's why they wonder if they will cope with the situation or not.

A continuous negative response to challenge can have a harmful effect on the happiness and health of a person. However, if a person aware of how to react to stressors then it helps him to reduce the negative feelings and it also helps to manage stress effectively.

Definition of Stress

1. According to Lazarus (1980), "stress is the result of transaction between person and environment. The way people appraise or construct their relationship with the environment is a function of cognition, or thought. These thoughts influence the way people feel."
2. According to Zimbardo (1988), "stress is the pattern of specific and non-specific responses an organism makes to stimulus events that disturbs its equilibrium and tax or exceed its ability to cope." (p. 496)
3. According to Monet & Lazarus (1977), "stress... consists of any event in which environmental demands, internal demands or both tax or exceed the adaptive resources of an individual social system or tissue system."
4. According to Selye (1956), "stress like relativity, is a scientific concept which has suffered from the mixed blessing of being too well known and too little understood."
5. According to Morse & Furst (1979), "stress is a mental or emotional, disruptive or disquieting influence of distress."
6. According to Chatterjee (1992), "stress is considered a response to a situation which demands that the individual adapt to a change physically or psychologically."
7. Ahmad (1998) integrated the ideas given by stress researchers (e.g., Cox 1978; Lazarus & Folkman, 1984; Singer & Davidson, 1986; Trumbal & Appley, 1986) and concluded "stress is a condition involving psychological and physiological responses resulting from transactions between the individual and his (her) environment which foster the perception and belief, sometimes even wrongly that his (her) bio-psycho-social resources are insufficient to meet the demand of a situation" (p. 108).

How to Manage the Stress?

Stress management is a complex task because each of the three different types of stress can present as single, repeated and complicated. So that they need different types of management, treatment interventions and psychological treatment because of the nature of a person's lifestyle, personality, environment, developmental history and resource management. Stress affects differently to different person. Some people may get stomachaches or headaches, while others may get depressed or angry or they lose sleep. People with continuous stress may get sick a lot also. Management of stress is an important phenomenon for a healthy lifestyle.

It is not easy to complete prevention of stress. The main aim of stress management is to identify the annoyance of a person, which are the things that cause maximum problems or demand the most of energy. During that one can succeed in dealing with the negative stress those things persuade.

The Centres for Disease Control and Prevention Trusted Source recommends the following, which helps to manage with stress:

- Taking care of yourself by getting plenty of sleep, exercising and by eating healthy food.
- Finding support by talking people to get rid of problems from chest.
- Connecting socially, as it helps to isolate a person from a stressful event.
- Taking a break from stressful things or events.
- Avoiding alcohol and drugs, as it may seem to help with stress in the short term, but can actually cause more problems in the long term.

According to the American Psychological Association (APA), there are three different types of stress — acute stress, episodic acute stress, and chronic stress. The three types of stress each have their own characteristics, symptoms, duration, and treatment approaches. In this discussion, we only discuss about episodic acute stress.

Meaning of Episodic Acute Stress

When acute stress occurs very often, it is called episodic acute stress. Episodic stress occurs when a person is taking too many tasks and submerging with all demands because of the inability to fulfil those demands. They may have many different calamitous situations, live in disorder and disorganization. Things like being late for meetings, work, or appointments happen because the car broke down or they forgot to get gas. They temporarily lost things because they are lacking concentration about what is happening around them and they failed to fix an episodic event that occurred prior to the next one. It seems like they believe that "What can go wrong, will go wrong." People who tend to worry habitually and often needlessly or gloomy or who always think the negative side of everything also tend to have episodic acute stress. When our bodily organs become stressful and overworked, we develop many diseases like heart problems, high blood pressures, possibly suffer a stroke and compromised immune systems.

Problems like short temper, irritation, feeling tense and anxious are the symptoms of episodic stress. Nowadays we are always in a hurry and appeared unexpected and aggressive towards people because of that our relationship becomes bad and after a short time our closed ones are feeling annoyed and stressed. We create an unhealthy atmosphere at home as well as at the workplace, and at other social background. There is nervous energy and for some of us if we do not have a state of confusion in our lives then we never know how to function without it.

They are always in a hurry, but always behind time. They seem constantly in the grasp of acute stress. Gradually, the workplace turns to a very stressful place for them because of their irritating nature. People with episodic acute stress may constantly suffer from negative health problems. People with this type of stress accept stress as a part of life so that they may face problems while changing their lifestyle.

Types of Episodic Stress

There are two types of personality that frequently present with episodic acute stress: (1) "Type A" personality, and (2) The "Worrier".

1. "Type A" personality: The cardiologists, Ray Roseman and Meter Friedman found Type A personality is the same as an extreme case of episodic acute stress. Type A personality have a competitive desire, immoderate restlessness and a sudden sense of time urgency. Such types of personality characteristics often create episodes of acute stress for the Type "A" individual. Roseman and Friedman also got knowledge about that the Type A's to be much more likely to develop coronary heart disease than Type B's, who show an opposite pattern of behaviour.

There are some physical symptoms of episodic acute stress which often found in people with type "A" personality are as follows:

- Heart disease.
- Migraines.
- Tension headaches.
- Hypertension.

2. The "Worrier": Another type of episodic acute stress comes from constant nervousness. People, who often worry especially about things that are not important see tragedy around everywhere and negatively predict disaster in every situation. According to "Worrier", the world is not satisfying, dangerous and a disciplinary place where something unpleasant is always about to happen. These "awfulizing" also tend to over inducing and tense but are more anxious and depressed than angry and aggressiveness. The person with worrier stress shows almost constant negative thoughts which caused episodic acute stress on physical and mental health. Their thoughts often filling with "what if....." statements that are with estimated negative outcomes. They are usually diagnosed DSM-5 with generalized anxiety disorder.

Effects of Episodic Acute Stress

The most common symptoms are alike to acute stress, but due to extended frequent overarousal or extended hyperarousal, there is ongoing damage and suffering. Following are some effects of episodic acute stress:

- Cognitive distress includes compromised processing speed, compromised attention/concentration mental fatigue and compromised new learning and new learning memory consolidation and retrieval.
- Emotional distress includes short-tempered, tense, impatient, anger or irritability, anxiety and depression.
- Muscular distress includes jaw pain, headache, tension, back pain, pulled muscles, ligament problems and tendons.
- Interpersonal relationships deteriorate includes the workplace becomes a very stressful place for them.

- Heartburn, stomach gut, acid stomach, bowel problems, constipation, diarrhea and irritable bowel syndrome (IBS).
- Rapid heartbeat, heart palpitations, high blood pressure, sweaty palms, headache, dizziness, migraine, insomnia, heart disease, cold hands or feet, chest pain and shortness of breath.
- Immune System Compromise includes allergies, asthma, frequent colds/flu and other immune system compromise illnesses.
- Episodic acute stress leads to more pronounced health issues such as high blood pressure and heart disease, and irritable bowel syndrome (IBS).

There are also some symptoms of episodic acute stress, which are the symptoms of extended overarousal: migraines, persistent tension headaches, chest pain, hypertension and heart disease.

Treatment of Episodic Acute Stress

Episodic acute stress requires involvement in so many tasks. Therefore, treatment of episodic acute stress is doing through lifestyle changes and professional help. The treatment needs professional help to extend over several months. But most of the people with this stress do not see anything wrong in their lives so they may not feel need for treatment.

Most of the time personality and lifestyle characteristics are so confirmed and habitual that the individuals see nothing wrong about their lifestyle settings. Individuals generally blame other people for their problems and external events. All the time they thought their way of interacting with others and their lifestyle patterns, and their ways of recognizing the world as an integral part of their personality and therefore most of the time are insane to search for a professional psychological help. Individuals can be very impervious to change their thinking patterns and behaviours. When the individual feel too much discomfort and physical pains and then they only seek psychological treatment. Sufferers of this stress can be brutal resistant to change but only if the promise makes of relief from pain and discomfort of their symptoms then it can keep them treatment and on track in their recovery programme.

Recognizing Effects on Family

Day by day, we begin to lose our traditional values, way of life; beliefs that related to our family and community because of our disordered and time-consuming life which tend to use shortcuts.

One most important thing that we are losing is the time we are spending with our family at the dinner table and in the kitchen when the food is preparing. However, in modern time most of the people prefer to buy frozen and prepared foods and eating fast foods in their daily life. We also reduce the time which we spend with doing family activities and replacing this family time with video games, internet service and other activities.

Our children become incurious because we do not have time to take them to the park and they do not participate in various school events like sports and concerts. Because of unhealthy lifestyle children can suffer, many consequences like weight gaining, feeling fatigue from consuming high sugared foods and inability to express their emotions.

Michael Watkins who is health director of the Grand Ronde Tribal Health Clinic shares his personal experience that "About two years ago, I was able to attend a tribal head start graduation where a nephew of mine was graduating and one thing that really stuck out to me as a tribal health director was how many children in our head start programme were obese and were on the road already to developing diabetes and other health chronic conditions in their life."

By this statement, we can say that there may be many reasons for becoming fat to the children but episodic stress is one of the reasons that affect the children.

Michael also shares some solutions for overcoming these problems that are as follows:

> "We were able to purchase the young man a tricycle that he was able to do on his own time at home along with his parents and incorporate the parents into the whole master plan. Through the aquatics programme at Dallas, Oregon, which is about a half-hour away from the tribe here, and we were able to enroll the child into swimming classes along with the mother, and try and incorporate the mother into transitioning the role of fitness over to the family."

> "Often the tribe does what is called Family Night out, fitness activities, and several have been family swim nights at the local aquatics centre where we have anywhere from 150 to 200 tribal members who go down for a night of activities at the swimming pool."

Conclusion

Based on the above discussions, we can say that stress is a condition where every person is struggling to manage challenges which they are facing in their daily life. Stress does not cure completely but it can be reduced. Therefore, stress is a very painful situation and world's half population is suffering from it. Stress is of three types and among them, episodic acute stress is quite dangerous. Episodic stress causes heart disease, high blood pressure and irritable bowel syndrome. Professional help can treat episodic stress but it takes a long time. But sometimes stress also plays an important role to motivate people because under pressure people doing work better and faster. Today's family system also creates episodic stress due to the nuclear family system and the development of technologies.

References

Ahmad, H. (1998). "Stress and disease", In Q. Hasan (Ed.), *Applied Psychology: Indian Perspective*. New Delhi: Gyan Publishing House, 105 117.

Chatterjee, A. (1992). "Commitment, cognitive appraisal and occupational stress", *Productivity*, 3.

discoveringourstory.wisdomoftheelders.org

https://blog.spire.io/2018/04/10/types-of-stress/

https://explorable.com/three-different-kinds-of-stress

https://spacioustherapy.com/3-types-stress-health-hazards/

https://www.healthline.com/health/whats-your-stress-type

https://www.medicalnewstoday.com/articles/145855.php

https://www.mygbhp.com/condition/stress/Top of Form

https://www.neurocorecenters.com/blog/understanding-your-stress-type-how-to-manage-it

https://www.psychologytoday.com/us/blog/open-gently/201812/the-three-types-stress

Lazarus, R.S. (1980). "The stress and coping paradigm", In L. Band and J. Rosen (Eds.), *Competence and Coping During Adulthood*. Hanover, N.H.: University Press of New England, pp. 28-74.

Monet, A. and Lazarus, R.S. (Eds.) (1977). *Stress and Coping*, New York: Columbia University Press.

Morse, D.R. and Furst, M.L. (1979). *Stress for Success: A Holistic Approach to Stress and its Management*, New York: Van Nostrand Reinholt Company.

Selye, H. (1956). *The Stress of Life*, New York: McGraw Hill.

Zimbardo, P.G. (1988). *Psychology and Life* (12th ed.). Glenview, IL: Scott, Foresman.

9
Cross-cultural Approach to Stress

Wahid Ahmad Dar

Introduction

In this chapter we have taken an anthropological approach to stress and its management. Here an attempt is made to anthropologise stress, which means moving away from psychology to take the cultural and sociohistorical context of Stress. Anthropological Approach can be distinguished from the physiological or psychological approach—its cross-cultural and comparative orientation. The study of cultural perspectives on stress started with the publication of '*Coming of age in Samoa*' by Margaret Mead (1928). Mead was the first anthropologist to delineate the role of culture in stress. Anthropologists and other cultural scientists have long debated the role of various cultural institutions and rituals in inducing and managing stress.

Historically psychology in general and stress and coping research in particular suffer from a very dangerous flaw, which relates to its inability to be responsive to cultural diversity. Most of the concepts in psychology of stress and coping have emerged from and grown out of research in western societies (Lazarus, 1999; Snyder, 1999). The issue with most of the psychological concepts has been that, most of them are being taken as dichotomous with one of them always considered better than other. Long ago personality anthropologists taught us that every culture has a unique personality make-up. The dominant personality make-up in a culture is called model personality. Following Raymond Cattle we argue that every culture has a unique psychological make-up to adjust to the environment. No value judgment is possible in personality anthropology, in saying that people in one culture have better psychological make-up than others. This will also mean that every culture has unique way to cope up with stress and a particular stress coping strategy endemic to a particular culture is good in that context only. Take an example of development of trust among children. While lack of trustfulness is seen as a developmental anomaly in children, some anthropologists assert that mistrust is a strategic adaptation in vulnerable environments ridden with conflict, as you won't allow your children walk with every stranger in such environment. When we go deep in the chapter, we will extend the same argument to locus of control, coping strategies like emotion focused vs. problem focused etc. In this context, the best thing we can do to reform stress and coping research is by asking question which are related to cross-cultural variations in stress and its coping and also about role of culture in stress. These questions could be like, what are the various types of stress inducing elements in a culture? What kind of socio-economic, political and behavioural factors induce stress? This can help us understand the kind of cultural changes needed for making a culture free of stress inducing elements. Wong, Wong & Scott (2006) call it the positive psychology of cultural transformations, which is a kind of meta coping strategy that can be employed from organizational level (Wong & Gupta) to national level (Wong, Wong & Scott, 2006). This macro cultural transformation as a national level strategy to cope with stress becomes more relevant in societies ridden with conflict, violence, poverty, and unemployment.

Cross-cultural research in stress and coping also becomes inevitable for the case of multicultural counselling. Unless a proper understanding of the cultural background of the client is not considered, multicultural counselling becomes an uphill task. Better understanding of the parties involved is possible only when a multicultural perspective to stress is taken into consideration. A counsellor has to take the other peoples worldviews into consideration (Wong, Wong & Scott, 2006).

Culture and Stress

Much of the psychological, mentalist and cognitive paradigms have created a notion of stress and its management which is often seen detached from its socio-cultural connections (Hofoll, 2004, p. 25). No doubt there may be stressors which are universal to human condition, like poverty, drought, conflict, discrimination but much of the stress in an individual's life is induced by practices unique to each culture from toilet training to life cycle rituals, from residential change to polygynous households, belief in malevolent gods, competition, and discontinuities between childhood socialization and adult roles (Spradley & Phillips, 1972). On this point psychoanalysts will argue that culture is an instutionalised system for releasing stress or culture is a symbol of conflicts residing deep in the unconscious of humans. For instance totems and taboos are emotional reactions death or other painful experiences of life. There are functionalist anthropologists who argue that culture is by itself an instrumental reality for coping with stressful events, like scientists at ISRO doing *puja* before a rocket launch in order to get rid of stress and anxiety for successful launch.

Stress being a field of interdisciplinary importance, many archeological anthropologists have tried to study the role of stress in human evolution. In this direction Goodman and co-workers (1984a), a model of stress needs special mention. It argues for the role stress plays in adaptation of human species. Environment is taken as the source of all the necessities of adaption as well as the source of stress. In this, cultural systems are potentially able to provide critical resources and to buffer individuals from environmental stressors. However, they are not always effective at buffering stress and may produce new threats. When stressors cross the buffering ability of cultural systems then a biological response becomes inevitable. Finally, if the biological response is not adequate, then the population's ability to survive may be challenged.

Some varieties of stress may in fact arise when an individual encounters an alien culture, anthropologists define it as 'culture shock'. Culture shock is a variety of stress which occurs in individuals suddenly landed in a foreign culture, it results from losing all familiar signs and symbols of social intercourse (Oberg, 2006).

Lazarus & Folkman's (1984) approach to stress and coping mechanism elaborates on problem focused and emotion focused strategies of coping behaviours. Lazarus & Folkman's (1984) research on stress and coping behaviours has been one of the dominant theoretical frameworks guiding studies in the field for more than three decades now. All studies following Lazarus and Folkman (1984) try to distinguish people on these two categories. Wong, Wong & Scott (2006) suggests researchers to focus on culture specific coping strategies and resources rather than on pre-established dichotomies which owe their origin strictly to western cultures. Since problem focused behaviours in coping are Eurocentric, scholars tend to emphasize and judge it as a better strategy than emotion focused one. Or scholars consider an emotion focused strategy related to poorer mental health (Lazarus & Folkman, 1984) which in reality is a culturally specific way of responding to stress. This is why an urgent need of the hour is to recognize the Eurocentric nature of modern psychology and apply reality-based approaches which are ready to accept the plurality of coping strategies and stress causing elements across various cultures (Wong, Wong & Scott, 2006; Snyder, 1999).

On the role of cultural elements in causing stress El-Islam (1975) found a specific type of culture bound neurosis syndrome among Arab women who cannot satisfy the social criteria of women's role fulfilment according to Qatari value systems. The syndrome is initiated, bound and maintained by socio-cultural expectations characteristic of Arabian culture. All our social world is subjectively construed and all our actions and motivations find their meaning in medium of culture. Therefore, most part of stress and anxieties in our life are in response to our inability to act in accordance with our social expectations, norms and values. Aranda & Knight (1997) provide a lively example of explaining the role of culture in process of stress and coping in Latino caregivers. They point out that caregivers of older Latinos face special challenges for caregiving of individuals at higher risk of chronic diseases. Ethnicity and culture play a significant role in the perception and use of family support and coping behaviours. For instance, the appraisal of stress among Latinos may depend upon the degree of family disruption, rather than on the interferences with the individual's perceived control on the circumstances. The breakthrough in understanding the relationship between stress and culture goes to Margaret Mead. Mead challenged Stanley Halls (1904) conception that Adolescence is the age of storm and stress. The problem with Hall's argument is that its inability to be universally applicable across various cultures (Arnett, 1999; Mead, 1928). Research shows that stress and identity crises during adolescence in western cultures is characteristic of capitalistic societies where an individual's choice at adolescence in choosing his vocation may have significant costs for his future life. Mead (1928) found that North American societies put an extra pressure on adolescents, which are related to taking critically important decision in life.

Laungani (1993) discussing the influence of culture on stress distinguished eastern and western cultures on four core value systems or factors, these include individualism and collectivism; cognitivism and emotionalism; free will and determinism; materialism and spiritualism. Based on these values or factors stress is induced in different ways. As Chun, Moos, & Cronkite (2006) use individualism and collectivism as examples of cultural constructs that can influence each component of stress and coping. In individualistic societies, many of the ongoing stressors may stem from pressure to be autonomous and independent. These stressors may be perceived by the individual during early adolescence when an individual is not ready to be autonomous so as to handle all responsibilities. Contrary to this in collectivistic societies, there is greater pressure to be symbiotic and interdependent (Chun, Moos, & Cronkite, 2006). These pressures could be in the form of sharing your earning among one's family members. Or these pressures could be in the form of the dilemma to stick a balance between one's own needs and needs of your fellows. Also based on some studies it has been found that individualistic cultures have people with internal locus of control than do collectivistic cultures. So the long debate classifying people on the type of locus of control may actually be cultural differences in attributing causes to the events (McGinnies, Nordholm, Ward & Bhanthumnavin, 1974).

Cultural Context for Stress Coping Mechanism

The field of stress and coping emerged long ago from the recognition of the dynamic interaction between person and environment (Lazarus & Folkman, 1984). Throughout the history of human race stress has been the permanent aspect of human life, people from different cultures have devised and different strategies to cope up with stress given the fact that humans cannot tolerate stress for too long. These coping strategies are therefore more likely than anything else to vary cross culturally. Lazarus and Folkman (1984) postulated that a person's internalized cultural values, beliefs, and norms influence the appraisal process of stressors and the perceived appropriateness of coping responses. Taken other way around these cultural factors delimit the coping options available to an individual in the face of stress (Kuo, 2011). Therefore, culture and situations form an important context to stress and coping research. But the dominant paradigms analyzing stress coping mechanisms have resulted in decontextualizing the stress and coping research as it does not give much consideration to the meaning of the events that occur in an idiosyncratic life context. In recent years, through insights from medical anthropology and ethnographic research across various native communities around the world, a more realistic approach to stress and coping research has given new direction to stress and coping research (Somerfield & McCrae, 2000). One of the most dominant factors in stress and coping is culture. Cross-culture approach to stress and coping is vital as far revealing the cultural differences in stress and copying mechanisms (Chun, Moos, & Cronkite, 2006). Ethnographic research has highlighted the shortcomings of applying general Decontextualized paradigms of stress and coping to many indigenous communities. An Anthropological approach takes into consideration the socio-historical context of people. Dinges & Joos (1988) identified environmental contexts and personal factors as potential mediators or moderators of stressful life events. Taking a lead Walters, Simoni & Evans-Campbell (2002) analyze American Indian's stress coping strategies in the face of colonization and impact of various stressors on substance use and associated health consequences. Their model for stress copying argues that relation between 'traumatic life stressors and adverse health outcomes are moderated by cultural factors that function as buffers, strengthening psychological and emotional health, decreasing substance use, and mitigating the effects of the traumatic stressors' (Walters, Simoni & Evans-Campbell, 2002).

Some scholars have been able to categorize cultures based on stress coping strategies or the way people respond to stress. The terms used for these types are primary control and secondary control. Orientation possibly more common in North America is somehow primary, and the orientation possibly more common in parts of East Asia is somehow secondary (Schulz & Heckhausen, 1999). Tweed, White, & Lehman (2004) argue that East Asian people are more likely to respond to stressful situations through internally targeted control attempts, that is, attempts to accommodate the self to the demand of the environment, and that people from Western English speaking backgrounds are more likely to cope through externally targeted control strategies, that is, attempts to control or alter the environment. What Schulz & Heckhausen (1999) mean by primary and secondary Tweed, White, & Lehman (2004) use the terms externally and internally targeted strategies respectively. The reason for these differences are several cultural variables, which may increase the likelihood of internal locus of control and may decrease the likelihood of external locus of control. The locus of control is directly related to the kind of coping strategy. As there are cultural differences in locus of control there are also cultural differences in coping strategies. Following Tweed, White, & Lehman (2004) we can hypothesize that in collectivist and spiritualistic cultures people will preferably adopt emotion focused, secondary and internally-oriented coping strategies and people living in individualistic and reason based cultures problem-focused, primary, externally-oriented problem strategies. Again Tweed, White, & Lehman (2004) argue that externally targeted control can destabilize the collectivist ethos surrounding an individual because of the potential for generating reactivity among others who prefer the status quo or who resist attempts to be changed.

Bjork, Cuthbertson, Thurman & Lee (2001) examined the ethnic differences in appraisal of stressors in Euro-, Korean-, and Filipino-American college students. Responding to the question of most stressful event they experienced in the past week on the degree of threat, challenge and loss. Korean-American students appraised their stressors as involving greater losses than did Euro-American students. Korean- & Filipino-American student's appraised stressors as more challenging than Euro-American students. Korean- & Filipino-American students were found to be using religious coping to greater extent.

Based on these experiences it could be argued that it is vital to bring a qualitative shift in stress coping research by contextualizing it and giving up some of the ethnocentric biases. The contemporary decontextualized stress and coping literature is replete with binary typologies of coping strategies like towards or away from problem (approach vs. avoidant), the primary focus of coping (problem vs. emotion), and the intensity of coping efforts (active vs. passive). Scholars particularly psychologists always advocate the use of one of the strategies over the other. Like some may advocate use of problem-focused strategy than emotion focused without paying attention to the context the individual is placed in. There are also some conceptual overlaps among these categories that create confusion for cross-cultural research on coping. More important, the inconsistent dichotomization is an indication that the current categorization of coping strategies does not adequately capture the full complexity of cultural variations in coping (Chun, Moos, & Cronkite, 2006).

Indian Perspective on Stress and Coping

Continuing the precedence that this chapter gives to cross-cultural variation in stress and coping an Indian perspective to stress and its coping will be discussed. As is already noted differences exist in appraisal, incidence, causes, and effects of stress, and in ways of coping across various cultures, it will be interesting to see an Indian perspective to stress. Palsane & Lam (1996) discussing Indian and Chinese perspective on stress and coping argue that since western societies particularly American society which is a melting pot of immigrants are based on reason, competition and individualism, their perspective on stress and coping differ than eastern societies where religion, spirituality tradition take more dominant position. As already noted that people in Indian subcontinent are more likely to focus on emotion focused coping strategies, apply an internal control to stressful events. There also have been semantic differentials in the terminology in east and west, the alternative terms used for stress in India are suffering, pain, and pressure etc. The Sanskrit term for stress is 'Dukha'. But *Dukkha* may not exactly resemble what we mean by stress in west (Palsane & Lam, 1996). The Urdu term for the same is 'Zehni Dabaw'.

Suffering in Indian tradition has been seen as an integral reality of life. Sufferings is one among the four noble truths in Buddhist philosophy (Davids, 1973). Among the followers of Buddhist tradition, who have internalized the philosophy of four noble truths, there is a greater tendency toward internally targeted control attempts when coping with stressful circumstances in life. According to Buddhism, which holds the philosophy of *Pratityasamutpada* (theory of dependent origination) sufferings are the result of desire which results in the perpetuating cycle of bondage, and the path to freedom from suffering is found in absence of desire (Chen, 2006), that means that stress or sufferings cannot be removed through external control of stressors, or not through direct efforts at symptom reduction or through active efforts to solve one's problems (externally targeted control) in the physical world but through an internally targeted control that is through removing desire from self. (see Tweed, White, & Lehman, 2004). In Hinduism also, the theory of *karma* entails that the cause of sufferings is *karma,* and theory of *karma* explains that the cause of bondage and therefore *Dukha* lies within the self. Therefore, philosophies like *Mimamsa* will emphasize meditation, devotion, *bhakti*, which all relate to self. Therefore, the appraisal of and response towards stressful circumstances is influenced by the religious beliefs of people. Religion being an important component of cultural system plays an important role in an individual's life. Kawa, Najar & Dar (2017) found that religiosity can help reduce the depression among the students.

Medical Anthropologists argue that accessibility and affordability are important considerations in health and well-being of people in India. Medicinal practice in India does have to pay attention to the issues of cultural plurality, economic affordability and accountable availability of medical services at the ground level. Diverse forms of health care practices in the form of various tribal, indigenous, localized, health and healing practices should be given adequate consideration and representation in mental health care system. The health models rooted in the culturally shared assumptions, ethical values, reasoning patterns and sensibilities should be given due consideration (Khare 1996). This is why a bottom up approach to understanding and managing stress is more viable option than a top bottom approach. Therefore, it is very critical that the research on stress and coping in India focusses on local and indigenous practices of coping and mental healing. Even localized forms of mental and spiritual healing practices and indigenous medical knowledge should be integrated in the formal curriculum of medical courses.

Recently in an empirical study it was found that in contemporary time's spirituality and religion form an important and integral aspect of health, healing and well-being in India (Mohan, Mohan, Roy & Basu, 2004). *Yoga* an Indian method to reducing stress and anxieties and maintaining balance in life is gaining worldwide recognition and resurgence (Mohan, Mohan, Roy & Basu, 2004). In India, the growing dependence on drugs have resulted into prompting health professionals to consider the role of *yoga* and meditation in curbing problem of drug abuse and other health related issues (Murthy, 1997). Also it was found by Kawa, Najar & Dar (2017) that religion in general more specifically the intrinsic religiosity among university students in India helps them to reduce the risks of depression. Religion as the essence of Indian culture has been restoring peace and happiness in the live of people in India through ages. Across the world such positive effects of religion and spirituality have been confirmed by a vast body of research (Mohan, 2001; Mohan, Mohan, Roy & Basu, 2004; Khan, & Steeves, 1993).

Discussing the relationship between psychoanalysis and Indian healing practices Kakar (1997) observes spiritual practices like meditation do have therapeutic value since both psychoanalysis and spiritual healing view mind as the centre that creates suffering and disturbance. He argues against those people who consider the indigenous spiritual practices as unscientific and irrational. The institution of *guru* forms an important institution of healing practice in India. Sacred places also play an important role in the process of healing. In fact, there is a wide spectrum of such resources that cater to the needs of people in trouble. *Gurus* and religious places play an important role in the process of emotional healing of people (Kakar, 1997). In all Indian traditions Hindu, Sufi etc., the role of sacred is very important. These traditions offer a glimpse of social values as well as the symbolic universe of the Indian society. In addition to the Western style biomedicine (allopathy), we have the Ayurveda, Siddha and Unani-Tibb systems. These systems employ different methods of healing (Kakar, 1982). Therefore, these traditions should form the important context of studying the process of stress and its management in India.

Conclusion

We could see in our present day world that stress and depression has taken troll of human population. Today we have professional mental health practitioners, psychiatrists, and counsellors etc. who help people manage and cope with stressful circumstances. Today economy is dominated by service sector and most of the people feel overburdened as far as there work is concerned. This phenomena of work overload has resulted into depression and blood pressure have become common. But it should not be surprising to know that stress has a long history with human race. Be it hunter gatherers, horticulturalists, agriculturalists, pastoralists etc. all societies feel stressful because of various pressures be it environmental or cultural. All cultures across the world have developed strategies to cope with stressors. In modern industrialized societies, we have professional mental health practitioners for dealing with stress. In traditional cultures, we have various cultural institutions for the same. For example according to Malinowski Trobriand islanders will perform some specific forms of rituals before going for fishing or hunt. Or like most of the death rituals performed in some societies are social mechanisms to deal with stress.

These we can take as examples of coping mechanisms at cultural level. We have discussed in this chapter how various cultures through the process of socialization shape the personality of their members in unique way. Every culture gives a unique psychological make-up to its members. This results into cross-cultural differences in appraisal of stress, coping strategies etc. Despite these realistic differences across cultures in coping mechanisms, historically psychological approaches to stress and coping have been decontextualized. Most constructs related to stress and coping are Eurocentric in nature. Like emotion focused approach to coping has been related to poor mental health.

The chapter argues for a bottom up, localized indigenous approach to stress and its management. This is particularly significant in organizational research, educational institutions etc., because it through recognizing the coping strategies cross-culturally that a better management of stress in multicultural organizations, classroom is possible. Better management in multicultural organizations is vital for employees' working efficiency.

An Indian perspective to stress has been discussed for valuing the rich Indian tradition of unity in diversity. The role of traditional healers, *Gurus*, *Pirs*, should be given due consideration. These traditional institutions should be properly researched to properly understand their role in stress reduction in present context in India. The role of sacred places in promoting the psychological well-being of people should also be properly analyzed and considered.

References

Bjorck, J.P.; Cuthbertson, W.; Thurman, J.W. and Lee, Y.S. (2001). "Ethnicity, coping, and distress among Korean Americans, Filipino Americans, and Caucasian Americans", *Journal of Social Psychology, 141*(4): 421-442.

Chen, Y.H. (2006). "Coping with suffering: The Buddhist perspective", In *Handbook of Multicultural Perspectives on Stress and Coping* (pp. 73-89). Springer, Boston, MA.

Chun, C.A.; Moos, R.H. and Cronkite, R.C. (2006). "Culture: A fundamental context for the stress and coping paradigm", In *Handbook of Multicultural Perspectives on Stress and Coping* (pp. 29-53). Springer, Boston, MA.

Dinges, N.G. and Joos, S.K. (1988) "Stress, coping, and health: Models of interaction for Indian and Native populations", *Am Indian Alask Native Ment Health Res,* 1, 8-64.

El-Islam, M.F. (1975). "Culture bound neurosis in Qatari women", *Social Psychiatry, 10*(1): 25-29.

Hobfoll, S.E. (2004). *Stress, Culture, and Community: The Psychology and Philosophy of Stress*. Springer Science and Business Media.

Kawa M.H.; Najar I.A. and Dar W.A. (2017). "A Study of Religious Orientation and Depression Among University Students", *Academic Social Research, 3*(4), pp. 35-41.

Khan, D.L. and Steeves, R.H. (1993). "Spiritual well-being: A review of the research literature", *Cerenex Pharmaceuticals Quality of Life: A Nursing Challenge*, 2, 3.

Khare, R.S. (1996). "Dava, Daktar and Dua: Anthropology of Practiced Medicine in India", *Social Science and Medicine, 43*(5): 837-48.

Kuo, B.C. (2011). "Culture's consequences on coping: Theories, evidences, and dimensionalities", *Journal of Cross-Cultural Psychology, 42*(6): 1084-1100.

Laungani, P. (1993). "Cultural differences in stress and its management", *Stress Medicine, 9* (1), 37-43.

Lazarus, R.S. (1999). *Stress and Emotion: A new synthesis*, New York: Springer.

Lazarus, R.S. and Folkman, S. (1984). *Stress, Appraisal and Coping*. New York: Springer.

McGinnies, E.; Nordholm, L.A.; Ward, C.D. and Bhanthumnavin, D.L. (1974). "Sex and cultural differences in perceived locus of control among students in five countries", *Journal of Consulting and Clinical Psychology, 42*(3), 451.

Mead, M. (1928). *Coming of Age in Samoa: A psychological study of primitive youth for western civilization.*

Mohan, Y.; Mohan, K.K.; Roy, G.; Basu, S. and Viranjini, G. (2004). "Spiritual well-being: An empirical study with yogic perspectives", *Journal of Indian Psychology, 22*(1): 41.

Oberg, K. (2006). "Cultural shock: Adjustment to new cultural environments", *Curare, 29*(2): 3.

Palsane, M.N. and Lam, D.J. (1996). "Stress and coping from traditional Indian and Chinese perspectives", *Psychology and Developing Societies, 8*(1): 29-53.

Snyder, C.R. (1994). *The Psychology of Hope. You can get there from here.* New York: Free Press.

Somerfield, M.R. and McCrae, R.R. (2000). "Stress and coping research: Methodological challenges, theoretical advances, and clinical applications", *American Psychologist, 55*(6), 620.

Spradley, J.P. and Phillips, M. (1972). "Culture and Stress: A Quantitative Analysis", *American Anthropologist, 74*(3), 518-529.

Tweed, R.G.; White, K. and Lehman, D.R. (2004). "Culture, stress, and coping: Internally-and externally-targeted control strategies of European Canadians, East Asian Canadians, and Japanese", Journal of Cross-Cultural Psychology, *35*(6): 652-668.

Walters, K.L.; Simoni, J.M. and Evans-Campbell, T. (2002). "Substance use among American Indians and Alaska Natives: Incorporating culture in an "indigenist" stress-coping paradigm", *Public Health Reports*, 117 (Suppl 1), S104.

Wong, P.T.; Wong, L.C. and Scott, C. (2006). "Beyond stress and coping: The positive psychology of transformation", In *Handbook of Multicultural Perspectives on Stress and Coping* (pp. 1-26). Springer, Boston, MA.

Wong, P.T.P. and Gupta, V. (2004). "The positive psychology of transformative organizations", In V. Gupta (2004). *Transformative Organizations* (pp. 341 360). New Delhi, India: Sage Publications.

10
Cognitive Stress

Rasna Shehrawat

Stress has been linked as a co-factor in 95 per cent of all disease processes. Stress factors broadly fall into four types or categories: physical stress, psychological stress, psychosocial stress, and psychospiritual stress.

Cognitive stress consisting of information overload, accelerated sense of time, worry, guilt, shame, jealousy, resistance, attachments, self-criticism, self-loathing, unworkable perfectionism, anxiety, panic attacks, not feeling like yourself, not feeling like things are real, and a sense of being out of control falls in category of psychological stress.

But whatever you might think is the cause of stress, the thing to remember is that really it originates in your brain. While these things might all be triggers of stress, the truth is that stress is actually *caused* by the way we perceive these events and these triggers. All stress is *cognitive* stress and when you recognize this, it becomes possible to keep it under control and to prevent it from spiraling out of control. Even if you didn't, then actually go through with it, you would already have that stress response and this would last for a while. You've entirely 'created' the stress in your mind. This is completely cognitive stress.

The point is that stress is not caused by reality but our *perception* of reality. Fortunately though, the cognitive nature of stress can also be a good thing because it means that you can remove that stress by changing the way you think about it.

This is the entire idea behind 'cognitive behavioural therapy' which is a form of therapy designed to change the way you think. It involves two processes. The first is identifying the thought patterns or cognitive distortions that are causing you to be stressed. Secondly, 'thought challenging' which means you challenge yourself on just how accurate or useful that thought is. By constantly repeating negative ruminations as you think about all the things that could go wrong, you will end up actually making yourself stressed for no reason. Instead then, you should try to replace those thoughts with more constructive thought patterns. The fact of the matter is that most of us worry *far more* than we need to. You've survived this long, so as long as you keep on doing what you're doing... you'll probably be okay. Stop putting yourself through cognitive stress and try restructure your thoughts in a positive and optimist manner.

Dr. Beck has detailed about the many different kinds of cognitive distortions that people commonly fall victim to. Explanations for ten of the more common distortions related to stress are as follows:

- **Catastrophizing** occurs when people expect a disaster or the worst to occur, even though the available evidence does not support such an assessment. For example, catastrophization is probably occurring when someone thinks to themselves, "My boyfriend/girlfriend broke up with me, and it is the end of the world! Nobody will ever want a relationship with me again in the future!"
- **Personalization** occurs when you develop a habit of overestimating your personal responsibility for causing things to happen and start thinking that everything people say or do is somehow a reaction to you. With personalization, if something bad happens we assume it is our fault; that we caused it to happen.
- **Externalization** occurs when we habitually refuse to see our role in causing things to happen and end up taking no personal responsibility and instead, blame other people and situations for our problems.
- **Filtering** occurs when people focus on only one part of a situation and form conclusions based only on that partial consideration rather than looking at the entire situation and forming a more holistic opinion. Filtering commonly occurs when people habitually focus on negative aspects of life by picking out a single negative detail and dwelling on it, while ignoring the positive elements that are also present.

- **Polarized thinking/splitting** describes a tendency some people have to view the world in extreme black or white terms rather than to allow for the possibility of a gray area or a mixture of characteristics. Polarized thinkers have difficulty with the notion of being "good enough" or a partial success. For them it is all or nothing, and if they make one mistake then they will have failed completely.
- **Overgeneralization** describes the tendency to form a general conclusion based on only a few pieces of evidence. For example, overgeneralization is occurring when someone fails one math test and then concludes that she is lousy at math. The rush to overgeneralize often involves a tendency to engage in filtering and personalization. That is, people who filter and only focus on negative outcomes while ignoring the positive information, and who blame themselves for a failure rather than considering how outside aspects of the situation may have affected it are likely to mistake their limited negative conclusion for a balanced picture of their entire situation. These people do not realize that by projecting that negative conclusion into the future, they are overgeneralizing, going beyond the actual facts and artificially limiting options for the future.
- **Mind reading** occurs when people make inferences about what other people are thinking based on their behaviour. People who engage in mind reading assume that they know what other people are thinking without bothering to check whether their assumptions are correct.
- **Control fallacies** involve a bias of viewing yourself as either more or less in control of your situation than you really are. They are related to tendencies towards personalization and externalization. People who personalize situations generally also believe they have control over those situations that they probably don't have, and *vice versa*, people who reject the idea that they can exert control over situations are more likely to see themselves as passive victims of other people's efforts to control them, and, as a consequence, to externalize.
- **A Fallacy of Change** occurs when someone believes that others will change their ways simply because that person wants them to, or because those other people "should" act differently. When fallacies of change are in place, people

blame, demand, withhold and bargain to try to achieve the desired changes in their partners.

- **Emotional Reasoning** occurs when people make decisions on the basis of what feels good rather than on the basis of a systematic review of the evidence. In emotional reasoning, we let our feelings guide our interpretation of reality. (*Source*: HARRY MILLS, PH.D., NATALIE REISS, PH.D. AND MARK DOMBECK, PH.D.)

Psychologist Aaron T. Beck originally came up with the theory of cognitive distortions in the 1960s, and many therapists since then have helped clients live more positive lives by hunting down their cognitive distortions and correcting them. (It's one of the tenets of a very successful and fast-working mode of therapy called cognitive therapy.

When you know what to be on the lookout for, it becomes rather easy to spot the cognitive distortions in others. It may be a little more challenging to spot your own, but it is possible. Doing so usually brings lasting positive change in the way you experience stressors in your life.

Stress: Symptoms, Signs, and Causes

Improving Your Ability to Handle Stress

The stress response is the body's way of protecting oneself. When working properly, it helps one stay focused, energetic, and alert. In emergency situations, stress can save one's life—giving one extra strength to defend oneself.

Stress can also help you rise to meet challenges. When you feel threatened, your nervous system responds by releasing a flood of stress hormones, and including adrenaline and cortisol, which rouse the body for emergency action. Your heart pounds faster, muscles tighten, blood pressure rises, breath quickens, and your senses become sharper. These physical changes increase your strength and stamina, speed your reaction time, and enhance your focus—preparing you to either fight or flee from the danger at hand.

Your nervous system isn't very good at distinguishing between emotional and physical threats. If you're super stressed your body can react just as strongly as if you're facing a true life-or-death situation. And the more your emergency stress system is activated, the easier it becomes to trigger and the harder it becomes to shut off. If you tend to get stressed out frequently—as many of us do in today's demanding world—your body may be in a heightened state of stress most of the time. And that can lead to serious health problems. Chronic stress disrupts nearly every system in your body. It can suppress your immune system, upset your digestive and reproductive systems, increase the risk of heart attack and stroke, and speed up the ageing process. It can even rewire the brain, leaving you more vulnerable to anxiety, depression, and other mental health problems.

Cognitive symptoms of stress overload:

- Memory problems
- Inability to concentrate
- Poor judgment
- Seeing only the negative
- Anxious or racing thoughts
- Constant worrying.

Cognitive Factors in Stress

Richard S. Lazarus developed his cognitive view of stress called the Cognitive-Mediational Theory of Emotions. It states that the severity of a stressor is mainly determined by how a person thinks about and evaluates the stressor. According to the eminent psychologist, there exists a two-step process in assessing the stressor's degree of threat/harm and how one should react to it.

Primary appraisal: Primary appraisal involves estimating the stressor's severity and classifying it as a threat—something harmful in the future, a challenge—something to be faced and conquered, or a harm that has already happened. If the stressor is perceived to be a threat, this will lead to increased stress reactions. The arising negative emotions will then inhibit the person's ability to handle it properly. On the other hand, if the stressor is seen as a challenge, it is possible to plan to meet that challenge, which is a less stressful and more positive approach. This makes coping with it more likely to be successful.

Secondary appraisal: After perceiving the stressor as a threat, we move on to secondary appraisal. This involves estimating the resources available for coping with the stressor. Such may include concrete resources like supplies, money, or people; and abstract resources like time, energy, information, social support, or skill. Despite assessing the stressor as a threat, the degree of stress will be significantly lower if resources are perceived as abundant or adequate than if resources are lacking or non-existent.

Does that mean we classify a stressor as a threat based on secondary appraisal—wondering if we can handle this situation? No. Again this depends on the person's perception of the stressor. He/she at first may feel like it is a threat, but during secondary appraisal may find adequate coping resources, physically or mentally.

Personality Factors in Stress

How one cognitively assesses a stressor depends on one's personality. For instance, highly anxious or aggressive people tend to create more stress for themselves than what may exist in the actual stressor. In fact, people who display positive emotions and relationships tend to live longer. This means that our personality dictates how much stress we take in, which would affect our health, which would determine our longevity.

Medical practitioners Dr. Meyer Friedman and Dr. Ray Roseman devised the Type A and Type B personality theory in the 1950s:

Type A: Type A people are workaholics: they tend to be competitive, irritable, ambitious perfectionists who despise wasting time. There is a never-ending sense of pressure and a desire to multitask beyond human capability. Often successful and just as often unsatisfied, they always seem to want to go faster and do more. They fuss over small things and do not tolerate even the slightest mistakes or distractions.

Type B: Type B people are not that competitive, tend to be easygoing and cool-tempered and exhibit great self-control. Preferring to take life at a slow and relaxed pace, they do not suffer from a bad temper or anxiety, and thus are calm, laid-back, and patient. They are still subject to stress, but during which are highly productive. They plan things in advance and do not complain much when faced with problems.

Type H: Yet again there is another personality type, coined by psychologist Suzanne Kobasa in 1979. She calls it the 'hardy' personality. These are Type A people who work hard, but feed on stress rather than let it feed on them. They have a deep sense of commitment to their values, beliefs, sense of identity, work, family and feel they are in control of their situations. Their primary appraisal is different. When things go wrong, they see it not as a threat, but always as a challenge. These are the "three C's of hardiness."

Remember, you can either let stress conquer you, ride on its back, say nothing, or make it your employee. Your personality dictates your actions.

References

Andries, F.; Kompier, M.A.J. and Smulders, P.G.W. (1996). "Do you think that your health or safety is at risk because of your work? A large European study on psychological and physical work demands", *Work and Stress*, 10:104-118.

Aldwin, C.M. (1994). *Stress, Coping and Development: An Integrative Perspective*, New York: Guildford.

Biondi, M. and Picardi, A. (1999). "Psychological stress and neuroendocrine function in humans: The last two decades of research", *Psychotherapy and Psychosomatics*, 68:114-150.

Burrows, D. (2002). "Memory overload: The effects of amount of information, rate of presentation and reorganization", *Cognitive Technology*, 7:20-30.

Burns, K.R. and Egan, E.C. (1994). "Description of a stressful encounter: Appraisal, threat and challenge", *Journal of Nursing Education*, 33:21-28.

Danboy, A.C. and Goldstein, A.G. (1990). "The use of cognitive appraisal to reduce stress reactions", *Journal of Social Behaviour and Personality*, 5:275-285.

Dutke, S. and Stoebber, J. (2001). "Test anxiety, working memory and cognitive performance", *Cognition and Emotion*, 15:381-389.

Wood, J.; Mathews, A. and Dalgleish, T. (2001). "Anxiety and cognitive inhibition", *Emotion*, 1:165-181.

11
Mathematical Anxiety

Hemlata Pande

Anxiety can be considered as the sensation of nervousness, tension, worry or uneasiness about a particular thing. In human beings, the presence of anxiety about some specific thing is normal, but if the presence of anxiety is so crushing that it affects one's mental health and the mundane normal life then the person can be assumed to suffer with anxiety disorder. Level of anxiety of a person about a particular object can be analyzed. Depression and anxiety disorders are analyzed under '*Psychoanalysis*'; Sigmund Freud was the founder of Psychoanalysis. The measure of anxiety is done with the help of noting the physical symptoms, monitoring the personal interactions and by means of certain questionnaires.

Nowadays in competitive academic surroundings, academic anxiety is common problem among children. Khemka and Rathod (2016) have mentioned that "Academic anxiety is a kind of anxiety which relates to the impending danger from the environments of the academic institutions including teacher and certain subjects like Mathematics, Science and English etc." Presence of anxiety cannot absolutely be considered as bad, when present in limited amount it helps in maintaining the students' punctuality, it increases their level of motivation and improves their performance however its presence beyond limit reversely affects their performance. "Students with anxiety disorder display a passive attitude in their studies such as lack of interest in learning, poor performance in exams, and on assignments." (Vitasari *et al.*, 2010).

Good proficiency of Mathematics is helpful not only for academic success but it is also beneficial in many problems of day-to-day life. The anxiety that interfere while solving the mathematical problems whether related to the academic mathematical problem or any other mathematical problem regarding to some real world problem (which can be solved with the help of Mathematics) is known as the Mathematical Anxiety. As mentioned in the book of Idris (2005) at page no. 51, Tobias and Weissbrod (1980) defined the Math anxiety as "the panic, helplessness, paralysis, and mental disorganization that arises among some people when they are required to solve a mathematical problem". Math anxiety can be seen in a number of children of each age group whether they are students of primary school, upper primary school, high school, students of intermediate school or they are college going students. Improper teaching methods, tests of limited time, and the chance of embarrassment are some of the causes of Math Anxiety and likewise some Myths as: *someone is God gifted with Math talent and I cannot do improperly, Mathematical talent is gender biased* and *an average student cannot do good in Math* etc. are also accountable for Math Anxiety.

Math anxiety is a serious problem for the young generation but when confirmed it can be reduced and can be removed. Different math anxiety scales depending on the ages of children have been defined by various researchers. "Abbreviated Math Anxiety Scale (AMAS)" developed by Hopko *et al.* (2003) is one of the prominent tools for measuring of Math anxiety. The AMAS depends on 9 item measure.

Some strategies can be useful to overcome the math anxiety which include:

In Mathematics learning one should always try to understand rather than to only memorize the mathematical notions.

The practice of Mathematics should always be done with positive attitude and the same problem should be solved by different methods.

Improvement in the quality of Mathematics teaching also helps. Teachers should try to teach Mathematics with the help of more and more examples from our surroundings of day-to-day life. Mistakes should be removed in such a manner that the process should not decrease the confidence level of students.

To maintain interest in the topics, the initial session for each new type of problem should be small, new things should be taught by variety of methods and the regular practice for different problems also helps in removing the level of anxiety.

More and more mathematical expressions should be used rather than to use more language forms.

While solving the Mathematical methods in case of failure, a clue about the result of the problem can be given rather than to forego it without answering and to take the help of calculators for complicated calculations is also beneficial practice.

And finally the fear of mistakes from one's mind should be removed.

References

Derek R. Hopko, Rajan Mahadevan, Robert, L. Bare, Melissa K. Hunt (2003). "The Abbreviated Math Anxiety Scale (AMAS) Construction, Validity and Reliability", *Assessment, 10*(2): 178-182.

Niti O. Khemka and Rajesh R. Rathod (2016). "A Study of Academic Anxiety of Secondary School Students", *TechnoLEARN, 6* (1): 31-34, June 2016.

Noraini Idris (2005). *Teaching and Learning of Mathematics*. Utusan Publications.

Prima Vitasari, Muhammad Nubli Abdul Waha, Ahmad Othman, Tutut Herawan and Suriya Kumar Sinnadurai (2010). "The Relationship between Study Anxiety and Academic Performance among Engineering Students", *Procedia Social and Behavioural Sciences*, 8:490-497.

Tobias, S. and Weissbrod, C. (1980). "Anxiety and Mathematics: An Update", *Harvard Educational Review, 50*(1):63-70.

STRESS MANAGEMENT

12
Stress Management
Techniques and Models

Mujibul Hasan Siddiqui and *MD Rajesh Ali*

What is Stress?

Stress is the "psychological, physiological and behavioural response by an individual when they perceive a lack of equilibrium between the demands placed upon them and their ability to meet those demands, which, over a period of time, leads to ill-health" (Palmer, 1989).

Stress is the reaction of the body for any change that needs an adjustment or response. The body responses to these changes with mental, emotional, and physical responses. Stress is an ordinary part of an individual. People can experience stress from their environment, their ideas, their thoughts. Even stress can occur during a mortgage, a promotion or even during the birth of a child of an individual.

A distress condition occurs due to no relief of stress. A distress condition is a negative stress reaction. Distress can disbalance of the internal balance of the body of an individual. Chest problems, elevated blood pressure, sexual problem, emotional problems, sleeping problems, headache problems, eye pain, etc. can be occur due to distress. Depression, anxiety, panic, worry, heart disease, accidents, cancer, lung ailments, suicide, and cirrhosis of the liver result from distress.

Sometimes people use tobacco, alcohol, drugs, shopping, sex, and internet to resolve the stress. People hopefully use these compulsive behaviours and substances to relieve stress but instead of relieving the stress they become more stressful and cause more problems. The distressed human being becomes spellbound in a ferocious circle and is trapped therein.

The environmental factors that trigger this reaction are called stressors. Noises, a speeding car, loud music, aggressive nature of men and women, terrifying moments in movies, are the examples of the stressor. The more stressor people experience, the more stress it gives.

Symptoms of Stress

Cambridge English Dictionary defines symptoms as "any feeling of illness or physical or mental change that is caused by a particular disease:

He's complaining of all the usual flu symptoms — a high temperature, headache, and so on". There are physical, emotional and behavioural symptoms of stress. The physical symptoms are as follows:

- Sweating.
- Eye pain.
- Chest pain.
- Cramps or muscle spasms.
- Fainting.
- Erectile dysfunction and loss of libido.
- Back pain.
- Sometime feel the headache.
- Heart problem.
- High blood pressure.
- Lower immunity against diseases.
- Nervous twitches.
- Pins and needles.
- Sleeping problems.
- Muscular aches.
- Stomach upset.

According to a 2012 study, childhood obesity is caused by stressors experienced by parents, for example, financial problems or single-parent household management.

Emotional reactions can include:

- Anger.
- Burnout.
- Anxiety.
- Concentration issues.
- Depression among men and women.
- Fatigue in body.
- Insecurity is the cause of stress among people.
- Poor memory.
- Bad temper.
- Impatience.
- Melancholy.

Behaviours linked to stress include:

- Some people take too much food and some people take too little.
- Sometimes suddenly people become angry outbursts.
- Taking out of society.
- Sometimes people take drug and alcohol.
- Taking too much tobacco.
- Problems in relation become the cause of stress.

Management

Management is an effective leadership process. It involves creative problem solving, motivating employees and making sure that the organization accomplishes its objectives and goals. In simple, management is the process of getting organizational goals by working with and through people and other organizational resources.

There are five functions of management—

- Planning.
- Organizing.
- Staffing.
- Directing.
- Controlling and coordinating.

Stress Management

Stress management is a broad field of techniques and psychotherapies.

It mainly aims at controlling the level of stress of an individual and improving the functions of the everyday life of a person. Stress has major negative consequences. In the words of Hans Selye, stress is actually distress or significant negative consequences. It produces numerous mental and physical symptoms which are the cause of depression or anxiety. Mental and physical problems are seen due to stress which pushes a person to become a person like depression.

In modern society, stress management plays a crucial role. Stress management means a happy and healthy life. It is one of the keys to a successful life in this scientific era. But life needs plenty of things. So it has a great demand to fulfil its goal and difficult to handle it properly. Instead of these difficulties, stress management provides a suitable way to overcome these problems.

It is hopeful to say that levels of stress are readily measurable. Several physiological tests are there for measuring it.

For reducing the levels of stress, the techniques of stress management are also found. These are used by health professionals and other persons also. The main aim of these techniques is to reduce the level of stress, provide positive feelings to work or promote ill-free health. If one person is bothering about the levels of stress then by using other techniques like exercise, maintaining routine, writing ideas and thoughts, fulfilling hobbies, speaking truth regularly can release stress. Two persons are not alike that's why every technique is not suited for everyone. Different stress managing techniques are needed for individual persons for a better solution. For example, two persons are going on a lonely path at night; one person feels fear while the other enjoys it. In another example, seeing the exam schedule of the board a student becomes panic while the other one becomes happy.

Everything must need evaluation. To evaluate the effectiveness of various stress management techniques, it is very difficult due to limited research on that field. Psychotherapy and other therapies are used as stress management techniques. Some have widely accepted for its effective treatment while others are less important due to low effectiveness among people.

There are many models of stress management, each with distinctive explanations of mechanisms for controlling stress. Much more research is necessary to provide a better understanding of which mechanisms actually operate and are effective in practice.

Definitions of Stress Management

- Stress management is a method of minimizing stress.
- Stress management defines stress accurately as a physiological response of an individual to an external stimulus that triggers the "fight-or-flight" reaction.
- Put simply, stress management is:
  "set of techniques and programmes intended to help people deal more effectively with stress in their lives by analyzing the specific stressors and taking positive actions to minimize their effects". (*Gale Encyclopaedia of Medicine*, 2008).

Stress can be minimized by doing **meditation, exercise**, and **yoga.** These are popular examples of stress management.

Stress occurs due to the pressure of an individual in everyday life. It is one type of tension or anxiety. The capacity to diminish or handle the emotional or physical effects of such anxiety is known as stress management skills.

The employers of various institutions and companies or organizations have been burdened with their legal responsibility. It is very difficult to maintain their physical health and mental state of mind.

Organizations give great emphasis on stress management.

Why is Stress Management Important?

A certain level of stress is always present in any person, organization or institution. As soon as the level of stress escalates to a point that it becomes perilous for the well-being of the institution or any workplace as well as employees, stress management becomes important. It has the following benefits:

- It enables a person to motivate employees better. A stressful situation can have a shocking effect on the spirits of workers. It is causing increased absenteeism and employee turnover. However, good stress management skills assist the morale of workers to stay together so that they are more motivated and better-paying attention to their works. Stress management skills motivate the employees for better performance.

- Reduce chances of workplace conflicts. In the workplace, different people come to work. So that they have different opinions, personalities, different backgrounds because two people are not alike. These are the reasons behind conflict and these are the reasons to increase the stress levels in the workplace. Good stress management skills can reduce this level of stress, build good reports between heads and their subordinates in any organization. It shatters the workplace relationships, undermining the overall culture. However, effective stress management skills put off such distractions and put up teamwork. It makes fun and easier in the life of people.
- It improves productivity even in stressful situations. Stress management skills are the main contributors to good productivity. Here the relationships between workplace and employee morale are considered. Much productivity depends on good relationships. Researches have shown that there is a lesser chance of complaints if the stress management skills are ideal where poor decision-making is seen in most stressful circumstances.

Seven Tips for Stress Management

Before discussing stress management techniques, there are several factors to consider.

The following seven tips are adapted from The American Psychological Association ("Check Out the Stress Tip Sheet" 2018) to support individuals with a stress management plan:

1. Understand Own Stress

Stress varies from person to person. By understanding what stress looks like to a person, that person can be better arranged, and arrive at for his stress management toolbox when needed.

2. Identify Stress Sources

What causes a person to be stressed? There may be family problems, social problems, and institutional problems. A client should identify the source causing it himself or herself.

3. Learn to Recognize Stress Signals

Stress is a psychological disease or disorder and every disease has its own symptoms like headaches, eye pain, stomach pain, low tolerance or a combination of the above 'symptoms'. A person should be aware of these symptoms of stress.

4. Recognize a Person's Stress Strategies

What is your go-to tactic for calming down? A person must set his strategies to handle the stress in a systematic and scientific way. These can be behaviours learned over years and sometimes aren't the healthy option. For example, some people can take over food for reducing stress. But it is not a good way to reduce stress. Some people cope with stress by self-medicating, reading the newspaper, reading good books or religious books whatever he or she loves to read or overeating.

5. Implement Healthy Stress Management Strategies

Sometimes people are applying unhealthy coping behaviours to overcome the stress like overeating or mobile chat to handle the problem. They must practice meditation or reading good books instead of wasting time with discussions with friends. Practical implementations become a person habitual for doing the right action at the right moment. The American Psychological Association advises that switching out one behaviour at a time is most effectual in creating positive change.

6. Make Self-Care a Priority

There is a proverb that 'charity begins from home'. A person must make time for himself first, and then put his well-being before others. This can feel selfish to start, but it is like the airplane analogy—we must put our own oxygen mask on before we can assist others. Well-being is needed first. For well-being a person must do the following things:

- Enough sleep.
- Food.

- Deep meditation.
- Exercise.

Self-care is group-care.

7. Ask for Support When Needed

Don't need to talk to each and every problem with others to reduce stress. It does not reduce the tension but this habit can increase his tension. He who feels not well can speak with a healthcare professional. It is needed for him and it can reduce his stresses unless to speak with others.

Techniques of Stress Management

The problem of stress can be resolved by resorting to some techniques like some guides or books related to stress management, e-resources, or by attending stress management counselling and by getting help by elder people, parents, and teachers. Psychotherapists and counsellors can minimize the stress of these people who have problems in group therapy sessions.

Stress management encompasses techniques intended to equip a person with effective coping mechanisms for dealing with psychological stress.

Causes of stress: Many things can trigger the stress reaction, including danger, threat, bad news, illness, as well as significant changes in one's life such as the death of a loved one.

Main techniques of stress management include:

- Self-understanding oneself or others (e.g. Type A—self-identification or Type B-personality)— understanding the strength or weaknesses.
- Self-management (e.g. becoming better-organized)—well manager.
- Conflict resolution—A better solution comes through active communication with people.
- Showing a more positive attitude can help a person to overcome stress.
- Meditation.
- Talking himself or herself.

- Regular exercise in the morning or evening time.
- Praying Salah or Namaz regularly.
- Yoga Nidra.
- Diet can be replaced.
- More rest is needed according to the demand of the body.
- Autogenic training is helpful to reduce stress.
- A person can engage himself with various social activities within society.
- Psychological treatment helps to reduce anxiety or tension. This therapy is called Cognitive therapy, based on behavioural activities.
- Cranial release technique.
- Fulfilling the hobbies.
- Mindfulness.
- Listening to music.
- Nootropics.
- Reading poetry or novels.
- Artistic expression.
- Fractional relaxation.
- Humour.
- Progressive relaxation.
- Spas.
- Somatics training.
- Spending time in nature.
- Proper time management is another stress management technique.
- Stress balls.
- Playing with own pets.
- Taking natural medicine.
- Clinically validated alternative treatments like go to swimming.
- Good decision.

Techniques of stress management will vary according to the philosophical paradigm.

Stress Prevention and Resilience

Stress prevention and resilience are the theory and practice of cognitive-behavioural therapy. Many techniques have traditionally been developed to handle the consequences of stress. Research is going on to reduce the drastic effects of stress on human life or their social life. Stress prevention and resilience is a subject closely related to psychological resilience-building. A number of self-help approaches to stress-prevention and resilience-building have been developed, drawing mainly on the theory and practice of cognitive-behavioural therapy.

Some common things have to discuss here to reach the goals of this chapter. These are as follows:

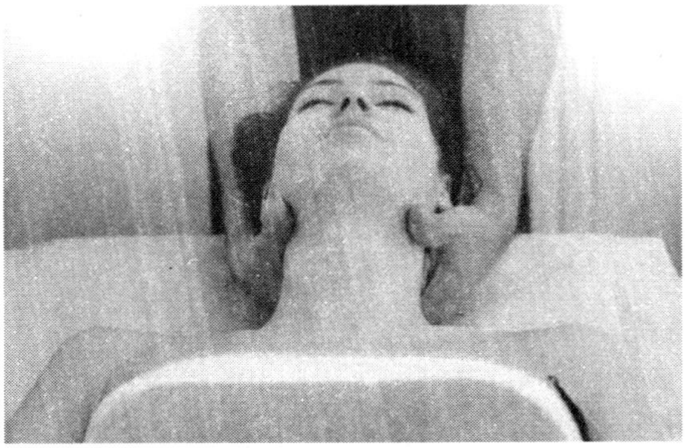

Yoga, massage, meditation or listening to music can help a person to reduce distress. It means it prevents stress.

Exercise: exercise is beneficial for human beings. Physical well-being and good mental sound depend on regular exercise.

Although a person reduces substances like drugs, alcohol, tobacco, and caffeine makes a person mad instead of preventing stress. People should avoid using this type of thing to reduce stress or stresses. There must be regular exercises to release tension.

Nutrition: An ill-health is occurs due to malnutrition matter. A healthy person must diet properly with healthy fruit and vegetables.

Prioritizing: focus on the most important task than less important on the basis of the demand for the work or situation.

Time: set a proper time for each and every work or task to be completed.

Talking Method: stress can be reduced by talking to family members, friends, colleagues or neighbours.

Breathing and relaxation: there must the proper provision of meditation, massage, exercise, and *yoga*. Breathing and relaxation techniques can help us.

Reducing the workload: in this technique, a person can reduce the workload by allocating the works or sharing the responsibilities.

Find the de-stressor: people can reduce stress by reading his or her favourite novel or magazine or by listening to music or spending time with a charming one.

Establishing support networks: good rapport is very effective. According to The APA, a social support network is— talking to siblings, family members, neighbours, and local community members, club members. Work in charity or religious organizations is an example of a support network.

Group work: working with groups can help a person to release the tension.

Online solution: there is also an online solution. It's a modern technical era. People can contact best doctors or psychiatrists through online sitting at home and can get medical or psychological solution for example, through stress management training, a doctor or psychiatrist can often help to release from anxiety or tension.

How to Improve Stress Management Skills?

Following are the measures of stress management skills which enhance the morale of each and every employee along with their performances in academic or professional life:

- *Identification of problem:* the better solution is depended on its identification of the problem. In any organization, two types of causes are there for stress. One is the personal problem or cause and the other is a workplace problem. To improve the stress management skills identification of problem which is the source causing should be the first step.
- *Priority Base:* after identifying the root cause of the problem, it is the duty of a person to make a list based on priority. It is the easiest way of improve stress management skills and the easiest way to handle the stressors one at a time.
- *Motivation level:* there must be a high motivation level to find out solutions. Motivation gives a person to overcome from various stressors. There are many ways where a person can boost up his morale for managing his stress. For example,

he can make a list of similar issues of a past time then he can recall how he did it. Here a person can keep a gift for himself if he can overcome the stressful situations successfully he will be awarded by himself. It is no matter that every stressor has a solution. Sometimes a person can not get a solution, then there is nothing to be worried about, it happens.

- *Role of exercise:* human beings are going through a lot of works from morning to night. He may face mental problems. Because he is facing a lot of issues in the surroundings where he lives. He needs active blood circulation that's why he can do *yoga*, exercise or praying *Salah* (namaz), the best exercise if he belongs to the Muslim community. These exercises give muscle relaxation. This will help a person from mental or physical stress.

Measuring Stress

Stress is measurable. It can measure through the psychological test. There is a scale of measuring stress i.e., The Holmes and Rahe Stress Scale. It is used to rate stressful life events. There is another scale named Depression Anxiety Stress Scales (DASS) based on self-report items. Blood pressure levels as well as galvanic skin response can also be measured to test stress levels, and changes in stress levels. A digital thermometer can be used to evaluate changes in skin temperature, which can indicate activation of the fight-or-flight response drawing blood away from the extremities. Cortisol is the main hormone released during a stress response and measuring cortisol from hair will give a 60- to the 90-day baseline stress level of an individual. This method of measuring stress is currently the most popular method in the clinic.

Effectiveness

From the above discussions related to stress management or stress management skills, it can be stated that stress management can help to:

- Get rid of or alter the source of stress.
- Revise the way you view a stressful event.
- Lower the impact that stress might have on your body.
- Learn alternative ways of coping.

- Stress management therapy pursues one or more of these approaches.
- Stress management has physiological and immune benefits.
- Positive outcomes are observed using a combination of non-drug interventions.
- Treatment of anger or hostility,
- Autogenic training.
- Talking therapy (around a relationship or existential issues) biofeedback cognitive therapy anxiety clinical depression.

Models

As per *Collins Dictionary*—

- A model is something that people use as a copy to understand the pattern of targeted goals.
- A model can be defined as a theoretical description, which is helpful in understanding the process or system of work.

According to the *Cambridge English Dictionary*:

- A way of doing something that can be used as an example or can be copied: *For example, He prefers the American approach to wealth creation over the European model.*

The common models are:

(a) The emergency response/fight-or-flight response by Walter Cannon (1914, 1932).
(b) General Adaptation Syndrome by Hans Selye (1936).
(c) Stress Model of Henry and Stephens (1977).
(d) Transactional (or Cognitive) Stress Model/Stress Model of Lazarus after Lazarus (1974).
(e) Theory of Resource Conservation by Stevan Hobfoll (1988, 1998; Hobfoll & Buchwald, 2004).
(f) Health realization/innate health model.

(a) The Emergency Response/Fight-or-flight Response by Walter Cannon (1914, 1932)

The fight-or-flight response is a physiological reaction of an individual or an animal. It takes place when humar beings or animals observe a danger to their survival. In short, this is a defensive response of living beings to be protected from any type of perceived danger. Following are some of the characteristics:

(1) This model was first introduced by Walter Bradford.
(2) According to this theory, animals react to threats that result in fighting or fleeing.
(3) Broadly speaking, some hormonal changes occur in the animal body. Due to the secretion of catecholamine-nor epinephrine and epinephrine in animal body fight or fleeing are observed.
(4) According to Amit Sood, professor of Medicine, Mayo Clinic College of Medicine, due to the effect of estrogen and testosterone hormones, animals react in stress as they react due to the effect of neurotransmitters dopamine and serotonin.
(5) This response is known as the first stage of "general adaptation syndrome" that affects and controls the stress responses found in animals like, vertebrates and other organisms.

The autonomic nervous system in animals plays a vital role in regulating digestion, respiratory rate, heart rate, pupillary response, urination, and sexual desire. This is the primary mechanism in controlling and managing the flight responses and its role is determined by two different elements.

(b) General Adaptation Syndrome by Hans Selye (1936)

In the General Adaptation Syndrome, a model is comprised of three components which explain the body's response to stress:

1. Alarm Stage

The Alarm stage is the first stage of General Adaptation Syndrome. In this stage, the body releases stress hormones like adrenaline, nor adrenaline, and cortisol due to which animals do unusual activities, and the danger or threat is called stressor.

For example, when a businessman suddenly comes to know about the major financial loss in his business, his mind and body go to the alarm stage. In such a situation, stress hormones release and cause stress, and the news of the loss of business is stressor here.

2. Resistance Stage

The resistance stage is the second stage. In this stage, the stress level reduces because, in the first stage, the body's capacity to defend minimizes since the body has responded to the stressor.

In this stage, the body remains on guard but is not stronger as it was in the first stage.

3. Exhaustion Stage

This is the third stage. The stress has been persistent for a longer period. In this stage, the body loses its ability to overcome the problems. Here in this stage, the body loses energy and unable to resolve the stressors and can cause serious health problems if not resolved immediately.

Therefore, the General Adaptation Syndrome Model by Hans Selye speaks about the biological changes and the process of adaptation in animals' bodies during stress.

(c) The Psycho Physiological Stress Model (Henry and Stephens, 1977)

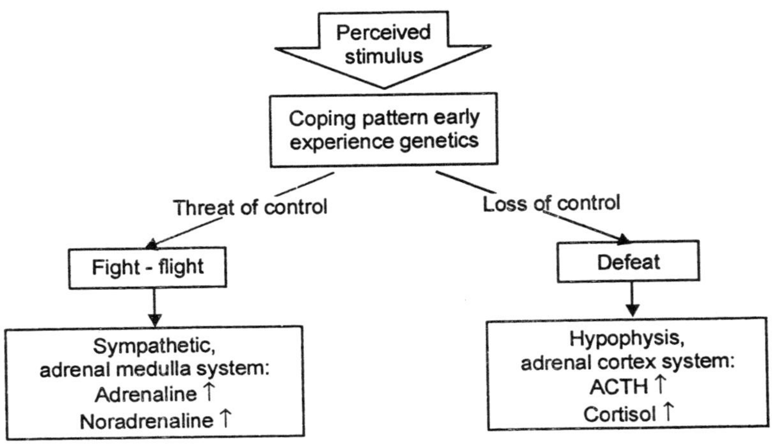

(d) Transactional Model

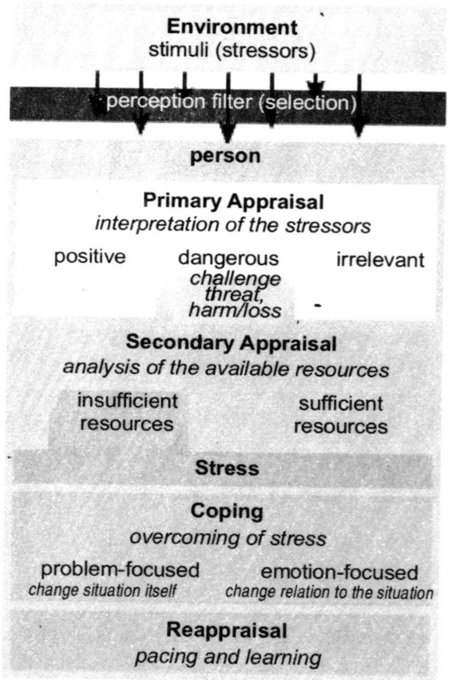

Fig.: Transactional Model of Stress and Coping of Richard Lazarus.

Richard Lazarus and Susan Folkman suggested in 1981 that stress can be thought of as resulting from an Şimbalance between demands and resources¿ or as occurring when Şpressure exceeds one's perceived ability to cope¿. Stress management was developed and premised on the idea that stress is not a direct response to a stressor but rather one's resources and ability to cope mediate the stress response and are amenable to change, thus allowing stress to be controllable.

Among the many stressors mentioned by employees, these are the most common:

- Conflicts in the company.
- The way employees are treated by their bosses/supervisors or company.

- Lack of job security.
- Company policies.
- Co-workers who don't do their fair share.
- Unclear expectations.
- Poor communication.
- Not enough control over assignments.
- Inadequate pay or benefits.
- Urgent deadlines.
- Too much work.
- Long hours.
- Uncomfortable physical conditions.
- Relationship conflicts.
- Co-workers making careless mistakes.
- Dealing with rude customers.
- Lack of co-operation.
- How the company treats co-workers.

There must be an effective stress management programme. It is necessary to identify the causing factors of stress among human beings. And one person must choose the best intervention methods to reduce stress. Lazarus and Folkman's interpretation of stress emphasizes the transaction between people and their external environment which is called the Transactional Model. The model contends that stress may not be a stressor if men do not identify the stressor as a menace but rather as positive or even challenging. Also, if the person possesses or can use adequate coping skills, then stress may not actually be a result or develop because of the stressor. The model proposes that people can be taught to manage their stress and cope with their stressors. They may learn to change their perspective of the stressor and provide them with the ability and confidence to improve their lives and handle all of the types of stressors.

(e) Theory of Resource Conservation by Stevan Hobfoll (1988, 1998; Hobfoll & Buchwald, 2004)

Conservation of Resources (COR) theory has given by Stevan Hobfoll, a well-known theory in the past 20 years. This theory emphasizes the objective elements of loss and threat. This theory focuses on objective reality and circumstances. Biological and cultural aspects are analyzed for the betterment of this theory. COR focuses on social appraisal rather than the personal appraisal. COR theory has also become a major theory in the field of burnout and the emerging field of positive psychology.

(f) Health Realization/Innate Health Model

The health realization/innate health model of stress is also founded on the idea that stress does not necessarily follow the presence of a potential stressor. Instead of focusing on the individual's appraisal of so-called stressors in relation to his or her own coping skills (as the transactional model does), the health realization model focuses on the nature of thought, stating that it is ultimately a person's thought processes that determine the response to potentially stressful external circumstances. In this model, stress results from appraising oneself and one's circumstances through a mental filter of insecurity and negativity, whereas a feeling of well-being results from approaching the world with a "quiet mind".

This model proposes that helping stressed individuals understand the nature of thought—especially providing them with the ability to recognize when they are in the grip of insecure thinking, disengage from it, and access natural positive feelings—will reduce their stress.

Types of Stress

The APA recognizes three different types of stress that require different levels of management. These are as follows:

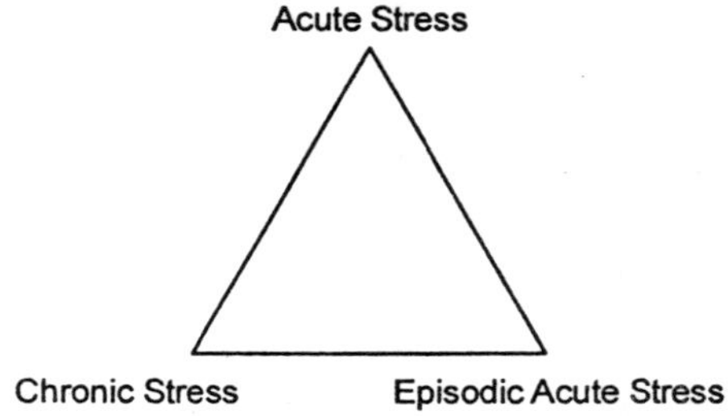

(a) Acute Stress

Acute stress is short-term stress. It is the most ordinary way that stress occurs. The events pressures of many programmes are the root cause of acute stress. Sometimes students feel anxiety due to the deadline for assignments in school. Sometimes the demand for society is the cause of distress.

For example, arguments are the root cause of stress among students in school. Upset due to family problems or personal problems are also the cause of stress. Basically, short-term effects are there like an upset stomach, headaches, pain in the body, etc.

Acute stress does not cause the same amount of damage as chronic stress (Long-term stress). But acute stress can become chronic and harmful due to repeated instances of this stress over a long period.

(b) Episodic Acute Stress

Episodic acute stress occurs due to frequent experience acute stress or who face frequent triggers of stress.

In society, some people give many commitments but cannot fulfil it. They have also poor organization or do not have such type of arrangement to reach the goal. They easily display irritation, become tense. This irritation breaks the relationship between people. Some people worry too much on a constant basis is the example of episodic acute stress.

Heart disease and high blood pressure is the cause of episodic acute stress.

(c) Chronic Stress

Chronic stress is the most harmful type of stress. It is long-term stress. Chronic stress can lead to memory loss, damage spatial recognition and produce a decreased drive of eating of an individual.

Chronic stress can occur due to family problem or dysfunctional family matter is the root cause of chronic stress. Ongoing poverty, divorce, an unhappy marriage can cause chronic stress. It occurs when human being never sees run away from the cause of stress and stops looking for solutions. Sometimes, it can be caused by a traumatic experience early in life.

Chronic stress can continue unnoticed, as people can become used to it, unlike acute stress that is new and often has an immediate solution. It can become part of an individual's personality, making them constantly prone to the effects of stress regardless of the scenarios they come up against.

Chronic stress can lead to violent actions, suicide, heart attacks, and strokes.

Conclusion

Stress is mental tension. It is caused by demanding, taxing or burdensome situations or circumstances. Stress doesn't just affect the human's mental state and mood; it affects a person's physical health as well. When a person is much stressed, a hormone called cortisol is released into his bloodstream, suppressing the functioning of our immune, digestive and reproductive systems. That is why it is so important to practice stress management in order to keep his mind and body healthy.

Stress management consists of making changes to one's live if he is in an invariable stressful situation, preventing stress by practicing self-care and relaxation and managing his response to stressful conditions when they take place.

The following table, from the WHO (2018) illustrates the advantages of workplace stress management:

Sl. No.	*To the organization*	*To the employee*
1.	A well-managed wealth and safety programme	A safe and healthy work environment
2.	A positive and caring image	Enhanced self-esteem
3.	Improved staff morale	Reduced stress
4.	Reduced staff turnover	Improved morale
5.	Reduced absenteeism	Increased job satisfaction
6.	Increased productivity	Increased skills for health protection
7.	Reduced health care/insurance costs	Improved health
8.	Reduced risk of fines and litigation	Improved sense of well-being

The following models (we have already discussed) of stress management have been playing a great role in reducing stress among human beings or animals— (a) The emergency response/fight-or-flight response by Walter Cannon (1914, 1932); (b) General Adaptation Syndrome by Hans Selye (1936); (c) Stress Model of Henry and Stephens (1977); (d) Transactional (or cognitive) Stress Model/Stress Model of Lazarus after Lazarus (1974); (e) Theory of resource conservation by Stevan Hobfoll (1988, 1998; Hobfoll & Buchwald, 2004); (f) Health realization/innate health model. People can consult with doctors as well as counsellors for better treatment.

References

Cannon, Walter (1932). *Wisdom of the Body*. United States: W.W. Norton & Company.

Felman, A. (2017). "Why stress happens and how to manage it", *Medical News Today*. Retrieved from: https://www.medicalnewstoday.com/articles/145855.php.

Freshwater, Shawna (2018). "3 Types of stress and health hazards", *Empathysites*. Retrieved from: https://spacioustherapy.com/3-types-stress-health-hazards/

"How to manage and reduce stress." *Mental Health Foundation*. Retrieved from: https://www.mentalhealth.org.uk/publications/how-manage-and-reduce-stress

Husain, A. and Ali, J. (2001). "Identifying stress sources, stress effects and coping behaviour among hockey players", In A. Husain (Eds.). *Stress Research and Stress Management*, 84-106.

Jahan, A. and Bhardwaj, B. (2001). "Assessing source of stress among school teachers", In A. Husain (Eds.). *Stress Research and Stress Management*, 107-131.

"Know your stress to manage your stress." (2014). *Life at Its Best*. Retrieved from: http://www.ppccfl.com/know-your-stress-to-manage-your-stress/

Kandola, A. (2018). "What are the health effects of chronic stress?" *Medical News Today*. Retrieved from: https://www.medicalnewstoday.com/articles/323324.php

"Stress Effects." *The American Institute of Stress*. Retrieved from: https://www.stress.org/stress-effects

"Stress and Stress Management" (2010). *Klinic Community Health Centre*. Retrieved from: https://hydesmith.com/de-stress/files/StressMgt.pdf

Sincere, S.M. (2012). "Three Different Kinds of Stress." *Explorable*. Retrieved from: https://explorable.com/three-different-kinds-of-stress

"Stress effects on the body." *American Psychological Association*. Retrieved from: https://www.apa.org/helpcenter/stress-body

https://my.clevelandclinic.org/health/articles/11874-stress

https://National Institute of Mental Health. Fact sheet on stress Accessed 12/9/2014.

https://www.medicalnewstoday.com/articles/145855.php#types

https://en.wikipedia.org/wiki/Stress_management#Models

https://www.cleverism.com/skills-and-tools/stress-management/

https://dictionary.cambridge.org/dictionary/english/stress-management

https://positivepsychology.com/stress-management-techniques-tips-burn-out/

https://www.collinsdictionary.com/dictionary/english/model

https://dictionary.cambridge.org/dictionary/english/model

https://home.cc.umanitoba.ca/~berczii/hans-selye/walter-cannon-fight-or-flight-response.html

https://explorable.com/general-adaptation-syndrome

http://www.noiseandhealth.org/viewimage.asp?img=NoiseHealth_2000_2_7_7_31745_1.jpg
https://psycnet.apa.org/record/2010-25086-007
https://dictionary.cambridge.org/dictionary/english/symptom
https://brainly.in/question/2543653
https://study.com/academy/lesson/what-is-stress-management-definition-benefits.html

13
Techniques of Stress Management

Qudsiya Jan and *Barkat Hussain Para*

Introduction

Education is the foundation on which a nation is built and prospers. The purpose of education is not just to possess skills and acquire a baggage of information; rather it is argued that the reason is to cultivate the fundamental faculties of learning, to define and pursue a purpose, to empower individuals to become active participants in the transformation of their societies, thus helps them to reach their full potential. It is rightly said by Lodge, "*Whatever broadens our horizon, deepens our insight, refines our reactions, and stimulates our thoughts and feelings educate us*." Every individual at different spheres of life has its own set of challenges and opportunities. Thus every individual has confounded to some amount of stress in his day-to-day life. There are many sources of stress for example stress is the result of a mismatch between demands and resources, our bodies react with the "fright, fight or flight" response—so basic in the animal world. When demands remain unfulfilled, the result is unproductive tension (Promod Batra, 1994). Stress is mental, i.e. it is always in our minds. Stress starts in the head. Stress is very harmful when it becomes a way of life. Stress is not dependent upon whether you are young or old, boy or girl, rich or poor, educated or uneducated, servant or master. Stress is not dependent where you live...whether in the USA or India or in a small town or village, in Aligarh or Hills of Kashmir. Again, a typical problem causing stress is "success" in our profession or business. Well, why should it? One can take failures and successes in stride. We can make our life either stressful or very simple depending upon what we choose. Before talking about the techniques of stress management, it would be better to know what stress is.

Stress

Stress is defined as any challenge that exceeds the coping abilities of the individual. Selye (1956) defines stress as any external event or any internal drive which threatens to upset the organism equilibrium. Wheeler (2007) viewed stress as a word of physics. He referred it to the amount of force used on an object. In real life, he related it as how certain issues that carry force are applied to humans. Financial difficulties, health issues, personal conflicts and work issues all carry pressure on physiology and psychology of a person. Life exists through the persistence of a complex dynamic equilibrium called homeostasis, which is constantly challenged by these internal or external adverse forces called stressors. These can be emotional or physical in nature. These stressors originate from the environment but most often they emerge from within in the form of worry, anxiousness, regret, discouragement, low confidence and self-esteem. In this arena of cut-throat competition, also students of all stages are affected by the unique challenges. They are expected to be the future elites in society. Due to the fast rhythm of life, problems are ever new and varied and they need to adapt themselves to different situations of life, thus the stress on them is considerable.

One of the oldest laws in psychology holds that, beyond a moderate level, increases in anxiety and worry erode mental abilities (Ramesar, Koortzen & Oosthuizen, 2009). Amongst all stressing issues, academic stress is mostly found in students. Kumar and Jejurkar (2005) as cited by Khan, Altaf & Kausar (2013) concluded that academic factors were mainly responsible for a higher level of stress among students. Academic stress refers to demands placed on students within the academic environment (Van Heerden-Pieterse, 2015). (Bojuwoye, 2002; Cotton, Dollard & De Jonge, 2002; Kausar, 2010) Cited in (Mason, 2017) stated that the concept of academic stress emerges as a prominent theme when considering factors that enhance low retention, high dropout and poor performance. Sarita (2015) stated academic stress, the unpleasant psychological condition, happens due to the educational expectations from parents, teachers, peers and family members for high academic achievement, prevailing educational as well as examination system, the overburden of homework etc. It is a frustrating condition which contains academic workload thus reduces the concentration and normal functioning ability of the student. (Hemamalini, Ashok & Sasikala 2018) while describing the sources of academic stress among high school students, Kouzma, N.M., and Kennedy, G.A., (2004) mentioned that Parental Pressure, Anxiety, inadequate resources, academic tests, self-imposed need to succeed, as well as that expected by others are the main sources of academic stress. Fear of examination, poor understanding of subjects, poor time management, academic competition, financial hardships, academic workload, poor academic evaluation procedures, and daily academic hassles are all sources of academic stress.

A great deal of empirical research revealed that academic stress has been deleterious to the student community and is linked to several outcomes such as poor adjustment, mental health problems, suicidal intention, and low academic achievement (Park, Kwon, & Shin, 2014). Stress-related disorders can impair cognitive functions thus affect the students physically, academically, socially and in this way affects the productivity and output the students make. Stress at the educational level leads to a lot of psychological problems in the form of decreased motivation, absenteeism for class and examinations, incompletion of all works etc. To overcome the deleterious effects of academic stress, the students have to utilize suitable coping techniques (Smith & Renk, 2007) as cited by Nakalema, G., & Ssenyonga, J. (2014).

Remember stress is inevitable. It has always been present and will continue to be present regardless of gender, age, social class, wealth, profession and the times in which we live. Stress is not necessarily harmful but can be an asset, as long as it is tolerable, by creating healthy competition among individuals. But since stress mostly leads to unpleasant consequences, and is inevitably present and cannot be avoided, it is important that stress and stressful situations be adequately managed by the individual (M.L. Bhatia, 1994).

Concept of Stress Management

Stress can be successfully managed (Lazarus & Folkman, 1984) explained that the concept of coping refers to cognitive and behavioural strategies persons use to manage situations that they perceive could potentially exceed their resources. Stress management is the ability to maintain and control when the situation, people and events make excessive demands (Bukhsh, Q., Shahzad, A., and Nisa, M., 2011). The reaction of the person is based upon the perception of an event or a situation. The way the individual formulates his mindset, i.e., if he views the situation negatively, he will feel stressed, overwhelmed and out of control; on the other hand, if he views a situation positively, then it is called Eustress, which is also known as good stress. Thus, depending on a person's explanatory style, stress could be viewed as either overpowering or motivational (Dweck, 2006; McGonigal, 2015; Seligman, 2006). Kalli & Shehu (2018) effectively explained that adverse consequences of academic stress can be managed if the students adopt more adaptive mechanisms when their performance begins to decline because of academic stress. Here it is important that the students must be aware of the symptoms and signals caused by stress. The bodily consequences of stress include diseases of heart and circulation, diseases of stomach, weakening of immune-system, psychiatric disorders and so on.

There are stresses in our lives which are unavoidable, so we must learn to change our reactions to them. Stress management is not a problem to be solved, it is an issue to be managed. Thus, the introduction of Stress Management Education into the curriculum could prove useful. It will help students to become trainers for managing stress. This trend will lead to empowering the students to get succeed in their academic and personal life. Encountering stress could help students to reinterpret stressors as opportunities for growth and personal development. It should be noted that stress management techniques apply not only to people who manifest disease or disorder but also to healthy people. After a thorough literature review, the following techniques were identified and are presented and briefly discussed here.

Stress Management Techniques

Autogenic Training: A self-relaxation procedure by which a psycho-physiological determined relaxation response is elicited. This relaxation technique was developed by Johannes Heinrich Schultz. And it aims to achieve deep relaxation and reduce stress. In this technique, the individual learns a set of six standard exercises that — with the use of visual imagination and verbal cues — make the body feel warm, heavy and relaxed. The person learns each exercise by reading about it or watching a teacher, then practising it for a few minutes several times a day. Mastering the exercises, either from a teacher or on one's own, usually requires 4 to 6 months. A meta-analysis of clinical outcome studies in Autogenic Training found that it is useful in a range of diverse disorders including tension headache/ migraine, mild to moderate essential hypertension, coronary heart disease, asthma bronchiale, somatoform pain disorder (unspecified type), Raynaud's disease, anxiety disorders, mild to moderate depression/dysthymia, and functional sleep disorders (Varvogli, L., and Darviri, C., 2011).

Relaxation Response: It was found by Herbert Benson of Harvard University in 1960. Just as stimulating an area of the hypothalamus can cause the stress response, so activating other areas of the brain results in its reduction. He defined this opposite state the "relaxation response." It is a simple practice that once learned takes 10 to 20 minutes a day to achieve relaxation. The important characteristics of a relaxation programme are:

- Repetition of a word, sound, prayer, thought, phrase or muscular movement, through which concentration is achieved.
- Passive return to the repetition when other thoughts intrude.

When an organism is stressed its physiological response is the fight-or-flight response, whereas when the body is no longer in perceived danger, and the autonomic nervous system functioning returns to normal, the relaxation response (RR) occurs. During Relaxation Response, the body moves from a state of physiological arousal, including increased heart rate and blood pressure, slowed digestive functioning, decreased blood flow to the extremities, increased release of stress hormones, and other responses preparing the body to fight or flight, to a state of physiological relaxation, where blood pressure, heart rate, digestive functioning and hormonal levels return to their normal state. This technique can reduce hypertension, improve cardiac rehabilitation and relieve medical symptoms (Varvogli, L., & Darviri, C., 2011).

Biofeedback: A process that enables an individual to learn how to change physiological activity to improve health and performance. Precise instruments measure physiological activity such as brainwaves, heart function, breathing, muscle activity, and skin temperature. These instruments rapidly and accurately 'feedback' information to the user. The presentation of this information often in conjunction with changes in thinking, emotions, and behaviour supports desired physiological changes. Over time, these changes can endure without continued use of an instrument. This training is done in the presence of qualified biofeedback therapists. The therapists work with their patients and explain to them the process of reading and then responding to the physiological information relating to their body using various biofeedback devices. When patients understand and practice this concept, after several sessions spanned in 3-6 months, they are then able to take control of their physiological functions like heartbeat rate, blood pressure, etc. They can also learn to observe the changes that happen when they apply the learning from the training. Biofeedback has been used successfully for the treatment of headaches, the control of high blood pressure, and type II diabetes (DM) (Varvogli, L., & Darviri, C., 2011).

Progressive Muscle Relaxation: It is a technique for reducing stress and anxiety by alternately tensing and relaxing the muscles developed by American physician Edmund Jacobson in the early 1920s. Jacobson argued that since muscle tension accompanies anxiety, one can reduce anxiety by learning how to relax the muscular tension. It involves the tensing and relaxing of muscle groups over the legs, abdomen, chest, arms and face. In a sequential pattern, with eyes closed, the tension of the individual place in a given muscle group purposefully for approximately 10 seconds and then releases it for 20 seconds before continuing with the next muscle group. The mental component requires that the individual focuses on the distinction between the feelings of tension and relaxation. With practice, the patient learns how to effectively relax in a short period of time (Varvogli, L., & Darviri, C., 2011).

Cognitive Behavioural Therapy (CBT): It was developed through a merging of behaviour therapy with cognitive therapy. It is time-limited psychological treatment for several health conditions such as anxiety disorders, major depression, and health problems such as insomnia, headache, and tinnitus among others. Briefly, CBT is a treatment approach that encompasses assessment strategies, cognitive and behavioural treatment techniques, and relies on collaboration between clinician and patient, who has the responsibility to complete homework assignments. Cognitive change and the resulting behavioural change relate to cognitive restructuring, which proposes that people are directly responsible for generating dysfunctional emotions and their resultant behaviours, like stress, depression, anxiety, something that can be prevented by changing thought patterns. Cognitive restructuring is the process of learning to disprove cognitive distortions, aiming to replace one's irrational, counter-factual beliefs with more accurate and beneficial ones. This is established by helping the individual gain awareness of detrimental thought habits, learn to challenge them and substitute life-enhancing thoughts and beliefs. It has been used successfully in the management of the cardiovascular disorder, diabetes, pain management, headaches, overweight and obesity.

Mindfulness-Based Cognitive Therapy: Mindfulness-Based Stress Reduction was pioneered by Jon Kabat-Zinn, Ph.D. and assisted by Saki Santorelli, Ph.D. and colleagues in 1979 at the University Of Massachusetts Medical Centre. It is a form of MBSR that provides information about depression and cognitive therapy based exercises that link thinking and its resulting impact on feeling. MBSR is a structured 8-week group programme employing mindfulness meditation in order to improve mental and physical suffering, associated with physical, psychosomatic and psychiatric disorders. MBSR is not a religion or dogma and is based upon a systematic procedure to develop an enhanced awareness of the moment-to-moment experience of one's mental process. The technique assumes that greater awareness of the here-and-now will provide clearer and more accurate perception, reduce negative affect and improve energy and coping. Systematic mindfulness training can influence brain areas involved in regulating attention, awareness, and emotion. MBSR offers psychological and health benefits for patients.

Problem-focused coping: It is directed towards altering, addressing or managing external stressors and it includes aspects such as drawing on social support and initiating problem-solving behaviours. It may prove to be the most appropriate when dealing with a stressor that is changeable (Lazarus & Folkman, 1984). It is usually posited as an adaptive, positive way of dealing with stress, especially when individuals view the stressful event as controllable (Folkman and Lazarus, 1988).

Emotion-focused coping: This technique is directed towards internal states, rather than external situations, that may have triggered a stress reaction and are more likely to be initiated when individuals appraise situations as harmful, threatening and potentially overwhelming. Examples of emotion-focused coping strategies are wishful thinking, minimising, and avoidance (Lazarus & Folkman, 1984). Emotion-focused methods of coping encompass more indirect methods to avoid the stressor or control its emotional impacts, such as ignoring, distancing oneself from the stressor, excessive worry, or anger (Folkman and Lazarus, 1988). Students who rely mainly on emotion-focused strategies in response to stress may be at greater risk for poor outcomes such as depression and substance use problems.

Problem-focused coping: It is directed towards altering, addressing or managing external stressors and it includes aspects such as drawing on social support and initiating problem-solving behaviours. It may prove to be the most appropriate when dealing with a stressor that is changeable (Lazarus & Folkman, 1984). It is usually posited as an adaptive, positive way of dealing with stress, especially when individuals view the stressful event as controllable (Folkman and Lazarus, 1988).

Live a Healthy Lifestyle: One should live a healthy lifestyle. Getting plenty of exercises, healthy eating, relaxation techniques such as meditation, prayer and breathing exercises; allowing time for vacations and breaks in between work, the arrangement of schedules for hobbies, extracurricular activities, fun activities, recreation and leisure. One should always take pleasure and enjoy work. It is observed that due to the increase use of social media the young generation become self-centred and only connect with the technology. It reduces the physical movement of the body and spending time with relatives and friends. All these create stress which increases the case of depression and suicide. It is necessary and suggestions to the young people that make objective planned and systematic use of technology within the limit and share your emotions with your loved ones. Research shows that those who are sleep-deprived have more trouble learning and remembering, and perform more poorly in many areas. Students can do much for their own stress management simply by eating a balanced diet and getting sufficient sleep. They can add to that by maintaining a schedule, including regular waking and sleeping hours (Nivethitha & Rita (2016).

Positive Learning Environment: A student's academic motivation and school connectedness also play stress-buffering roles and are associated with low levels of depression, anxiety and perceived stress among high school students (Gilman and Anderman, 2006). Students may be guided regarding proper time management. Thus, a student should set up an appropriate time schedule for all the tasks and must have a routine to do all kinds of tasks. He has to decide what things are more important that need to be done and what are the things that carry lesser priority and can wait. Regular study habits and adequate preparation can help students to avoid stress (Waghachavare, *et al.,* 2013). Teaching techniques and college environments should be adapted to the needs of the students. Teachers may identify the symptoms of stress in students and provide counselling services to help them cope with it. The departmental committee may be formed which should educate the students about how to identify and manage stress (Bukhsh, Shahzad, & Nisa, 2011). The productive utilization of existing student welfare systems, development of more 'student-friendly' environments and regular periodic extracurricular activities with universal participation can prove to be useful stress-busters. The promotion of healthy dietary and lifestyle habits should be encouraged. Learning Stress among students may also be reduced by utilization of good study skills, which involves remaining calm, focused and organized (Varvogli, L., & Darviri, C., 2011).

Practice Facing Stressful Moments: It is vital to think about a situation that causes stress and practice how to effectively deal with it. If a person knows that speaking in front of the group or making a presentation causes stress then he should practice or do the rehearsal in advance with a trusted friend or a fellow student. If taking exams to cause stress or a particular subject causes stress then it is recommended that individuals should practice taking tests at home as well as focus thoroughly upon the subject area when there are no time pressures.

Examine Your Expectations: One should set up proper goals and objectives that he wants to achieve and have to make sure that expectations are rational; one should watch out for self-confidence and work hard towards the achievement of goals and objectives. In order to manage stress, an individual has to develop positive thinking and be satisfied with what he has and what he wants to accomplish.

Creating a Social Network: Loneliness is an extreme and distressful state of mind and it can cause stress amongst individuals of all age groups, children, young adults, middle-aged people and older persons. In order to curb the stress of loneliness, it is essential to create a social network and communicate with the people around. It is necessary to develop a support system of friends and relatives that one can talk to when it is required. For example, a working person who works five days a week from morning until evening, he has weekends to take out time for himself and over the weekend he socializes with friends and gets engaged into recreational activities.

Learn to Accept Change as a Part of Life: Changes and transformations do occur in life in all kinds of activities, family, job, education, career, location and so forth. All these changes do lead to stress, but an individual should understand that changes are a crucial part of one's life and should learn to accept them wholeheartedly, he should think of changes in a positive manner and not form negative opinions about them.

Proper Time Management: Developing a schedule and managing time properly indicates goals and priorities. Students should always try to plan ahead and avoid procrastination; it will help them to manage stress effectively. Hence, students should always make a 'To-Do list' or a planner and keep track of deadlines and schedules and learn to say 'No' so that they can beat stress.

Being Organized: Students should always develop a good study environment where they can concentrate, focus and get things done. Moreover, if they are well organized, they can bring the peace of mind that comes from knowing where everything is, remembering deadlines and test dates, and clearing the mind of some of the mental clutter.

Stress Management Counselling Help: Stress management counselling help allows you to explore the underlying causes of your stress and anxiety. It examines your thoughts, feelings and behaviours that contribute to stress. It helps in to gain self-understanding and insight, including identifying stress triggers. It offers tailor-made coping strategies to manage stressful situations. It improves your ability to handle pressures and your reactions to them.

Conclusion

To de-stress himself man needs to capitalize his strength and repair his weak link. Stress is a mental process which starts from womb and continues until death. Throughout our whole life, we face very difficult situations. Life throws a various curve and hard balls to us. Thus, stress management is a matter of concern to all of us. After surveying the literature of many scholars, psychologists and other professional, it was found that various techniques can be used to de-stress yourself. These techniques are very useful to manage our emotions in the right direction.

Stress is like a rose bush! It depends on how we look at it. We might see the rose bush as a treacherous plant, its branches covered with sharp thorns with some rose flowers at the ends. Or we might see the rose bush as all roses with a few thorns underneath and even these thorns crumble when you hold the bush forcefully with a gloved hand! Life is full of problems, some of them very prickly indeed. We can magnify the problems. Or we can reduce them to brain-teasers and solve them one by one with better ideas. We can fall victim to stress, or make it work for you. As of last we can conclude that our minds are acres of land where we can either grow happiness or grow stress, unfortunately, it is a human tendency to grow stress if deliberate efforts are not made to plant our SEEDS (Stores, Examples, Exhibits, Demonstrations, and Sayings) of happiness. And like a piece of land, unless tilling, seeding, watering, fertilizing and weeding are done as required, we are bound to get nothing but weeds! Happiness is harvest; stress is weeds.

References

Batra, P. (2009). *Simple Ways to Manage Stress*, New Delhi: Vijay Batra; Think Inc. G-42 & G-44, Nizamuddin (West).

Bukhsh, Q.; Shahzad, A. and Nisa, M. (2011). "A Study of Learning Stress and Stress Management strategies of the students of postgraduate level: A case study of Islamia University of Bahawalpur, Pakistan", *Procedia-Social and Behavioural Sciences*, 30:182-186.

Dweck, C. (2006). *Mindset: The New Psychology of Success—How we can learn to fulfil our potential*, New York, N.Y.: Ballantine Books.

Hemamalini, R.; Ashok, V. and Sasikala, V. (2018). "A Study on Stress Management and its Impact among Students", *Sciences*, *7*(3): 101-110.

Kalli, K.A. and Shehu, A.B. (2018). "Effects of Stress on the Academic Performance of Students of Tertiary", *International Journal of Humanities, Art and Social Studies (IJHAS)*, *3*(3).

Khan, M.J.; Altaf, S. and Kausar, H. (2013). "Effects of Perceived Academic Stress on Students' Performance". *FWU Journal of Social Sciences*, *7*(2).

Kouzma, N.M. and Kennedy, G.A. (2004). "Self-reported sources of stress in senior high school students", *Psychological Reports*, 94: 314-316.

Lazarus, R.S. and Folkman, S. (1984). *Stress, Appraisal and Coping*. New York, N.Y.: Springer Publishing Company.

Leonard, N.R.; Gwadz, M.V.; Ritchie, A.; Linick, J.L.; Cleland, C.M.; Elliott, L. and Grethel, M. (2015). "A multi-method exploratory study of stress, coping, and substance use among high school youth in private schools", *Frontiers in Psychology*, 6, 10-28.

Mason, H.D. (2017). "Stress-Management Strategies among First-Year Students at a South African University: A Qualitative Study", *Journal of Student Affairs in Africa*, *5*(2): 131-149.

Nakalema, G. and Ssenyonga, J. (2014). "Academic stress: Its causes and results at a Ugandan university", *African Journal of Teacher Education*, *3*(3).

P. Nivethitha, S. Rita (2016). "A Study on Stress Management Among Student Community", *International Journal of Engineering Sciences and Research Technology*, *5*(11): 480-483.

Park, M.; Kwon, Y. and Shin, H. (2014). "Coping strategies as a mediator between gifted students academic stress and school adjustment", *Korea Youth Research*, *21*(8): 1-25.

Ramesar, S.; Koortzen, P. and Oosthuizen, R.M. (2009). "The Relationship between Emotional Intelligence and Stress Management", *SA Journal of Industrial Psychology*, *35*(1): 39–48.

Sarita, S. (2015). "Academic stress among students: Role and responsibilities of parents", *International Journal of Applied Research*, *1*(10): 385-388.

Seligman, M.E.P. (2006). *Learned Optimism: How to Change Your Mind and Your Life*, New York, N.Y.: Vintage Books.

Van Heerden-Pieterse, E. (2015). *Life Skills: My Journey, My Destiny*.

Wheeler, C.M. (2007). *Ten simple solutions to stress: How to Maintain Tension and Start Enjoying Your Life*, New Harbinger Publications, 2.

14
Transforming Stress Through Awareness, Education and Emotional Resilience

Shabana A. Memon

Introduction

Stress is a feeling of being under abnormal pressure. This pressure can come from different aspects of the day-to-day life. The term "stress" continues to be used in several fundamentally different ways (a) as an environmental condition, (b) as the appraisal of an environmental situation, (c) as a response to the environmental condition that results in physical, psychological and behavioural disturbance, and (d) as an interactive term indicating the relationship between environmental demands and the person's capacity to meet these demands, such as an increased workload, a transitional period, an argument you have with your family or new and existing financial worries. During these situations one may feel threatened or upset and the body might create a stress response. This may cause a variety of physical symptoms, change the way one behave and lead to experiencing more intense emotions.

The generally accepted definition of stress today is 'interaction between the situation and the individual'. It is the psychological and physical state that results when the resources of the individual are not sufficient to cope with the demands and pressures of the situation. Thus, stress is more likely in some situations than others and in some individuals than others. Stress can undermine the achievement of goals, both for an individual and for an organisation.

This chapter will introduce you to what is stress, what are the symptoms of stress and what simple steps one can take, to reduce stress. Nothing is worth your health; nothing is worth poisoning yourself into stress, anxiety and fear. SO DEAR STRESS, LET'S BREAK UP.

1. Stress Awareness

A. What is stress?

We all know what it is like to feel stressed, but it's not easy to pin down exactly what stress means. When we feel stressed emotionally, our body releases hormones called cortisol and adrenaline. This is the body's automatic way of preparing to respond to a threat (sometimes called the 'fight or flight' response); but if one is constantly under stress, these hormones remain in our body, leading to the symptoms of stress. These hormones can reduce blood flow to our skin and reduce our stomach activity. Cortisol releases fat and sugar into our system to boost our energy. As a result, one may experience headaches, muscle tension, pain, nausea, indigestion, dizziness, have palpitations or suffer from various aches and pains. In the long-term, this may put oneself at risk from heart attacks and stroke.

Stress may also be defined as a state of mental or emotional strain caused by adverse circumstances. Stress is a natural reaction to many situations in life, such as work, family, relationships and money problems. The actual or perceived threat to an organism is referred to as the "stressor" and the response to the stressor is called the "stress response." Although stress responses evolve as adaptive processes, it is observed that severe, prolonged stress responses might lead to tissue damage and disease. Being under pressure is a normal part of life. It can be a useful drive that helps us to take action, feel more energized and get results. A moderate amount of stress can help us perform better in challenging situations, but too much or prolonged stress can lead to physical problems. Thus, it is important to manage our stress and keep it at a healthy level to prevent long-term damage to our body and mind.

When we say things like "this is stressful" or "I am stressed", we might be talking about:

- **Situations or events that put pressure on us** — for example, situations where we have lots to do and think about, or times when we don't have much control over what is happening.

- **Our reaction to being placed under pressure** — the feelings we get when we have demands or expectations placed on us that we find difficult to fulfil.

Stress is not a psychiatric diagnosis, but it is closely linked to one's mental health in two important ways:

- **Stress can cause mental health problems, and make existing problems worse.** For example, if you often struggle to manage stress, you might develop a mental health problem like anxiety or depression.
- **Mental health problems can cause stress.** Your coping strategy with the day-to-day symptoms of mental health problem can become an extra source of stress.

B. Common Signs and Symptoms of Stress

We all experience stress differently in different situations. Sometimes, one might immediately recognize their feeling of stress, but other times they might keep going without recognising the symptoms. Stress can affect both physically and emotionally and affect the way one behaves. When it is affecting one's well-being, health and life, it is important to tackle it as early as possible.

Common signs of stress are—

- Frequent headaches, jaw clenching or pain.
- Gritting, grinding teeth.
- Stuttering or stammering.
- Tremors, trembling of lips and hands.
- Neck ache, back pain, muscle spasms.
- Light headedness, faintness, dizziness.
- Ringing, buzzing or "popping sounds."
- Frequent blushing, sweating.
- Sudden attacks of life threatening panic.
- Chest pain, palpitations, rapid pulse.
- Frequent urination.
- Diminished sexual desire or performance.
- Feeling of anxiety, worry, guilt, nervousness.
- Increased anger, frustration, hostility.
- Depression, frequent or wild mood swings.
- Increased or decreased appetite.
- Rapid or mumbled speech.

- Excessive defensiveness or suspiciousness.
- Problems in communication, sharing.
- Social withdrawal and isolation.
- Constant tiredness, weakness, fatigue.
- Frequent use of over-the-counter drugs.
- Weight gain or loss without diet.
- Increased smoking, alcohol or drug use.
- Cold or sweaty hands, feet.
- Dry mouth, problem in swallowing.
- Frequent colds, infections, herpes sores.
- Rashes, itching, hives, "goose bumps."
- Unexplained or frequent "allergy" attacks.
- Heartburn, stomach pain, nausea.
- Constipation, diarrhea, loss of control.
- Insomnia, nightmares, disturbing dreams.
- Difficulty in concentrating, racing thoughts.
- Trouble in learning of new information.
- Forgetfulness, disorganization, confusion.
- Difficulty in making decisions.
- Feeling overloaded or overwhelmed.
- Frequent crying spells or suicidal thoughts.
- Feelings of loneliness or worthlessness.
- Little interest in appearance, punctuality.
- Nervous habits, fidgeting, feet tapping.
- Increased frustration, irritability.
- Overreaction to petty annoyances.
- Increased number of minor accidents.
- Obsessive or compulsive behaviour.
- Reduced work efficiency or productivity.
- Lies or excuses to cover up poor work.
- Excessive gambling or impulse buying.

C. Causes of Stress

Feelings of stress are normally instigated by events happening in your life which involve:

- Being under lots of pressure.
- Facing big changes.
- Worrying about something.

- Not having much or any control over the outcome of a situation.
- Having responsibilities that you are finding overwhelming.
- Not having enough work, activities or change in your life.

There might be any one big reason causing stress, or stress can also be caused by a build-up and accumulation of small challenges. This might make it more difficult for you to identify what is making you feel stressed.

Feeling of stress in different situations can also depend on:

- **Your perception of the situation** —how you interpret things; positively or negatively, depending upon your past experiences, your self-esteem.
- **How skilled you are at dealing with pressure.**
- **Your emotional resilience to stressful situations**— A situation that doesn't disturb you in any ways might cause a lot of tension to someone else leading to stress.

Few life events which may cause stress are—

Personal Issues

- Illness or injury.
- Pregnancy and becoming a parent.
- Long-term health problems.
- Organising a complicated event, like a family holiday.

Friends and Family

- Getting married.
- Going through a break-up or getting divorced.
- Difficult relationships with parents, siblings, friends or children.
- Being a carer for a friend or relative who needs lots of support.

Employment and Study

- Losing a job.
- Long-term unemployment.

- Starting a new job.
- Retiring.
- Exams and deadlines.
- Difficult issues at work.

Housing

- Poor housing conditions.
- Shifting a house.
- Problems with neighbours.

Money

- Worries about money or benefits.
- Poverty.
- Debt.

One can also get stressed just by troubling himself about things like—

- **Fear and uncertainty:** When one regularly hears about the threat of terrorist attacks, global warming and toxic chemicals on the news, it can lead to a stressed feeling. Fears can also be felt by being worried that one may not finish the task in hand, or won't have enough income to meet the expenditures incurred.
- **Attitudes and perceptions:** One's attitude towards a particular situation can determine whether it causes stress or not. For example, if some stock of raw material is stolen from your shop and you take the attitude, "It's OK, my stock was insured and it will be reimbursed by the insurance company", you will be less stressed than if you think, "My stock is stolen and I will never get it back! What if the thieves come back to my shop to steal again?"
- **Unrealistic expectations:** If one expects to be perfect and do everything right all the time, he is destined to feel stressed when things don't go as per his expectation. No one is perfect and this fact should be accepted.

Your stress level will differ based on your personality and how you respond to the situations. Some people take things very lightly and let everything roll off their back. To them, work stresses and life stresses are just minor bumps in the road of life. Others literally worry themselves sick. When you are considering your own stress and how to develop effective stress management techniques, it is very important to start with identifying what is the origin and source of that stress. Few steps to take when feeling stressed—

1. Realise When it is Causing You a Problem

- Try to connect the dots between feeling tired or ill and the stress you are faced with.
- Look out for stress symptoms such as tense muscles, over-tiredness, headaches or migraines.

2. Identify the Causes

- Try to identify the underlying causes.
- Sort the possible reasons for your stress into three categories:
  (a) Those with a practical solution,
  (b) Those that will get better with the passage of time, and
  (c) Those which are not in your control and you cannot do anything about.

Try to release the worry of those in the second and third category above and let them go.

3. Review Your Lifestyle

- Is it that you unnecessarily take on too much?
- Are there things you are doing which could be delegated over to someone else?
- Can you do things in a more leisurely way?

To zero down on the answers to these questions, you may need to prioritise things you want to achieve and re-arrange your life; this will help to release the pressure that comes from trying to do everything at the same time.

D. Stress Effects

A number of emotional and physical disorders have been linked to stress including depression, anxiety, heart attacks, stroke, hypertension, immune system disturbances that increase susceptibility to infections, host of viral linked disorders ranging from the common cold to AIDS and certain cancers, as well as autoimmune diseases like rheumatoid arthritis and multiple sclerosis. In addition stress can also have effect on the skin (rashes, hives, atopic dermatitis, the gastrointestinal system (GERD, peptic ulcer, irritable bowel syndrome, ulcerative colitis) and can contribute to insomnia and degenerative neurological disorders like Parkinson's disease. In fact, it is hard to think of any disease in which stress cannot play an aggravating role or any part of the body that is not affected.

Common Effects of Stress

At times one may not recognize the stress symptoms and take it to be illness which is creating the nagging headache or decreased productivity at work. But in actual it may be stress. Stress symptoms can affect our body, our thoughts, feelings and behaviour. Being able to recognize the common stress symptoms can give an indication to manage them. Stress, if left neglected can be a reason of many health problems, such as rise in blood pressure, tightens muscles, heart disease, tense stomach, obesity and diabetes.

Common Effects of Stress on Our Body

- Headache.
- Muscle tension or pain.
- Chest pain.
- Fatigue.
- Change in sex drive.
- Stomach upset.
- Sleep problems.
- Rapid Heartbeat.
- Aches and Pains.
- Frequent Colds.
- Skin Complaints.
- Indigestion.

- High Blood Pressure.

Common Effects of Stress on Our Mind

- Memory Problems.
- Poor Judgment.
- Inability to Concentrate.
- Brain Fog.
- Indecision.
- Starting many tasks but achieving little.
- Self doubt.
- Increased negativity towards life.
- Post-traumatic stress disorder.

Common Effects of Stress on Our Mood

- Moodiness.
- Irritability.
- Fatalistic Thinking.
- Panic.
- Cynicism.
- Anxiety.
- Feeling Overwhelmed.
- Frustration.
- Restlessness.
- Lack of motivation or focus.
- Irritability or anger.
- Sadness or depression.

Common Effects of Stress on Our Behaviour

- Overeating or undereating
- Sleeping too little or too much.
- Angry outbursts.
- Increase intake in alcohol, cigarettes and caffeine to relax.
- Isolating yourself from others.
- Demotivated.
- Loss of sense of humour.

One of the difficulties with stress is that it contributes to manifest itself differently. Different people experience stress in different ways. Stress targets the weakest part of our physiology or character; if you are prone to headaches or eczema, this will intensify. If you have low levels of patience or tolerance for others, this will be the first area to be affected under times of stress. Keep this in mind that stress isn't avoidable but it is manageable. One should be alert enough to identify stress-related problems as early as possible, so as to tackle them better.

Thus, when stress is properly managed, it can be useful to increase one's concentration, it contributes to creativity, increases productivity and helps to develop new skills: but for that one must learn to manage it effectively.

2. Stress Management Education

When something occurs that causes stress, one's sympathetic nervous system reacts, triggering a series of physiological responses that can change from moment to moment. This fight-or-flight response, as it is known, ultimately has one main aim and that is to keep one safe by reviving one up, heightening one's focus and putting one on alert. The adrenal glands release the stress hormones, including adrenaline and cortisol, setting off a cascade of emotional and physical symptoms designed to help one get oneself to safety. The body's fight-or-flight stress response is vital for keeping one safe from harm, but if it comes into action because of trivial events, it can have detrimental effects.

Stress management enables one to understand that stress is a part of everyone's life. Stress management is an important skill that everyone needs in order to improve themselves as problem solvers and to be more in control of their lives. Effective stress management helps to break the hold of stress on our life, which may make one feel happier, healthier and more productive. The ultimate goal is a balanced life, with time for work, relationships, relaxation and fun.

A. How to Deal with Pressure?

Even though there are things happening in your life that you cannot control, still lots of practical things can be done to manage the amount of pressure you are undergoing. But remember stress management is not one-size-fits-all. That is why it is important to experiment and find out what works best for you. The following stress management tips can help.

a. Identify Your Triggers/Sources of Stress in Your Life

Working out what triggers stress for you can help you anticipate problems and think of ways to solve them. Even if you can't avoid these situations, being prepared to face them can help. Take some time to reflect on events and feelings that could be contributing to your stress. You could consider:

- **Issues that come up regularly** and that you are too much worried about
- **One-off events that are on your mind** such as shifting a house or writing an exam.
- **Ongoing stressful events** like having problems at work.

Remember that not having enough work to do or no change in your life can be just as stressful as having too much work activities to deal with.

b. Organise Your Time

Making some adjustments in the way one organises time can help one feel more in control of any tasks one is facing and will enable to handle pressure better.

- **Identify best time of the day** and do the important tasks that need the most energy and concentration at that time. For example, a person might be a morning person or an evening person.
- **Make a list** of things one has to do. Arrange them in order of importance and try to focus on the most urgent first. This may help one to push back some tasks until one is feeling less stressed.
- **Vary activities,** balance interesting tasks with more mundane ones, and stressful tasks with those one can do more easily and calmly.
- **Try not to do too much at once**. If one takes on too much or too many task, one might find it harder to do any of the tasks effectively. Thus leading to more stress and pressure on oneself.
- **Take breaks and take things slowly.** This might be difficult to do when one is feeling stressed, but it could make one more effective and productive.

c. Accept the Things You can't Change

There may be lots of things in your life that you cannot change nor do anything about it, you can use some practical ways, like read some books on issues like family and personal life, mental health, work life, student life and finances. At times though not easy, it is wise to accept that there are some things that you probably cannot do anything about and thus you need to focus your time and energy on something more productive than worrying about those thing you have no control of.

B. Acts to Manage Stress

If you have stress symptoms, taking steps to manage your stress can have numerous health benefits. Explore stress management strategies, such as:

1. Eat Healthy— There is a growing amount of evidence showing how food affects our mood and how healthy diet can improve it. One needs to ensure that their diet provides adequate amounts of nutrients such as essential vitamins and minerals, as well as water.

2. Beware of smoking and drinking alcohol — Try to avoid smoking and drinking alcohol, as they often make problems worse.

3. Exercise—Try and integrate physical exercise into your lifestyle, just going out and getting some fresh air, doing some light physical exercise, can really help.

4. Take time to relax—Strike a proper balance between responsibility towards others and responsibility towards yourself. Set aside time for hobbies, such as reading a book or listening to music. It is okay to prioritise self-care. Taking a break is important for good mental health.

5. Be mindful—Mindfulness is a mind-body approach to life that helps to pay attention to our thoughts and feelings, thereby increasing our ability to manage difficult situations and make wise choices. It can also reduce the effects of stress, anxiety and related problems.

6. Get some restful sleep—Struggling to sleep is a common problem when you are stressed. It can impact on your physical and mental health. Amend your environment, make small changes to your lifestyle to help improve your sleep.

7. Don't be too hard on yourself— Remember that having a bad day is a universal human experience. If you feel you have failed, don't beat yourself up. Act as if you are your own best friend. Do take a few minutes each day to appreciate yourself, socialize with family and friends.

3. Emotional Resilience

Emotional resilience refers to one's ability to adapt to stressful situations or crises. Resilience is not a quality that you either possess or do not possess; there are varying degrees of how well a person is able to handle stress. More resilient people are able to "roll with the punches" and adapt to adversity without lasting difficulties; less resilient people have a harder time with stress and life changes, be it major or minor. Taking steps to look after your well-being can help you deal with pressure and reduce the impact that stress has on your life. This is sometimes called developing emotional resilience. The ability to adapt and bounce back when something difficult happens in your life. It has been found that those who deal with minor stresses more easily can also manage major crises with greater ease, so resilience has its benefits for daily life as well as for the rare major catastrophe.

Characteristics of Resilient People

- **Emotional Awareness:** People with emotional awareness understand what they are feeling and why. They also understand the feelings of others better because they are more in touch with their own inner life.
- **Perseverance:** Whether they are working toward outward goals or on inner coping strategies, they are action-oriented, they trust in the process and do not give up.
- **Internal Locus of Control:** They believe that they, rather than outside forces, are in control of their own lives. These traits are associated with less stress because people with an internal locus of control and a realistic view of the world can be more proactive in dealing with stressors in their lives, more solution-oriented and feel a greater sense of control, which brings less stress.
- **Optimism:** They see the positive in most situations and believe in their own strength. This can shift how they handle problems from a victim mentality to an empowered one and thus more choices open up.

- **Support:** While they tend to be strong individuals, they know the value of social support and are able to surround themselves with supportive friends and family.
- **Sense of Humour:** People strong in emotional resilience are able to laugh at life's difficulties. This can be a huge asset, as it shifts one's perspective from seeing things as a threat to seeing them as a challenge and this alters how the body reacts to stress. They also get a good laugh more often and this brings benefits as well.
- **Perspective:** Resilient people are able to learn from their mistakes, they see obstacles as challenges and allow adversity to make them stronger. They can also find meaning in life's challenges rather than seeing themselves as victims.
- **Spirituality:** Being connected to spiritual side has been connected with stronger emotional resilience.

Tips to Developing Emotional Resilience

1. Be Optimistic

- Looking on the bright side keeps you going.
- Balance a positive outlook with a realistic view of the world.
- Be realistic, disengage rapidly from problems that appear to be unsolvable and turn your attention to problems that can be solved.

2. Face Your Fears

- Neuroscience says there is only one real way to deal with fear: you need to face it, head on.

3. Have a Moral Compass

- Having a keen sense of right and wrong helps one to adjust to life.
- Altruism-selflessness, concern for the welfare of others and giving to others without any expectation stands as a pillar of one's "moral compass."

4. Practice Spirituality

- It is seen that religious beliefs are the most powerful forces in explaining a tragedy which lead to stress and in explaining our survival.

5. Have Resilient Role Models

- Great role models provide a positive example and to follow their beliefs, attitudes and behaviours inspires one to stay emotionally healthy.

6. Keep Your Brain Strong

- Keep growing your mind, learn to learn and adapt to new information about the world.
- Be lifelong learners; seek opportunities to become more mentally fit. This will keep you sharp and benefit you with the whole host of positive health.

7. Be "Cognitively Flexible"

- Use a number of ways to deal with stressful situations, be flexible; flexible in the way you think about challenges and flexible in the way you react emotionally to stress.
- Substantial evidence exists for 'effectiveness of humour' as a coping mechanism. Humour reduces the threatening nature of stressful situations.

8. Make Some Lifestyle Changes

- Practice being straightforward and assertive in communicating with others—Be prepared to tell a NO on unreasonable or unrealistic demands of people.
- Use relaxation techniques—If you know that a certain activity helps you feel more relaxed, make sure you set aside time to do it.
- Develop your interests and hobbies—Finding an activity that is completely different from the things causing you stress is a good way to get away from everyday pressures.

- Make time for your friends—Chatting to friends about the things you find difficult can help you keep things in perspective. Laughing and smiling with them will also produce hormones that will help you to relax.
- Find balance in your life—This may help you spread the weight of pressures in your life and make everything feel lighter and bearable.

9. Look After Your Physical Health

- **Get good sleep**— Being well-rested can increase your ability to deal with difficult situations.
- **Be more physically active**—Physical activity is important for reducing stress levels.
- **Healthy diet**—What you eat and when you eat, make a big difference to how good you feel.

10. Give Yourself a Break

- Reward yourself for achievements — Even small things like finishing a piece of work or making a decision. You could take a walk, read a book, treat yourself to food you enjoy or simply tell yourself "well done".
- Get a change of scenery—You might want to go outside, go to a friend's house or go to a café for a break; even if it is just for a short while.
- Take a break or holiday—Spending time away from your normal routine or a day in a different place can help you relax and feel refreshed.
- Resolve conflicts—Speaking to a manager, colleague or family member about problems in your relationship with them can help you find ways to resolve them and move forward.
- Forgive yourself—When you make a mistake, or don't achieve something you aimed for, remember that nobody is perfect.

11. Use Your Support Network

- Friends and family—Sharing your feelings with people close to you, can make a big difference and they might be able to help you out. Friends and loved ones are a big support when life gets hard.

- Support at work—Our brains need social support to function optimally, don't worry that talking to your manager or colleagues about your stress will be seen as a sign of weakness. Your well-being is important and responsible employers will consider it seriously.

12. Find Meaning in What You Do

Resilient people don't have jobs, they have callings. They have a mission and purpose in life that gives meaning to the things they do. So when times are difficult, they feel a greater purpose is behind them, and this is what pushes them forward.

4. Treatments for Stress

Though stress is not a medical diagnosis, still specific treatments are there for it, if you are experiencing lots of signs of stress, there are treatments available that could help.

A. Talking Treatments

Talking with a trained professional can help you learn to deal with stress and make you be more aware of your own thoughts and feelings.

Common types of talking treatments which can help with stress are:

- Cognitive Behavioural Therapy (CBT), helps you understand your thought patterns, recognize your trigger points and identify positive actions you can take.
- Mindfulness Based Stress Reduction (MBSR), combines mindfulness, meditation and *yoga* with a focus on particularly reducing stress.

B. Medication

Feelings of stress are a reaction to things happening in your life, not a mental health problem, so there is no specific medication for stress. However, there are various medications available which can help to reduce or manage some of the signs of stress.

For example. doctor might offer to prescribe:

- sleeping pills or minor tranquillisers if you are having trouble in sleeping.
- antidepressants if you are experiencing depression or anxiety.
- medication to treat any physical symptoms of stress, such as irritable bowel syndrome (IBS), or high blood pressure.

C. Ecotherapy

Ecotherapy is a way of improving your well-being and self-esteem by spending time in nature. This can include physical exercise in green spaces or taking part in a gardening or conservation project.

D. Complementary and Alternative Therapies

You may find certain alternative therapies which may help you manage feelings of stress. These might include acupuncture, aromatherapy and massage.

The Bottom Line

Stress is something that most people will experience at one point or another. It can take a toll on many aspects of health and has a wide range of symptoms, including reducing energy levels and triggering headaches or chronic pain. There are many ways to help relieve stress, such as practicing mindfulness, exercising and doing *yoga*. A professional counsellor or therapist can help you identify sources of your stress and coping tools. But if you are not sure that it is stress only, if you have chest pain, especially if it occurs during physical activity or is accompanied by shortness of breath, sweating, dizziness, nausea or pain radiating into your shoulder and arm, get emergency help immediately. These may be warning signs of a heart attack and not simply stress symptoms. Speak to your doctor, they can check your overall health and help you access treatments.

Many people feel too embarrassed to openly discuss their experience with stress therefore we need to familiarize ourselves with the behavioural symptoms of stress so that we can understand what they are going through and help them to identify it early and take proper action and suitable help.

If you do not end up identifying a method to handle your stress then it eventually can lead to a heightened sense of dysfunction. This may result in increased anxiety or a sense of depression because you're not mastering your world. Remember it is not the load that breaks you down, it's the way you carry it.

It is worthwhile to end with a quote:

> **Life is All About Balance**. You don't always need to be getting all stuff done, sometimes it is perfectly okay, and absolutely necessary, to shut down, kick back and do nothing.

References

Byrd, O'Brien, T. and DeLongis, A. (1997). "Coping with Chronic Stress: An Interpersonal Perspective." In B.H. Gottlieb. (Eds.). *Coping with Chronic Stress*. Springer Science+Business Media: New York.

Crum, A.J., Salovey, P. and Achor, S. (2013). "Rethinking stress: The role of mindsets in determining the stress response." *Journal of Personality and Social Psychology*, *104* (4), 716-733.

Gray, J.A. (1988). *The Psychology of Fear and Stress* (2nd Ed.). Cambridge University Press: New York

Rita Agarwal (2001). *Stress in life and at work*, Response Books (A division of Sage Publication India Pvt Ltd.).

D. Vernon Coleman (1992). *Stress Management Techniques*, IBH Publishers Pvt. Ltd.

https://www.mind.org.uk/media/1993364/how-to-manage-stress_2015.pdf

https://www.ncbi.nlm.nih.gov/pmc/articles/PMC2568977/

https://www.linkedin.com/pulse/understand-five-components-stress-daniel-goleman

https://positivepsychologyprogram.com/stress-management-techniques-tips-burn-out/

https://explorable.com/stress-management

https://ebrary.net/2885/management/models_stress_management_transactional_model

https://www.selfgrowth.com/articles/models-for-stress-management

http://www.heart.org/en/healthy-living/healthy-lifestyle/stress-management/3-tips-to-manage-stress

https://oem.bmj.com/content/59/1/67

https://www.webmd.com/balance/guide/causes-of-stress#1

http://www.gostress.com/stress-sources/

https://www.mayoclinic.org/healthy-lifestyle/stress-management/in-depth/stress-symptoms/art-20050987

https://www.helpguide.org/articles/stress/stress-management.htm

15
Spiritual Intelligence in Reducing the Job Stress

Kounsar Jabeen

Introduction

> "All earthly delights are sweeter in expectation than in enjoyment; but all spiritual pleasures more in fruition than in expectation." (*Francois Fenelon is about Spirituality*)

Spiritual intelligence is the most significant type of intelligence because of its ability to influence change in people, societies, and cultures. In the opinion of Hosseini *et al.* (2010), "spirituality can be viewed as a form of intelligence because it predicts functioning and adaptation and offers capabilities that enable people to solve problems and attain goals." According to Srivastava & Misra (2012), "Spiritual intelligence assists people in any context (corporate, community or family) to develop their spiritual awareness, capacity and intelligence, and also to use that intelligence to be more effective as an individual, and to expand their capacity to make a greater contribution to the endeavours of others. Spiritual intelligence helps individuals toward adopting a positive outlook and in achieving inner peace." Sisk (2008) revealed that "spiritual intelligence, using a multisensory approach to access one's inner knowledge to solve global problems, could be an integrating theme to create global awareness among teachers and students." Spiritual intelligence not only brings out self-awareness but also develops various qualities such as holism and humanity. It teaches us to act upon principles and to live a value-led life. Spiritual intelligence is individual mental ability it appears to connect the personal to the transpersonal and the self to spirit. In addition to self-awareness, it implies awareness of person's relationship to transcendent, to each other, to the earth and all beings.

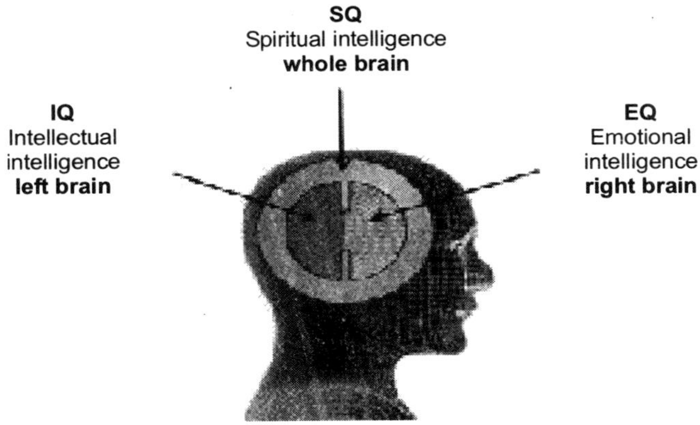

https://www.bing.com/images/search?q=images+of+spiritual+itelligece&form=HDRSC2&first=1&cw=1129&ch=511#CA!Share

Both IQ and EQ work with the confines of existing information and the known. Only SQ is capable of thinking beyond the known. To think a brand new thought or see a higher truth in a situation; SQ operates through knowledge of the spiritual laws on which our world is founded. When our IQ, EQ, and SQ work together we are able to fully manifest our potential in the world. Human beings are essentially spiritual in nature.

Importance of Spiritual Intelligence

Spirituality is a worldview and a way of life based on the belief that there is more to life than what meets the senses, more to the universe than just purposeless mechanics, more to consciousness than electrical impulses in the brain, and more to our existence than the body and its needs. It usually involves the belief in a higher form of inteligence or consciousness running the universe, as well as life after death.

This contemporary world is characterized by a lack of emotional and spiritual intelligence as most of us worship materialism, emotional, social and physical gratification. Consequently we turn to food, drink, drugs, sex to try to fill ourselves up and to get rid of the emptiness that we feel and that we observe. There tends to be a lack of inner peace and meaning in our lives. We are beginning to realize that spiritual intelligence has the power to change our life, civilization, the planet and the course of history. Wolman (2002) reported that spirituality is concerned with the fundamental issues of life and death, which make possible for us to make connections to the world and to each other that give our life happiness and purpose.

From Islamic point of view, the importance of spiritual intelligence is obvious as it gives direction in our life in critical moments, when we feel we are inferior or week.

وَلَا تَهِنُوا وَلَا تَحْزَنُوا وَأَنتُمُ الْأَعْلَوْنَ إِن كُنتُم مُّؤْمِنِينَ ﴿١٣٩﴾

"Don't become weak, nor be sad, you will be superior if you are indeed true believers". (surah ale-Imran, verse 139)

Our younger generations who do not find a spiritual philosophy of life become disorganized and even distractive. It is the spiritual intelligence with which we can solve problems of meaning within a wider context. It is the working with our inner glow that is in line with our deepest desires. This is uniquely human and it allows us to change the rules and modify the situations.

لَا يُكَلِّفُ اللَّهُ نَفْسًا إِلَّا وُسْعَهَا

"Allah does not charge a soul except [with that within] its capacity".

Dimensions of Spiritual Intelligence

Spiritual intelligence has been classified into the following dimensions according to Zohar and Marshall (1999):

The inner self: comprises the personal inner sense of "wholeness" deriving from honesty and consistent of character. It also includes the motive to realize all of one's potentialities the pursuit of communion with, identity with, or conscious awareness of an ultimate reality, divinity, Spiritual truth or God through direct experience, intuition, instinct or insight.

The inter self: Relating and awareness of how one influences others. As being helpful to other people with little or no interest in being rewarded for one's efforts. This is distinction from merely helping others. An ethical doctrine that holds that individuals have a moral obligation to help others.

Biostoria: Is the story of one's life.

Life Perspectives: living in alignment with the sacred manifesting love for and trust in life.

Spiritual Actualization: Creativity/flexibility is a mental and social process involving the generation of new ideas or concepts or new associations of the creative mind between existing ideas or concepts. Creativity is fuelled by the process of either conscious or unconscious insight. An alternative conception of creativeness is that it is simply that act of making something new.

Value Orientation: Value orientations are based on the assumption that individuals pursue different goals when making decisions for which the outcomes affect others. Spiritual intelligence exists in work and life environments. Spirituality in work refers to making work as a part of spiritual life, finding opportunities to express yourself, bringing ethical values to working environment, ethical beliefs (other than religious beliefs) that forms their senses of right and void and developing the feeling that life is sacred. Generally, these beliefs concentrate on the tendency to be the best in workplace, in helping others and in sensing the connection with work and co-workers. With these ideas into action, individuals gain a sense of holiness in their deeds and world (Zohar, D., & Marshall, 2000). The role of educational organizations is provoking and stimulating staff, using a spiritual perspective and setting the cultural ground based on human values so that empowered employees with high efficiency.

Stress

Stress is the body's reaction that changes the physical, mental or emotional adjustment or response as defined in certain amount of stress is normal and necessary for survival (Middle Brooks, J.S. & Audage, N.C., 2008). Stress which has major effects on individual's attitudes, behaviour and interpersonal relationship, is a case formed by the mixture of several factors. Due to the creation of stress people need to be affected by the surrounding they live in (Rice, 1999). People's mental and emotional status, their way of life, financial status determines the level of being affected by these changes. Now in society stress related diseases increase day by day, so the people and institution are confronted with significant problem has been faced

(Rice, 1999). Stress is the multidimensional phenomenon which determines the dynamic relationship between the individual and the environment (Beddoe & Murphy, 2004). Some kind of stress can be effective on increasing and enhancing the individual performance. Facts point out the most of human successes are formed in stressful situation, but high rate of stress would be harmful for numerous consequences, including mental and physical illnesses, sleep disorder, restiveness, irritability, absentmindedness, irregular tiredness, reduced individual's resistance and regular infections, headaches, poor attentiveness, memory destruction and reduce in problem-solving ability (Beddoe & Murphy, 2004). Overcome the stress by using these stress management practices like Yoga relaxation, progressive muscle leisure, breathing exercise, contemplation mental metaphors and spiritual intelligence (Daubenmier *et al.*, 2007). Spiritual intelligence play very important role to reducing the any job stress and motivate us. Vaughan (2003) says, spiritual intelligence depends on the capability to observe the things from more than one point of view and identify the relationship between perception, belief and behaviour.

Job Stress

Occupational stress can be wearisome to the most employees. It is a major health problem and faces the serious challenges to the effective operation of any organization and any institution.

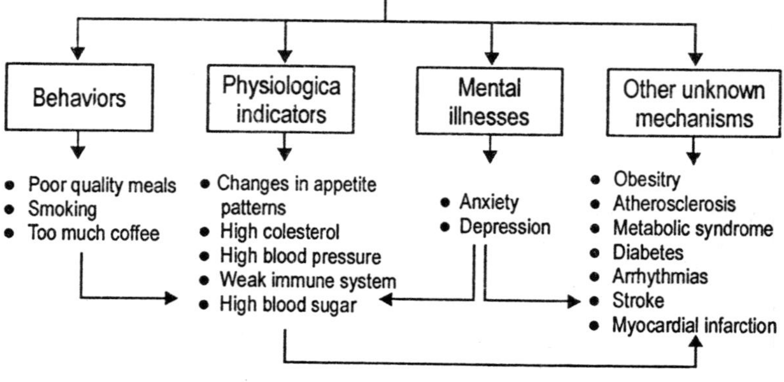

Spirituality is an effort that is used in an organizational culture to develop a positive surrounding. Spirituality when recognized and incorporated in leadership practice could contribute to human resources well-being and the well-being of their organizations (Rani *et al.*, 2013). Past few years, the interest of spirituality in workplace has been growing (Garcia-Zamor, 2003). Since the late 1990s publications such as *Wall Street Journal, Business Week, Fortune* and others have reported arising the numbers of employees yearning for the meaning and purpose at work, for the spiritual dimension to organizational life (Duchon & Plowman, 2005). Religion gives or guides a better way of life for its follower. Religious and spiritual dimensions can be shaping the most important factors of human experience (Kripner & Welch, 1992).

Spirituality in Workplace

Workplace spirituality is the dominant view among writers and scholars. Some attempt distinguishes between the spirituality and religion to be analytically and empirically (Bell & T. Taylor, 2001). Spirituality in workplace is an effort to get associated to this divine principle in the context of workplace (Dhiman, 2007). Giacalone and Jurkiewicz (2003) says, workplace spirituality elaborate the framework of the organizational values and also promotes the employees experience and joy. Ashmos and Duchon (2000) elaborate the definition of spirituality at work as the acknowledgment in which employees have inner life that nourishes and is nourished by the meaningful work that take place in the context of society. Whether we acknowledge or not, Spirituality is the experienced part of the workplace. Power of management can be nurtured by spirituality in workplace.

Conclusion

In the light of the discussion of the importance of Spiritual intelligence and its relationship with stress, it could be concluded that spiritual intelligence helps an individual to reduce the stress. Few studies had also suggested that there is negative relationship between the two variables individuals with high spiritual intelligence are more capable to show control over their emotions and for them it is easy to reduce the stress.

References

Aldwin, C.M. (1994). *Stress, Coping, and Development: An Integrative Perspective.* New York, US: Guilford Press.

Beddoe, A.E. and Murphy, S.O. (2004). "Does mindfulness decrease stress and foster empathy among nursing students?" *Journal of Nursing Education, 43*(7): 305-312.

Daubenmier, J.J.; Weidner, G.; Sumner, M.D.; Mendell, N.; Merritt-Worden, T.; Studley, J. and Ornish, D. (2007). "The contribution of changes in diet, exercise, and stress management to changes in coronary risk in women and men in the multisite cardiac lifestyle intervention programme", *Annals of Behavioural Medicine, 33*(1): 57-68.

Dhiman (2007). *Spirituality in Workplace*, Personhood Press.

Duchon, D. and Plowman, D.A. (2005). "Nurturing the spirit at work: Impact on work unit performance", *The Leadership Quarterly, 16*(5): 807-833.

Garcia Zamor, J.C. (2003). "Workplace spirituality and organizational performance", *Public Administration Review, 63*(3): 355-363.

Hosseini, M.; Elias, H.; Krauss, S.E. and Aishah, S. (2010). "A Review Study on Spiritual Intelligence, Adolescence and Spiritual Intelligence, Factors that May Contribute to Individual Differences in Spiritual Intelligence, and the Related Theories", *International Journal of Psychological Studies*. Vol. 2(2)

Krippner, S. (1992). *Spiritual Dimensions of Healing*. Irvington Pub.

Middlebrooks, J.S. and Audage, N.C. (2008). *The effects of childhood stress on health across the lifespan.*

Rani, A.A.; Ghani, A.A. and Ahmad, S. (2013). "The impact of spiritual intelligence in reducing job stress: Case studies in Malaysia University of East Coast of Malaysia", *Macrotheme Rev., 2*(4): 183-192.

Rice, P.L. (1999). *Stress and Health.* Pacific Grove, CA: Brooks/Cole Publishing.

Sisk D. (2008). "Engaging the spiritual intelligence of gifted students to build global awareness in the classroom", *Roeper Review, 30*(1): 24-30.

Srivastava, A. and Misra, S. (2012). "Is Spiritual Quotient a better tool of success: Spirituality in the new World Order", *EXCEL International Journal of Multidisciplinary Management Studies*. Vol. 2(1): ISSN 2249 8834.

Vaughan, F. (2002). "What is spiritual intelligence?", *Journal of Humanistic Psychology, 42*(2): 16-33.

Wolman, R. (2001). *Thinking with Your Soul: Spiritual intelligence and why it matters*, New York: Harmony, *10*(1): 3-26.

16
A Multi-Dimensional Study of Stress

Effects and Coping Strategy

Maliha Batool and *Dada Ab Rouf Bhat*

Introduction

In everyone's life there is a common experience, i.e., stress. At everyone's personal level words like migraine, anxiety, headaches, depression, feeling out of control, time pressures, overwork, cannot sleep, panic attacks etc. are used in day-to-day life. In short it is the most common human phenomenon which is applied to psychological and physiological pressure experienced by the people. It has become a part of everyone's life and with the advent of industrial growth, urbanization, science and technology, modernization, and automation. And this experience has been increasing.

Definitions of Stress

According to **Australian Psychological Society**— Stress can be defined as a feeling of being overloaded, tense, wound-up tight and worried.

According to **Skinner**, "a reaction of a particular individual to a stimulus event.

Eliot opines "stress may be viewed as the body's response to any real or imagined event perceived as requiring some adaptive response and/or producing strain.

As per **Steinberg and Ritzmann** "stress can be defined as an underload or overload of matter, energy or information input to, or output from, a living system."

Further as per **Palmer**, "Stress is the psychological, physiological and behavioural response by an individual when they perceive a lack of equilibrium between the demands placed upon them and their ability to meet those demands, which, over a period of time, leads to ill-health."

Many people consider stress as something that happens to individual that may harm or provide encouragement wholesome consider it as what happens to our body in response to an event stress within limits is productive but if it goes beyond can be harmful. Mostly, stress is regarded as a negative experience for the individual but stress at all the times is not harmful but sometimes it helps to motivate to get a task finished or perform well. Stress that can have positive effect can be referred to as eustress. Eustress is very necessary in everybody's life.

But stress taken in excess can be harmful as it interferes with the persons' ability to get on with our normal life for too long. While talking respect to behavioural outcomes of stress it provokes depressive symptoms (Monroe and Simons, 1991), whereas other in some cases it may generate anxiety symptoms as well (Finlay-Jones and Brown, 1981). Even if the degree of severity is not taken into consideration, stress mainly promote huge physiological and behavioural disturbances which involve psychiatric disorders along with to immune system dysfunction ((Brown, 1993; Herbert and Cohen, 1993).

Depending upon the intensity of stress, we cannot assume that those who persons with less stress are totally anti-thesis to those taking more stress but those taking major stress can be the person who take minor stress on some problematic situations (Lazarus, 1990; Ravindran *et al.*, 1997).

The World Labour Report, produced by the U.N.'s International Organization, states, *"Stress has become one of the most serious health issues of the 20th century and a worldwide epidemic."*

Characteristics of Stress

Stress is helpful to prepare the body to face danger. Take place inside the brain with the symptoms both physical and psychological. Stress for short-term stress can be helpful, but if it has long-term stress it is linked to various ailments. Stress does not affect physically but it the slows normal bodily functions like the digestive and immune systems. Certain body changes during stress are blood pressure and pulse rate rise, a heightened state of alertness prevents sleep, immune activity decreases, the muscles become tense, breathing is faster, the digestive system slows down.

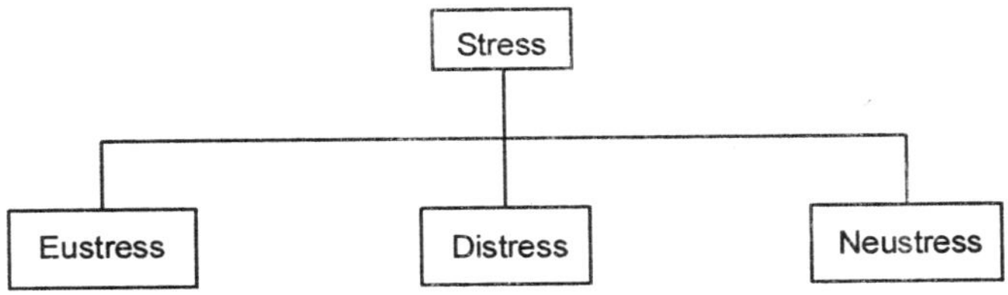

Broadly stress can be categorised into three types:

Eustress: Eustress is mostly a good type of stress and this type of stress arise in any situation or circumstance in which a person finds motivation in itself providing positive boost to him, e.g. meeting a sports player, actor that inspires a person to go in the field in which he can specialise, falling in love which provides pleasure and joy. Providing pleasure and joy is the reason, it is not considered as a threat.

Neustress: Neustress is neutral type of stress and describes sensory stimuli which have neither good nor bad consequential effect e.g. if we are living in J&K news of Tsunami/flood in Kerala may fall in this category.

Distress: Distress is synonym of actual stress and is mostly considered as bad as its intensity can stay for an hour, hours, day, few days, months etc.

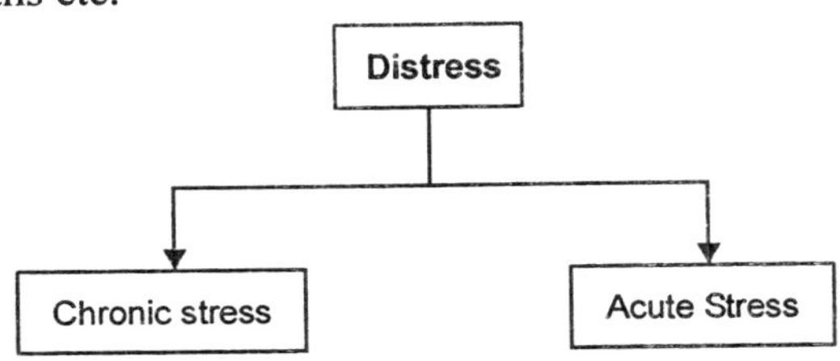

It can be of two types: chronic stress which is mostly prolonged, may not disappear easily and is unbearable for e.g. when someone's father is alcoholic and quarrels with the family members it is difficult to end all relations with that person and in such circumstances it is to live with him too difficult to leave him alone in the streets, another example of chronic stress is when a husband commits domestic violence to his wife and she bears which is commonly observed in India. The second type of stress is acute stress disappears quickly and is quite intense, an example of acute stress is while driving if someone overtakes that might result in accident.

Fig. 16.1: Signs.

From Fig. 16.1, we can say that persons with stress can be identified with signs of stress like: being irritable, over-burdened, impatient or wound, aggressive, neglected or lonely anxious, nervous or afraid, one's thoughts are racing and he/she can't switch off. Along with this person with stress is uninterested in life, a sense of dread, unable to enjoy himself, worried about his/her health, usually depressed, the person loses his/her sense of humour etc. Stress can take place from daily routine annoyances to unexpected calamities. In reaction to stressors, a series of neurochemical, behavioural, and immunological changes take place that may serve in an adaptive capacity.

Symptoms of stress are presented in Fig. 16.2.

Two-way Relationship between Mental Health and Stress

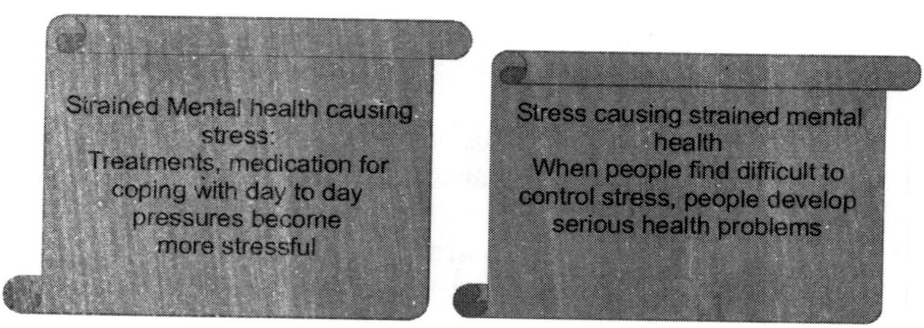

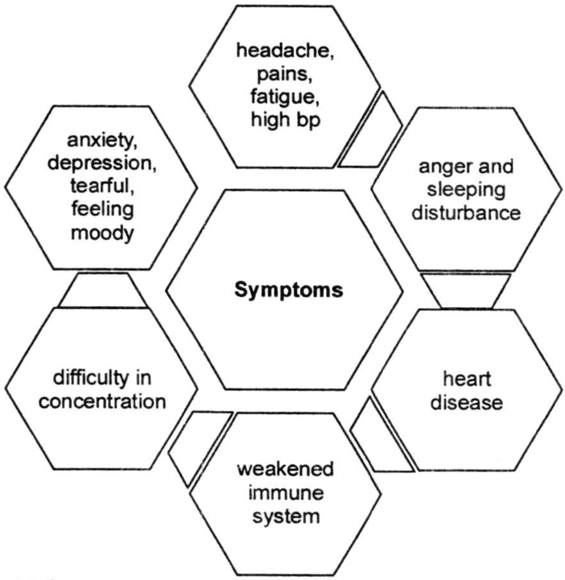

Fig. 16.2: Main Symptoms.

Causes of Stress

Stress can arise due to any reason at any time, at some time it can be sudden or at some it can be influenced by some past event (Summers, 2001).

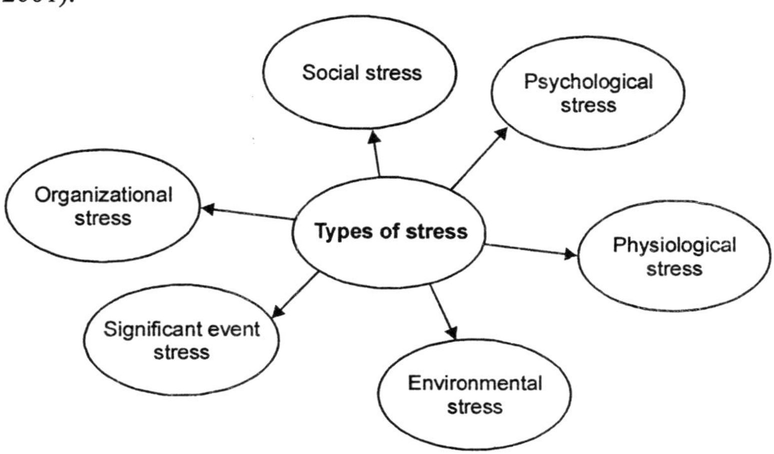

Social stress: It involves the stress that stems out from one's relationships with others and from the social environment in general. Being a social being there are demands of the different social roles that we occupy like parent, spouse, caregiver, and employee, while performing same roles multiple stressors may arise. According to appraisal theory of emotion, stress mainly arise when a person evaluates a situation which is personally relevant and perceives that he or she does not have the resources to cope or handle the particular specific situation. It may involve some life events which can be defined as abrupt, some severe life changes that require an individual to adapt quickly (financial problems, job interviews, presentations, disagreements, sexual assault, sudden injury, deadlines, divorce, demands for your time and attention, loss of a loved one, and co-parenting).

Physiological Stress: It involves the situations and circumstances that affect our body and can result in physiological stressors e.g. illness, accidents, lack of exercise, ageing, growth of adolescence, menopause, giving birth, poor nutrition, and sleep disturbances.

Psychological Stress: It involves the emotional and physiological reactions experienced by an individual to a situation which the demands goes beyond their coping resources e.g. stressful situations arise due to death of a loved one, marital problems, abuse, some health problems, family related problems like the partition related problems and financial crises.

Environmental Stress: It involves the environmental factors like noise, crowding, pollution, traffic, crime, unsafe and substandard housing.

Significant Event Stress: Certain events like the death of mother, friend, insult at the public place etc. can result in stress.

Organisational Stress: Work overload, lack of control over work and lack of participation in decision-making, long hours worked, and pressure, the effects of these on personal lives, poor social support, over restrictions in the management side etc.

At present people in many businesses, mostly workers face stress because of longer working hours have been expecting more from their IT personnel without any commensurate increase in remuneration. These are not being able to take a vacation or having any sort of cut short due to regular IT related problems that has been identified as a major problem relating to the retention of employees. Stress in the present scenario in IT sector come to the workers via sector's strategies, to the changes in external environment, role ambiguity, role conflict and work overload, IT personnel are often subject to increased user demands. More pressure comes from active or passive strategies like the downsizing or re-structuring or meeting the supply and demand gap for IT professionals and similarly boundary spanning is also contributing factor to role conflict and ambiguity among IT personnel. It is making environment stressful to the workers and the daily changing nature of work and uncertainties at the workplace which are inherent in the business environment are mainly the primary determinants of stress among IT personnel. The inability to cope with the pressure in a job at the workplace. (Bartol & Martin, 1982; Ivancevich *et al.* 1983; Guimaraes and Igbaria, 1992; Li and Shani, 1991; McGee, 1996; Sethi *et al.* 1999; Moore, 2000). Similarly, Baroudi (1985) and Guimaraes and Igbaria (1992) have also reported that.

Problems Associated with Stress

Pain of any kind, Sleep problems, Depression and anxiety, Heart disease, autoimmune diseases, digestive problems, thinking and memory problems, skin conditions, reproductive issues, eczema, weight problems, etc.

How to Cope-up with Stress?

> "People are disturbed not by a thing, but by their perception of a thing." — *Epictetus*

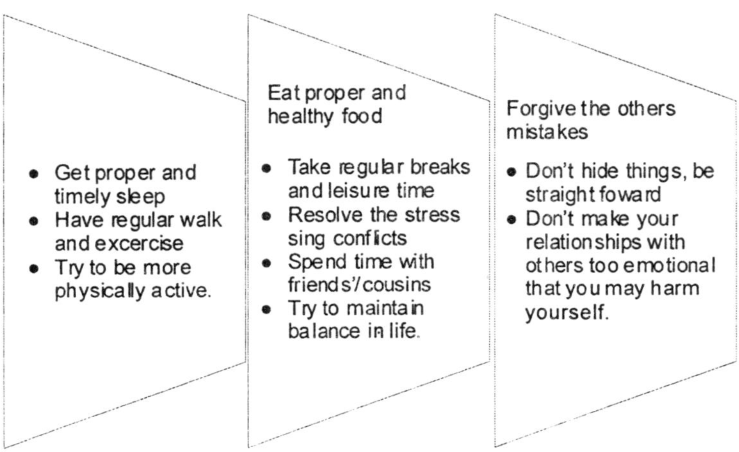

At the individual level: If a person is aware of the fact that he/she get easily stressed. He/she should take steps like—talking to friends, remove the negative thinking people i.e. "stress carriers" from his/her peer group, get proper sleep, eat healthy, well-balanced meals, exercise regularly, avoid drugs and alcohol, share your problems, take a break, watch comedy shows. If news events result in your stress take a break from watching or listening the news, if you are spiritual being, pray; speak to God, to a higher power, and believe in your inner guide.

Exercise daily, a lot of studies show that maximal exercise does reduce intensity of stress. High doses of exercise is not only beneficial for health but also relieve the mental fatigue including stress and the most important aspect of exercise is that it reduces the blood pressure and anxiety (Bartholomew, J. 2000; Rejeski *et al.*, 1991; Hobson and Rejeski, 1993).

> "The greatest weapon against stress is our ability to choose one thought over the another"—*William James*

At family level: Intensity of stress can be decreased by taking care of the person who usually faces the same, use the words like "We are with you", "Don't take tension", "We can do it", "Together everything will be fine" etc. ***As parents Talk*, listen, and encourage expression of your children,** take care if children are behaving in any way out of the ordinary, avoid abuse, neglect, or other such behaviour that make children feel that they are not cared. Is there any change in behaviour, **take care if** children sleeping more or less etc.

At the organisational level: As the organisation knows that the work in the enterprise is possible if the workers, managers and the whole staff coordinate. The enterprise should take care of things that they should not be overburdened by work and if this happens the situation will get worsen. So the organisation should take steps like providing leisure time, bonus, slack etc. so that the staff do not feel the burden.

Stress Management

If anyone experiences physical symptoms that is related to stress, it is important to take immediate steps for managing that stress and there is urgent need to consult doctor in order to be sure one is/are doing well to safeguard his or her health. There is need of creating a proper stress management plan in order to reap the benefits of being healthy. Effective stress management can help in reducing the stress level in one's life and can make one healthier, happier and more productive so that one can get a suitable balanced life, relationships, relaxation, time for work, fun and reduce the intensity of pressure can successively to meet challenges in day-to-day life. In simple words, a successful stress management can be helpful in removing or altering the source of stress, altering the way one looks at a stressful situation, reduces the impact that stress might have on one's body and can be helpful to make other learn the alternative ways of coping with stress.

It can be of three levels:

At Primary-level: In this type of stress management technique or intervention stress is totally eliminated and reduced in intensity at the source of stress. The main motive is to prevent the stress level at work, in all the levels the focus is mostly at individual level than team and peer group and the organization.

At Secondary-level: It aims to develop stress resistance and helps in developing adaptive capacity in persons via education and training. This helps involve reducing the intensity of stress by interventions i.e. to response directed, here the role to group of workers, individual employees is recognized in case of response to signs of stress.

At Tertiary-level: It involves the direct intervention like the rehabilitation of the stressed and distressed employees and symptom directed.

Conclusion

In nutshell we can say that stress although is a universal truth but this situation is not such that cannot be cured.

"Be the change you wish to see in the world."—*Gandhiji*

By taking steps at individual, family level and even at organisational level if steps are taken which can relieve such condition that create stress. If stress is being felt by a student, student should practice some aspects like study as much, learn more to study more effectively, find ways to calm down, try to mimic test taking conditions, watch your diet, get enough sleep, exercise regularly, make sure you have plenty of time etc.

As the social being, there is need of social support: One need to call a friend, send an email. When anyone shares one's feelings with another person, it helps a lot to relieve stress. This needs one important thing that the person whom one share things is the one whom one trusts and whom one feel can validate and understand him/her.

Make connection to God by meditation: Meditation and mindful prayer help the mind and body to relax and focus. Mindfulness can help people see new perspectives, develop self-compassion and forgiveness. When practicing a form of mindfulness, people can release emotions that may have been causing the body physical stress. Much like exercise, research has shown that even meditating briefly can reap immediate benefits.

At organization level, steps should be taken to recognize the things that create the high costs of mismanaged stress at the workplace and how to achieve enhanced level of effectiveness and well-being among the workers. So, it means at both individual coping and organizational change can combat the problems related with stress.

References

Baroudi, J.J., (1985). "The impact of role variation variables on IS personnel work attitudes and intentions", *MIS Quarterly*, *9*(4): 341-356.

Bartholomew, J. (2000). "Stress Reactivity After Maximal Exercise: The Aspect of Manipulated Performance Feedback", In Endurance Athletes. *Journal of Sports Science*, (18): 893-899.

Bartol, K. and Martin, D. (1982). "Managing Information System Personnel: A Review of Literature". *MIS Quarterly*, *6*(1): 49-70.

Brown, G.W. (1993). "Life events and affective disorder: Replications and limitations", *Psychosomatic Medicine*, 55:248-259.

Cartwrite, S. (2000). "Taking the pulse of executive health in UK. Academy of Management Executive", *14*(2): 16-24.

Finlay, R. and Brown, G.W. (1981). "Types of stressful life events and the onset of anxiety and depressive disorders", *Psychological Medicine* 11:803–816.

Ganster, D.C.; Fox, M.L. and Dwyer, D.J. (2001). "Explaining employee health care costs: A prospective examination of stressful job demands, personal control, and physiological reactivity", *Journal of Applied Psychology*, 86: 954-964.

Guimaraes, T. and Igbaria, M. (1992). "Determinants of turnover intentions: Comparing IC and IS personnel", *Information Systems Research*, *3*(3): 273-303.

Herbert, T.B. and Cohen, S. (1993). "Stress and immunity in humans: A meta-analytic review", *Psychosomatic Medicine*, 55:364-379.

Hobson, M.L. and Rejeski, W.J. (1993). "Does the dose of acute exercise mediate psychophysiological response to mental stress?", *Journal of Sport and Exercise Psychology*, 15:77-87.

Ivancevich, J.M.; Napier, A.H. and Wetherbe, J.C. (1983). "Occupational stress, attitudes and health problems in the information systems professional," *Communications of the ACM*, *26*(10): 800-806.

Lazarus, R.S. (1990). "Theory-based stress measurement and commentaries", *Psychological Inquiry*, 1:3-51.

Li, E.Y. and Shani, E.B. (1991). "Stress dynamics of information systems managers: a contingency model", *Journal of Management Information System*, *7*(4): 107-130.

Monroe, S. and Simons, A. (1991). "Diathesis stress theories in the context of life stress research: Implications for the depressive disorders", *Psychological Bulletin*, 110:406-425.

Ravindran, V.; Merali, Z. and Anisman, H. (1997). "Dysthymia: A biological perspective", In: Licinio, J.; Bolis, C.L. and Gold, P. (eds.) *Dysthymia: From Clinical Neuroscience to Treatment*, Washington, DC: World Health Organization, pp. 21-44.

Rejeski, W.J.; Gregg, E.; Thompson, A. and Berry, M.J. (1991). "The aspects of varying doses of acute aerobic exercise on psychophysiological stress responses in highly trained cyclists", *Journal of Sport and Exercise Psychologyra*, 13:188-199.

Selye H. (1974). "Stress without distress", *Philadelphia*, PA: J.B. Lippincott Co.

Sethi, V.; Barrier, T. and King, R.C. (1999). "Examination of correlates of burnout in information systems professionals", *Information Resources Management Journal*, *12*(3): 5-13.

Sklar, L.S. and Anisman, H. (1981). "Stress and cancer", *Psychological Bulletin*, 89:369-406.

Summers, C.H. (2001). "Mechanisms for quick and variable responses", *Brain Behav. Evol.* 58.

17
Befriending Stress

Anjum Ahmed

> "Check your thoughts, challenge them and change them."
> — Dr. Hopley

'Stress' the word and its concept which is deeply entrenched in our vocabulary. At a very early stage we observe and we are taught that adult life is invariably 'stressful'. It comes with the package of us being the supreme creation. If we are not under stress it could mean that we are either not challenging ourselves or we are not leaving our comfort zones as a result we are not striving to become the best versions of ourselves.

History has it that the stress only came to be defined as a concept and the object of scientific attention in the 1950s. A golden age of the welfare state, probably a drastic increase in leisure time and growing criticism towards work and its ethic. This no doubt illustrates how only recently the global world has come to acknowledge the phenomena. And how freshly familiar we are with understanding its implications for our bodies and mind. Selye (1965) gave the original meaning of stress as "the non-specific responses of the body to any demand for change". According to Li, Cao & Li (2016) stress has been preserved and further developed in psychology, the general notion that stress is equivalent to a health crisis which can lead to cardiovascular diseases as well as anxiety and depression has trickled down into the general public to remain there until this very day.

When we are 'stressed' we say it when we mean that life feels like it is going out of hand and we have no control over it. When we feel we don't have what it takes to handle a heavy workload. And sometimes when tragic events strike our lives a loss of loved ones, a divorce, an accident, loss of wealth or job etc. It is believed that "stress" pushes people into psychological states which feels uneasy, bizarre and unnatural. As a result which renders living in the present and finding inner peace challenging and difficult. This simplification, however, is an indicator of how little we are familiar on the concept of 'stress'. How the inner brain works and the role belief plays in shaping our physiological responses.

No matter stress has such a bad reputation partly it is because of its misconception. In a general sense 'stress' is only but a conditioned response to a stressor (a stressful event or situation). It means that the belief a person holds about the way one respond to it will determine whether it will be physiologically harmful and to what extent.

Hence, psychology backed with empirical data cries for our attention. It also implores us to actualize our definition by stirring in some fresh knowledge or research findings that could potentially transform our lives.

In 1956, the famous Hungarian endocrinologist Hans Selye published 'The Stress of Life'. It sets the concept of stress and stressor (to distinguish between the stimulus and the response) at the foreground of psychological research.

Almost two decades later, in 1974, Selvy redefines the terminology to establish a clarification between two different types of stress: ***eustress***, and ***distress***. By combining the Greek prefix eu-, (meaning good) with stress, eustress became the term used to define "***good stress***" in opposition with "***bad stress***". By making the distinction between good stress (eustress) and bad stress (distress), Selye sought to show that stress, while being a reaction to a stressor, should not be always linked to negative scenarios.

On the contrary, he professed that eustress had, in fact, a range of health, mental and physical benefits on individuals, and can be fairly easily be remarkably distinct from distress only basing itself on its characteristics. According to Mills, Reiss and Dombeck (2018), the following are the distinguishing characteristics:

- It stimulates and motivates.
- It only lasts in the short term.
- It is perceived as something within our coping ability.
- It feels intriguing and exciting.
- It increases one's attention, focus and performance.

On the other hand, following attributes are associated with distress, or negative stress:

- It can last in the short as well as in the long term.
- It sparks anxiety and concern.
- It is perceived as something that goes beyond our coping abilities.
- It feels undesirable and unpleasant.
- It decreases one's attention, focus and performance.
- It can lead to mental and physical ailment.

The Psychology behind 'Good Stress'

McGonigal (2008) explained that stress as we know it is essentially the outcome of the primal reaction known as *fight-or-flight*, which evolution has endowed humans with to *fight against* or *flee from* a potentially life-threatening danger. Different mechanism of the reaction come into play. Firstly as soon as a stressful event occurs, an immediate response in the autonomic nervous system is triggered or initiated. A stress response arises, which in turn activates the sympathetic nervous system and floods the body with hormones such as cortisol and norepinephrine (McGonigal, 2008). These hormones heighten the senses which increases the heart rate and blood pressure, plunging the brain into a state of hyper-awareness. The part of the brain in authority for emotional calm and physical relaxation, the parasympathetic nervous system, is overpowered. This neurological cocktail of hormones and the hyperactivity of brain areas, in turn, results in a sudden burst of energy and focus, coupled with emotions such as anger, aggression, and anxiety.

This reaction is most assuredly very beneficial for situations involving a real danger. Unfortunately, it has remained as a basic element of human psychological processes, which activates whenever someone is confronted with what is subjectively perceived to be a **stressful situation**.

As such, whether the situation is actually life-threatening or not, the hormonal release is the same, which explains why it is possible for us to experience such intense physical symptoms at the mere thought of something stressful.

This is in some ways as a handicap often struggle to cope with the behavioural and emotional outcomes of the response. It is true that the fundamental neurological functioning of the process cannot be altered, something can be done about the stressor (the 'thing' that triggered the stress in the first place).

Since the stressor is often only a ***perceived stressor*** as opposed to a real one, the way one personally relates to the stressor typically determines the intensity and the emotional framework within which it is experienced.

This is where 'good stress' or eustress kicks in. Eustress, in someway, is a kind of tamed stress, which neurologically unwinds the same way as other types of stress but is channelled in such a way that individuals who experience it feel good about it.

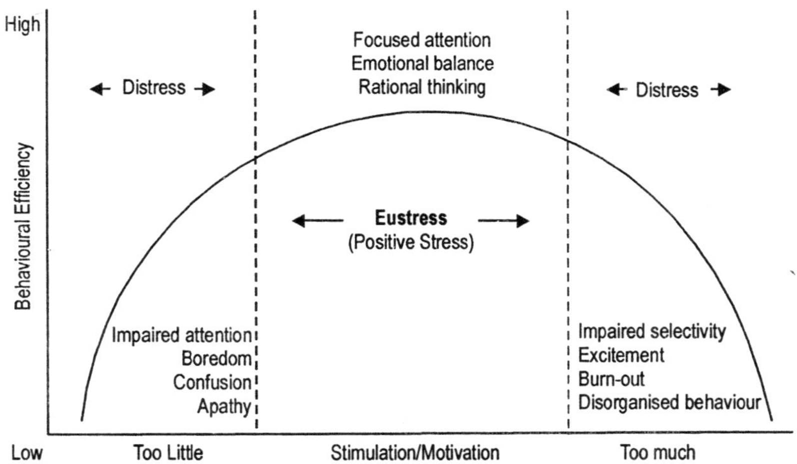

Fig. 17.1: The Stress Diagram (McGonigal, 2008).

As Fig. 17.1 illustrates that the good stress (eustress) reveals itself through focused **attention,** rational thinking and emotional balancing, as opposed to distress, which covers the areas of impaired attention, apathy, confusion, and boredom etc. Distress can also cover areas as impaired selectivity, excitement, burn-out and last but not the least, disorganized behaviour. This distinction is crucial as it sets the line between what may be considered to be **Flow**. A flow is a productive equilibrium in which skills are balanced with a healthy dose of challenge, and a state with all the psychological ingredients that could potentially have disastrous adverse effects on anyone's life.

One question we have in our mind is that is it possible to transform distress into eustress? The answer is yes. Easy said than done. For a convincing answer, we have to dive into what research findings have to say. Suedfeld (1997) points out, some societally traumatic instances such as war, natural disasters or plague can simultaneously cause stress and distress in an individual. On the one hand, distress would express itself around the anxiety triggered by possible traumatic events, financial anguish as well as a concern for other people's well-being.

It is observed that on the other, eustress would be triggered by positive forms of social engagement, resourcefulness and assistance to members of one's community (Suedfeld, 1997), provoked in part by the release of the oxytocin hormone during the stress response, which propels people to seek and provide support to others (McGonigal, 2014).

According to Mills, Reiss, and Dombeck (2018) there exists a range of stressors which tend to be experienced positively by most people, most of the time are as follows:

- Marriage.
- Newly found romantic relationship.
- New job.
- Buying or constructing a house.
- Travelling to different places.
- Having a child.
- Exercising.
- Going on a holiday.
- Taking a decision to buy something that is expensive.
- Learning a new hobby.
- And even retirement.

The essential point to note is that as long as the pushing of this boundary feels pleasurable or enjoyable, then it is eustress. If it doesn't feel acceptable, even in a remote sense, then it is just plain distress. It is crucial to look out for sign and listen to our body because what feels good often does something satisfying as well (most of the time). Indeed, there are a few researches in psychology which have shown that those who experience eustress on a regular basis reap a number of positive health benefits. Subjective well-being goes through the roof, which in the long-term, has a range of positive consequences on physical and mental health (Brule & Morgan, 2018).

How can a Teacher Maintain and Befriend Eustress?

Teaching job entails a lot of stress when it comes to handling students (the kind of teacher-student ratio that persist in Indian school), managing parents and satisfying the management of the school. With some practice a teacher can increase his/her sense of satisfaction and calmness without changing anything else in their life. Because our thinking is automatic, something natural and it becomes invisible. We forget we are thinking and accept our thoughts as reality. Rather than noticing thoughts and deciding if we want to respond to them, we usually assume they are absolutely true and react to them instantly. It's important for our brain to scan for utility, accuracy and fairness.

The first rule to remember is we should be controlling our thoughts. If there is a disturbing thought, try diffusing with the counter thought phrase "there goes another one" and let the thought go rather than being lured into the details of your thought.. If we have to learn to redirect our thinking. If it is not important, let go of it. This is where we can start breeding positive attitude Give ourselves kindness by thinking. Nurturing positive attitude not only helps you to manage your personal and professional lives, it has health benefits too. Research has it that people with positive attitudes are less likely to be hospitalized and tend to live longer. Older adults with a positive attitude about ageing may be more resilient to stress. For older adults, stress often centres on relations with family or friends, while for younger people it may more often be related to work.

Think of a positive attitude like a survival tool: carry it with you at all times for emergencies.

Secondly, it is important to surround ourselves with positive people if possible. One might be surrounded by colleagues with negative attitude. It is vital to remember that *'He who wants a rose must respect the thorn'*. In most cases shunning away for these personalities is not possible, view it as a opportunity to develop patience and tolerance. Otherwise it will have detrimental effect on our thoughts and health. Try to find people and connect with them who are passionate about their job, have new ideas, and are interested in lots of other things besides work. Fill your mind with positive input.

Language is another imperative aspect to be considered. The structure of language affects a person's view of the world, and the way they think. Taken to the furthest extent, our language actually limits or delineates how we are able to perceive the world as given by the Sapir-Whorf hypothesis (1929). At the incipient level, the language we use everyday, both in thought and spoken word, has a cumulative effect on how we think about ourselves, our work, and those around us.

We cannot become an optimist overnight. Practice positive self-talk. Start by not saying anything to oneself that you wouldn't say to anyone else. Here are some examples of negative self-talk and how one with the help of language can swirl into a positive thinking:

1. I have never done it before. – It is an opportunity to learn something new.
2. It is too complicated. – Let me tackle it from a different angle.
3. I don't have the resources. — Necessity is the mother of invention.
4. There is no way it will work. – Let me can try to make it work.
5. It is too radical a change. – Let us take a chance.

Having a bleeding heart, a courteous nature and being empathetic is the first and foremost quality of a teacher. Being kind to others makes one happy. Research has it that if we are being nice to others on a regular basis, it will become a cycle of generosity and happiness that makes one feel good as well as causes those you are nice to, to feel happy as well. Including the administrators, parents, colleagues and students.

Be accountable of your actions. Refusing to take responsibility for one's actions and situation, or not taking control of how one responds, kills a positive attitude immediately. If you are at fault or in some way responsible, refusing to acknowledge it means you cannot correct the behaviour and it will happen again in the future. As a result one also sets oneself up for a victimhood mindset in which things happen to them again and again. Taking responsibility for your action helps you to see life as something you have some control over rather than at the mercy of fate. It is like the equation: E + R = O (event + response = outcome). How one respond has an effect on the outcome, even when events are out of their control.

A teacher has to be curious and embrace learning. A mind that is closed to learning new things grows stagnant and negative. Change, new ideas, or any additional task becomes arduous to someone like that. A teacher should be willing to learn and curious about many things. One's attitude will be positive because one is forward-looking and wanting to understand instead of closed off. Being curious about a new situation or what's going on tends to develop mindful skills that is, aware of the present moment, and that tends to force out negative attitudes.

Conclusion

A good support system and a healthy sense of self-esteem are essential elements which helps to keep stress levels as low as possible. We all respond differently physically and mentally to different stressors because we have different ideas and psychological associations with these. Positive attitude emerged as one the supreme factor that helps us to befriend stress as eustress. One of the worst killers of a good attitude is going through life thinking people owe us. Negativity is the standard state of existence if we think the world owes us. Positive self-talk, reaffirming statements to ourselves reminding us of our achievements can be extremely powerful and slowly disintegrate negative thoughts or beliefs that lie at the roots of certain stress responses. The best way to go is ultimately for us to try finding different methods and see what works and what doesn't for us in that particular circumstance. The next time one talks about their stress, let's hope that we will not be referring to the 'distress' kind of stress, but our prolific eustress, instead.

References

Brulé, G. and Morgan, R. (2018). "Working with stress: can we turn distress into eustress?", *Journal of Neuropsychology and Stress Management, 3*, 1-3.

Gardner, W.L. and Schermerhorn, J.R. (2004). "Unleashing individual potential", *Organizational Dynamics, 3*(33):270-281.

Gavin, J.H. and Mason, R.O. (2004). "The Virtuous Organization: The Value of Happiness in the Workplace", *Organizational Dynamics, 33*(4): 379-392.

Jones, J.G. and Hardy, L. (1990). Wiley series in human performance and cognition. Stress and performance in sport.

Keller, A.; Litzelman, K.; Wisk, L.E.; Maddox, T.; Cheng, E.R.; Creswell, P.D. and Witt, W.P. (2012). "Does the perception that stress affects health matter? The association with health and mortality", *Health Psychology, 31*(5):677.

Le Fevre, M.; Matheny, J. and Kolt, G.S. (2003). "Eustress, distress and interpretation in occupational stress", *Journal of Managerial Psychology, 18*(7):726-744.

Li, C.T.; Cao, J. and Li, T.M. (2016, September). "Eustress or distress: An empirical study of perceived stress in everyday college life", In *Proceedings of the 2016 ACM International Joint Conference on Pervasive and Ubiquitous Computing: Adjunct* (pp. 1209-1217). ACM.

McGonigal, K. (2008). "Tame your stress", *Yoga Journal*, 275, 82.

McGonigal, K. (2013). *How to make stress your friend.* Ted Global, Edinburgh, Scotland, 6, 13.

Mills, H.; Reiss, N. and Dombeck, M. (2018). *Types of Stressors* (*Eustress vs. Distress*). Retrieved from https://www.mentalhelp.net/articles/types-of-stressors-eustress-vs-distress/

Rosch, P. (2018). *Hans Selye: Birth of Stress*. Retrieved from https://www.stress.org/about/hans-selye-birth-of-stress/

Sapir, Edward. (1958). *Culture, Language and Personality*. Berkeley: University of California Press.

Selye, H. (1956). *The Stress of Life*, McGraw-Hill Inc., US.

Selye, H (1965). "The Stress Syndrome", *The American Journal of Nursing*, 97-99.

Spector, P.E. and Jex, S.M. (1998). "Development of four self-report measures of job stressors and strain: Interpersonal conflict at work scale, organizational constraints scale, quantitative workload inventory and physical symptoms inventory", *Journal of Occupational Health Psychology*, *3*(4):356.

Suedfeld, P. (1997). "Reactions to societal trauma: Distress and/or eustress", *Political Psychology*, *18*(4):849-861.

World Health Organization and Commission of the European Communities. (1986). *Environmental Health Criteria* (No. 53). World Health Organization.

WHO (2018). *WHO: Stress at the workplace*. Retrieved from https://www.who.int/occupational_health/topics/stressatwp/en/

Whorf, B.L. (1940). "Science and Linguistics", *Technology Review* (1940) 35: 229-31, 247-8.

Wilding, M. (2018). *Please Stop Telling Me to Leave My Comfort Zone*. Retrieved from =https://anxymag.com/blogs/home/comfort-zones-melody-wilding

STRESS IN HUMAN LIFE

18
Stress in Adolescents
Stressors and Techniques to Cope

Agrita Bisht and *Sunita Godiyal*

Introduction

The word stress is quite common in our everyday life and we use this word in daily basis to explain our mood without understanding its exact meaning. Etymologically the word 'stress' is derived from the Latin word 'strictus', meaning 'to tighten'. In the world of physics, stress is defined as a force per unit area and strain is said to be the deformity that occurs in a solid due to that applied force. If we apply this same physical meaning of stress in the living organisms, it is conceptually similar to the demands faced by organisms and their responses towards it.

In the field of biological science, the term stress is coined by a Hungarian-Canadian endocrinologist Hans Selye in 1936. According to Selye, "stress is the non-specific response of the body to any demand for change". Stress is the most common problem faced by the majority of population. He explained the model of stress based on physiology and psychobiology as *General Adaptation Syndrome* (GAS). He also defined a system which prepares the body to cope with stress and named it *hypothalamic-pituitary-adrenal axis* (HPA axis). In his experiments on laboratory animals he subjected them to various noxious physical and emotional stimuli and noted that they all exhibited the same pathological changes in the body. These noxious agents were later termed as stress by him. He also found that persistent stress in animals resulted into various diseases which are similar to the human, such as heart attacks, stroke, kidney diseases etc. Positive stress is called 'eustress' and the negative is called 'distress'.

In simple words stress can be defined as a way our body responds at the time of some threat or danger. It is the body's way to protect us from upcoming crises. Generally, each one of us faces some kind of stress on daily basis in our life and it is also said that a little stress is indeed good for survival. But too much stress, which remains for longer period of time could negatively affects our physical and mental health. At the time of stress our body responds in an amazing way by triggering fight-or-flight response. This stress response is marked by physiological changes, which also includes endocrine and nervous changes that helps in preparing a human or an animal to react or to retreat. The fight and flight response is characterized by anxiety, increase in heart rate, increase in blood sugar etc.

Adolescence and Stress

Etymologically, the word adolescence is derived from the Latin word 'adolescere' meaning 'to grow up'. Generally, it is described as the period between 13 and 19 years of age and is considered as the transition age from puberty towards adulthood. Adolescents are stereotyped as rebellious, distracted and moody; they behave in this manner because they experience numerous physical, neural, cognitive and socio-emotional changes. It is the main reason they behave in such manner as these changes make it difficult for them to take decision. This transition period brings issues related to self identity, independence, choices regarding school, peer pressure, romantic interests etc. There is also a change observed in the parent-child relationship. The learning experiences in the teenage works as a foundation stone for adulthood and various mental health issues like depression and anxiety which an adult face later in their life starts manifesting at the early age of adolescence.

It's a general belief that children are too young to be stressed and only adults experience stress. Children are not stressed as they don't have to work, manage home and pay various bills. But even very young children do feel stress and not only children, even animals feel stress various time. Although little amount of stress is essential and can be really helpful for children, but too much negative stress could lead to serious long term psychological damage. Here are some general stressors and some modern day's technological stressors that affects the adolescents on regular basis and add to their daily stress:

General Stressors in the Life of Adolescents

1. Competition

Competition, in a healthy way, is very essential in the life of human beings. A good and healthy competition at school level helps to inculcate various valuable skills like resilience, motivation and other important interpersonal skills. One can only learn these skills in a competitive environment as it make them to see the same things from others' point of view. Competition makes a person strong enough to face even the failure with pride and acceptance. But competition, when not taken in a healthy manner, can result in various serious problems. Excessive stress and anxiety are the major causes of competition. People face competition at every stage of their life, whether at childhood or adulthood. While facing the competition, the student can suffer from low self-esteem which can lead to depression and emotional turmoil. Sometimes failure in competition results in hopelessness and could also lead into suicidal tendencies. The pressure of achieving well grades and remain in the top slot in the class is making adolescents vulnerable towards various mental health issues like stress, depression and anxiety.

2. Homework

Homework is considered as a crucial part of school curriculum as it helps to consolidate what is taught in the school. It helps to broaden the imagination of the child as it provides opportunities to think beyond what is taught in the classroom. But too much homework could affect the social life of a child and results in lack of sleep and exhaustion (Lohman & Jarvis, 2000). Excess of anything is harmful, same goes with the homework. In a research conducted by Verma, Sharma and Larson (2002), homework is found to be the most negative context of schoolwork experience and is considered to be associated with anger, stress, irritability and boredom more than that of class work. Koumza and Kennedy (2002) in their study on senior high school students of Australia found a significant and positive correlation between the hours of home work and stress. They also found positive as well as significant correlation of hours of homework with mood disturbance.

3. Parental Pressure

In India, parental pressure is one of the major stress causing factors among the students. This stressor is very common in the board examination aspirants. Whatever parents had failed to achieve during their school days, they expect their child to achieve it all. This way poor child is burdened under their parents' wishes and is obliged to follow them (Byrne, D.G. *et al.*, 2007). The pressure of achieving best grades is so high that parents are often tend to neglect physical activities like sports, which may be the personal interest of their kids. In a study conducted on Indian high school students by Deb, *et al.* (2015), the data was collected from the students of grade 11 and 12 of three government aided and three private schools. Here the researchers found a positive relation between the stress and the parental pressure.

4. Poor Grades

Poor grade in the examination is nightmare for the students, especially when there is parental pressure. Fear of not achieving good grades creates very much stress in the daily life of students (Crystal, *et al.*, 1994). Also stress during exam can also result in poor grades. So, bad grades and stress both are interrelated with each other because one can result into other and *vice versa.* Abouserie (2006) in his study concluded that examination and the result of examination is the biggest cause of stress among the students. Limited amount of stress or positive stress (eustress) works as a self-motivation for students and helps in a positive manner. But many times students are so worried for their grades that they are unable to focus on their studies, this fear for result works as distress or negative stress. This negative stress is very harmful and affects the performance of the students in the examination.

5. Financial Status

Financial condition is a very effective stressor for college going students. Although during adolescence, finance is not a big issue for the students since parents are taking care of all their expenses. But when the economic condition of the family is poor, this too adds as a stressor in the young students (Flanagan & Eccles, 1993). When family struggles with day-to-day needs, the child also suffers the same and this affects his studies. Parental education is associated with the socio-economic status (SES) of the family. Good education increases the probability of earning good money and thus increasing the socio-economic condition of the family. Finkelstein, *et al.* (2007) concluded in their study that lower SES increases stress in the adolescents. In another study conducted by Goodman *et al.* (2005), the level of stress was found higher among the students belonging lower SES families.

Modern Technology as Stressors among Adolescents

1. Mobile Phones

Talking about the modern technology, mobile phone comes first before all the other gadgets. They are very closely associated to the life of almost everyone of us. The emergence of the mobile phones over the last decade has influenced our lives in both positive as well in negative ways. On one hand, the mobile phones has made various day-to-day tedious task very easy but on the other hand it negatively affects our mental health (Thomee, S. *et al.*, 2011). Nowadays mobile phones have become as crucial as oxygen for all of us, whether child or adult. Excessive use of mobile phones from a very early age is making the students more prone to mobile phone addiction and hampering their mental health. Separation from phones for few minutes can make an addicted child very anxious and stressed. Dr. Gladius *et al.* (2018) studied mobile phone usage on sleep disturbance, stress and academic performance on medical students and they found that 72.40 per cent of the study participants had poor sleep quality, 66.50 per cent had moderate stress and 14.80 per cent had severe stress. Gupta, Garg and Arora (2015) in their study concluded that overuse of mobile phones results in various negative impacts such as psychological health, sleep and academic performance of students.

2. Social Media

One of the main reasons among the students for sticking with their mobile phones is the constant desire to be remaining active at various social media platforms. Although social media is a great platform to stay connected to our far away family, friends and to the people who care about us. But excess of anything is always bad. This excessive use of social media platforms like Facebook, Twitter, Instagram etc. gave birth to various new stressors like FOMO (Fear of missing out), comparison stress etc. (Beyens, I., *et al.*, 2016). Excessive use of social media can contribute to stress and other negative emotions. Aydogan and Buyukyilmaz (2017) studied the stress and anxiety levels of the students in relation to their type and rate of social media use. They found out that the social media usage, frequency and duration of use, increases students' stress' and anxiety level.

Excessive engagement in social media disturbs the sleep patterns which also results in stress. A recent study by Schuur, Baumgartner and Sumter (2018) states that the social media use and social media stress were positively related to sleep latency and daytime sleepiness. Excessive internet use is linked to depression, people who are internet addicted shows high level of depressive symptoms (Morrison and Gore, 2010).

3. Video Gaming

It is a debatable topic that if video games work as stressor in the life of students or not. Well various researches shows that playing video games can actually work as stress boosters and contribute in stress relief. Playing video games can be fun but excessive gaming could contribute in stress, especially when they are violent in nature (Lynch, P.J., 1999). In another research it was found that playing excessive video game increases the risk of obesity among the youngster (Mario, S., *et al.*, 2014).

4. Video Streaming Services

Video streaming services are online video viewing platform. Here the user can view online movies, TV shows etc. without being downloaded on the host computer. The content here is sent in a compressed continuous stream form and is played as it arrives. Netflix, Hooq, Amazon prime video, Hotstar, Voot, Sony Liv, Eros Now, Jio cinema etc. are some of the famous video streaming services widely used by the young generation of India. These services provide entertainment anytime anywhere, all you need is a smart phone or laptop with internet connection. Free internet services have worsened the situation even more. People are developing compulsive tendencies to watch various shows whole day long avoiding various physical activities and social life. Spending hours in front of the screen contributes in increasing anxiety and irritability. This is a recent developing trend contributing as the daily stressors in the life of humans. Researches also show that delay in the streaming creates much higher stress than been stuck in the heavy traffic.

How to Identify a Stressed Student?

When in stress our body secretes the stress hormone called cortisol. And when a child is in prolonged stress this hormone level increases in the body which ill affects the brain and its functioning. It hampers the mental and cognitive development of the child. If the child with overly stress is not identified in time and remained unaddressed for a long period of time, the stress can convert into chronic stress. This chronic stress could be a permanent and irreversible damage to the mental health of the child. So it is very essential in the part of parents and teachers to identify such children in time and help them to overcome such situation. Below is the list of some signs a child will exhibit if he/she is in stress:

1. **Mood Swings**—There are some days when you are very happy and feeling high, then suddenly you start feeling low and the soon up again. This type of sudden changes in the mood in a single day when starts affecting us and the others around us, then it is not normal and termed as mood swings. This becomes very common when a person is stressed.
2. **Aggression**—Too much stress can be direct cause of aggression. A stressed person may always remain irritated and in anger. If a child in a class is in stress, he will show anger to his classmates, siblings and parents.
3. **Disinterest in studies, playtime and leisure activity**—A child in stress not only loses his interest in his studies but even in his playtime and other leisure activities. He prefers to stay home doing nothing than going out in field to play with his mates.
4. **Negative thinking**—Having negative thoughts about himself and about his future is also a sign of a stressed child. He starts focusing in his weaknesses leaving his strengths aside and is always in fear of failure.
5. **Rebellious nature**—Sometimes a stressed child could show a rebellious behaviour at home or at school. He will rebel

against the people or norms with which he is not agreeing. This rebellious nature sometime can cause very serious harm.

6. **Headaches**—Although there could be numerous reason behind a headache. But it is an important physical symptom of a stressed person. Stress can trigger headaches and migraine. These types of headaches are termed as stress headaches.
7. **School absenteeism**—With the lack of interest in studies, a child tends to take leave or start bunking from the school. Child does not want to remain in between groups of people and rather prefer to stay alone by himself.
8. **Overeating or loss of appetite** — Change in the eating habits is another sign of a stressed person. Some people gets involved in overeating and some face loss of appetite, these changes are due to cortisol (stress hormone). Both excess and less intake of food always has adverse effect on the health of the individual.
9. **Disturbed sleep patterns**—Lots of stress also negatively affect our sleep cycle. An individual having stress will find it difficult to sleep at night due to anxiousness and worrying. Less sleep or improper sleep boost the stress hormone in the body. Disturbed sleep at night will ruin the upcoming day and the individual will feel exhausted and unable to concentrate on his work.
10. **Sudden drop in performance**—Continuous worrying, anxiety and negative thoughts due to stress affect the overall performance of an individual. Even a very bright child in the class can suddenly become dull.

Techniques for Reducing Stress

After identification of the stressed child, it is important to identify their possible stressors and provide them proper knowledge of various techniques to overcome stress in life. Once the child gets familiar with the various techniques he could become aware and can cope with the stressful situation in future. It is very essential in the part of parents and teacher to make the child capable enough to understand their stress and cope with it. Various stress management techniques which are proven methods for curbing stress are enumerated below:

1. Aromatherapy

Aroma stands for the fragrant scent that pleases our senses. So aromatherapy is a type of treatment which uses various fragrant essential oils to sooth and calm our senses. Here natural plant extracts are used in three ways — aerial diffusion, direct inhalation and topical applications in massage, baths etc. which helps in improving psychological and physical well-being. This therapy has gained a lot of attention in recent years. Aromatherapy helps in the reduction of "cortisol", the stress causing hormone. In an article by Sharma, Adhav and Vaswani (2016), explained a detail account on aromatherapy and how it works as a brain tonifier. According to them aromatherapy helps in enhancing mood and encourage the sense of general well-being. Seo Ji-Yeong (2009) in a research also found aromatherapy as effective stress management tool. Aromatherapy is a reliable, affordable and effective therapeutic solution for relieving stress which is now worldwide (Dave and Yadav, 2013).

2. Classical Music

Music has a soothing power and acts as a powerful tool for stress management (Scheufele, 2000). Listening to music can have a relaxing effect on our body and soul, especially slow and classical music. Good classical music helps us in many ways by slowing the pulse and heart rate, lowering the blood pressure and decreasing the stress causing hormone. Thoma *et al.* (2013) in their research studied the effect of music on human stress response. This research was conducted on sixty healthy female volunteers and the findings shows, listening to music impacted their psychobiological stress system. One of the other research of Linnemann *et al.* (2015) also found out that listening of the classical music was effective in reducing subjective stress level and explains the physiological mechanisms of stress reducing effect of music.

3. Yoga

Yoga is the gift from India to the world. It is a proven mind and body practice involving various physical poses, breath control and meditation. It helps in the overall health including physical as well as emotional aspect of human body. It makes the practitioner self-aware about the connection of body, mind and soul and thus calms the senses.

With the regular practice of *yoga* we can train our body and mind to counter stress (Pascoe and Bauer, 2015) and make a balance with the day-to-day activity of our life. Prashad (2004) explains that regular *yoga* practitioners are more resilient to various stressful conditions and thus reducing risk towards various cardio-respiratory diseases.

4. Meditation

Called *Dhyana* in Hindi language, meditation is a technique of focusing our attention to a single point. Meditation helps to detach ourselves or our attention from distracting and negative thoughts. It works as a great stress buster and relaxes our body and mind (Peterson and Pbert, 1992) by bringing us back to the present from the bad experiences of past or from the worries of future. Making habit and sincere indulgence in only 10 minutes of meditation can do wonder to our life. Coppola and Spector (2009) conducted a research on 31 practitioners of a mental meditation technique called Natural Stress Relief Meditation. After four weeks of regular practice of this meditation, significant reductions of anxiety were found in them. Meditation contribute in our mental health as it makes us feel refreshed and ready to face the daily challenges of our life with better healthy perspective.

5. Exercise

Exercise is a physical activity which helps in the overall fitness and health of a person. It can be any bodily movement with greater level of intensity than usually done as daily activity. Regular exercise helps to achieve a good level of physical fitness and reduction of the risk of various diseases due to obesity, hypertension, diabetes etc. (Warburton, Nicol and Bredin, 2006). It also helps to strengthen the vital organs like heart and lungs. Niebauer and Cooke (1996) studied the cardiovascular effects of exercises and came to the conclusion that physical exercises slows the rate of progression of vascular diseases and also reduces the cardiovascular morbidity and mortality. Exercising increases one's self-confidence, contributes in relaxing and improves mood, improve sleep cycle and thus helping to cope with stress, anxiety and depression.

6. Laughter Therapy

Laughter is an excellent way to lessen the stress and this method to minimize stress is called laughter therapy. It works as a great stress buster by decreasing stress hormone (Bennett and Lengacher, 2008) and triggers the body to release the natural feel-good chemicals called endorphins. These endorphins are very helpful for sound mental and physical health and could also provide temporarily pain relieve to the person. For all these reason, laughter is considered as the best medicine. Mora-Ripoll (2010) in his work on therapeutic value of laughter concludes that laughter has positive and quantifiable effects on health. The importance of laughter is even recognized by the ancient Indian *rishis* and *yogis* and laughter has also included in *Yoga* in the form of an *aasana*.

7. Guided Imagery

Guided imagery is another method of relaxation and stress relief (Gruzelier, 2002). This method involves the concentration of the mind on some positive mental place or mental image. This method helps us to visualize and connect to some positive images thus leaving all the tensions and anxiety behind. It can also be called as guided meditation in which an expert initially guide us by creating soothing and peaceful environment thus helping to connect the person with himself. Apostolo and Kolcaba (2009) conducted a ten days experiment on sixty short-term hospitalized depressive patients. They used guided imagery technique on them for next ten days. The pre- and post-result on test scales of depression, anxiety and stress gave a significant difference, thus concludes that this technique is quite helpful in curbing stress over time.

Conclusion

To conclude, stress is experienced by all of us at certain point of life. Some of us can easily cope with it while for some it is difficult. Life of a modern day child especially adolescent, with so much work load, academic pressure, parental pressure and day-to-day increased proximity with new technologies is full of stressors. It is the duty of the parents and teachers to get alert if any early signs of stress are noticed by them. Find the cause of their stress and provide them proper stress management through various techniques like *yoga*, aromatherapy, meditation etc. These techniques if learnt and followed regularly will not only curb stress but also add to a wholesome development of the personality of the child. Doing exercise daily followed with meditation will contribute in the physical, mental and emotional health of an individual by making him more focused and energetic for his work.

For parents it is also very essential to make their child to understand the fact that, it is good to set standards high but not always expecting perfection. This way child will develop a sense of positive self-esteem, without developing any unrealistic expectation. On the other hand in the case of chronic stress, it is essential to seek out professional help since parents or teacher do not always have the required resources to deal with the stress.

References

Abouserie, R. (2006). "Sources and levels of stress in relation to locus of control and self-esteem in university students", *Educational Psychology, 14*(3): 323-330.

Apostolo, J.L.A. and Kolcaba, K. (2009). "The effect of guided imagery on comfort, depression, anxiety and stress of psychiatric inpatients with depressive disorders", *Archives of Psychiatric Nursing, 23*(6): 403-411.

Aydogan and Buyukyilmaz (2017). "The effect of social media usage on students' stress and anxiety: A research in Karabuk University Faculty of Business", *International Journal of Multidisciplinary Thoughts, 6*(1): 253-260.

Bauer, I.E. and Pascoe, M.C. (2015). "A systematic review of randomized control trails on the effect of yoga on stress measures and mood", *Journal of Psychiatric Research,* 68: 270-282.

Bennett, M.P. and Lengacher, C. (2008). "Humor and laughter may influence health III. Laughter and health outcomes", *Evidence Based Complementary and Alternative Medicine, 5*(1): 37-40.

Beyen, I., Frison, E. and Eggermont, S. (2016). "I don't want to miss a thing: Adolescents fear of missing out and its relationship to adolescents social needs, Facebook use and facebook related stress", *Computers in Human Behaviour,* Elsevier, 64: 1-8.

Byrne, D.G., Davenport, S.C. and Mazanov, J. (2007). "Profiles of adolescent stress: The development of the adolescents stress questionnaire", *Journal of Adolescence,* 30: 393-416.

Coppola, F. and Spector, D. (2009). "Natural stress relief meditation as a tool for reducing anxiety and increasing self actualization", *Social Behaviour and Personality: An International Journal, 37*(3): 307-311.

Crystal, D.S., Chen, C., *et al.* (1994). "Psychological maladjustment and academic achievement: A cross-cultural study of Japanese, Chinese and American high school students", *Child Development*, 65: 738-753.

Dave, V. and Yadav, S. (2013). "Aromatherapy for stress relive", *International Journal of Research and Development in Pharmacy and Life Sciences*, *2*(3): 398-403.

Deb, S., Strodl, E. and Sun, J. (2015). "Academic stress, parental pressure, anxiety and mental health among Indian high school students", *International Journal of Psychology and Behavioural Sciences*, *5*(1): 26-34.

Finkelstein, D.M., *et al.* (2007). "Socioeconomic differences in adolescent stress: The role of psychological resources", *Journal of Adolescent Health*, *40*(2): 127-134.

Fisher, S. (1994). "Identifying video game addiction in children and adolescents", *Addictive Behaviours*, 19, 545–553.

Flanagan, C.A. and Eccles, J.S. (1993). "Changes in parents' work status and adolescents' adjustment at school", *Child Development*, 64: 246-257.

Gladius, J.H., *et al.* (2018). "A study of mobile phone usage on sleep disturbance, stress and academic performance among medical students in Tamil Nadu", *International Journal of Community Medicine and Public Health*, *5*(1): 365-368.

Goodman, E., *et al.* (2005). "Social disadvantage and adolescent stress", *Journal of Adolescent Health*, *37*(6): 484-92.

Gruzelier, J.H. (2002). "A review of the impact of hypnosis, relaxation, guided imagery and individual differences on aspect of immunity and health", *The International Journal on the Biology of Stress*, *5*(2): 147-163.

Gupta, Garg and Arora (2015). "Pattern of mobile phone usage and its effects on psychological health, sleep and academic performance in students of a medical university", *National Journal of Physiology, Pharmacy and Pharmacology*, *6*(2): 132-139.

Kauzma, N.M. and Kennedy, G.A. (2002). "Homework, stress and mood disturbance in senior high school students", *Psychological Reports*, *91*(1): 193-198.

Linnemann, A., *et al.* (2015). "Music listening as a means of stress reduction in daily life", *Psychoneuroendocrinology*, 60, 82-90.

Lohman, J.B. and Jarvis, P.A. (2000). "Adolescent stressors, coping strategies and psychological health studied in the family context", *Journal of Youth and Adolescence*, 29, 15-43.

Lynch, P.J. (1999). "Hostility, Type A behaviour and stress hormones at rest and after playing violent video games in teenagers", *Psychosomatic Medicine*, *61*(1): 113.

Mario. S., *et al.* (2014). "Frequent video game playing in young males is associated with central adiposity and high-sugar, low fiber dietary consumption", *Eating and Weight Disorders*, *19*(4): 515-520.

Mora-Ripoll, R. (2010). "The therapeutic value of laughter medicine", *Alternative Therapies in Health and Medicine*, *16*(6): 56-64.

Morrison, C.M. and Gore, H. (2010). "The relationship between excessive internet use and depression: A questionnaire-based study of 1,319 young people and adults", *Psychopathology*, 43: 121-126.

Niebauer, J. and Cooke, J.P. (1996). "Cardiovascular effects of exercise: Role of endothelial shear stress", *Journal of American College of Cardiology*, *28*(7): 1652-60.

O'Reilly, M. (1996). "Internet addiction: A new disorder enters the medical lexicon", *Canadian Medical Association Journal*, 154: 1882-1883.

Peterson, L.G. and Pbert, L. (1992). "Effectiveness of meditation based stress reduction programmes in the treatment of anxiety disorders", *The American Journal of Psychiatry*, *149*(7): 936-943.

Prashad, O. (2004). "Role of yoga in stress management," *The West Indian Medical Journal*, *53*(3): 191-194.

Scheufele, P.M. (2009). "Effect of progressive relaxation and classical music on measurements of attention, relaxation and stress responses", *Journal of Behavioural Medicine*, *23*(2): 207-228.

Schuur, Baumgartner and Sumter (2018). "Social media use, social media stress and sleep: Examining cross-sectional and longitudinal relationships in adolescents", *Health Communication*, 1-8.

Sharma, R., Adhav, R. and Vaswani, P. (2016). "Aromatherapy as a brain tonifier: A review", *The Pharma Innovation Journal*, *5*(4): 108-111.

Thoma, M.V., *et al.* (2013). "The effect of music on the human stress response", *PLoS ONE*, *8*(8): 1-12.

Thomee, S., Harenstam, A. and Hagberg, M. (2011). "Mobile phone use and stress, sleep disturbances and symptoms of depression among young adults — a prospective cohort study", *BMC Public Health*, 11(1): 1-11.

Verma, S., Sharma, D. and Larson, R.W. (2002). "School stress in India: Effects on time and daily emotions", *International Journal of Behavioural Development*, *26*(6): 500-508.

Warburton, D. ER., Nicol, C.W. and Bredin, S. SD. (2006). "Health benefits of physical activity: the evidence", *Canadian Medical Association Journal*, *174*(6): 801-809.

Yeong, S.J. (2009). "The Effect of Aromatherapy on Stress and Stress Responses in Adolescents", *Journal of Korean Academy of Nursing*, *39* (3): 357-365.

19
Stress Among Trainee-Teachers

Sangeeta Pawar

Introduction

Stress is one of the most prominent factors that have enormous influence on an individual's personal and academic life. Stress is body's mechanism of responding to a challenge or threat. It results into change in certain physiological processes such as secretion of hormones, change in heart beat, rise in blood pressure etc. It usually occurs when an individual feel pressure to adapt to their environment. A non-fulfilment of demands, resulting into stress leads to lowering of self-esteem, poorer health habits, poorer self-management choices (Lok & Bishop, 1999), and impaired memory (Vondras, *et al.*, 2005). Significant levels of stress found among students, increased mental health problems, resulting in devastating impacts, gained attention of researchers in educational settings.

Stress is the condition typically characterized by symptoms of mental and physical tension or strain, as depression or hypertension, which can result from a reaction to a situation in which a person feels threatened or pressured (Chaplain, R.P., 2008). The individual responds to the stress affect the individual as well as their habitat. According to Gunnell, *et al.* (2009) stress is related to both external and internal factors; the external factors include the physical environment, job, relationships with others, home, and all the situations, challenges, difficulties, and expectations confronted with on a daily basis. Internal factors determine body's ability to respond to, and deal with, the external stress-inducing factors includes nutritional status, overall health and fitness levels, emotional well-being, and the amount of sleep and rest. Because of the overabundance of stress in our modern lives, we usually think of stress as a negative experience, but from a biological point of view, stress yield neutral, negative, or positive experience. Thus stress has driven evolutionary changes (the development and natural selection of species over time) and the species that adapted best to the causes of stress (stressors) had survived and evolved was evident in plant and animal kingdom (Caplan, *et al.*, 1975). Stress has a great impact on an individual's energy level (Brown, *et al.*, 2002).

There are many types of stress that are distinguishable by the symptoms and sensations that the individual feels, how they react and how long these feelings persist among other variables. They are acute stress; chronic stress; panic disorder; agoraphobia; post-traumatic stress disorder; childhood separation anxiety or adult separation anxiety; social anxiety disorder; generalized anxiety disorder; obsessive compulsive disorder; phobias and acute stress disorder (Manthei, *et al.*, 1996).

Stress among Teachers

In educational process, the teacher occupies a very significant place. A teacher is the medium through which goals and objectives of development can be actualized. For this, the teacher must possess sound mental and physical health as it is directly related with his/her working efficiency. Teaching is a profession wherein changing programmes and policies tend to increase the level of stress in teachers. The psychological conditions of a teacher such as feelings of inferiority, insecurity, non-satisfaction, non-compliance to the demands, anxiety, stress and strain, fear, worry, tension etc. all have bearing on students learning. Teachers experience higher level of stress in the present time due to overcrowded classes, heavy syllabus and inadequate facilities, demand of dynamism more focus on results and increasing workload of non-academic work. The stress experienced by different occupation types and job roles has been discussed in many papers for example, teachers (Travers and Cooper, 1993), healthcare (Cooper *et al.*, 1999), nurses and social workers (Kahn, 1993), and the ambulance service (Young and Cooper, 1999).

Teaching is recognized as one of the most stressful professions (Johnson, *et al.,* 2005), besides this psychological distress among teacher-trainees is less-well recognized. This is probably because the stress of teacher-training is seen by some as a normative part of becoming a qualified teacher (Murray-Harvey, *et al.*, 2000). However, this assumption is increasingly being challenged. For example, Chaplain (2008) found high levels of stress among 38 per cent of teacher-trainees. Despite the study by Chaplain (2008), there remains a relative lack of research interest in the level of stress of teacher-trainees worldwide and especially in developing countries. This limited research interest is surprising given the large number of studies showing increased psychological distress among qualified teachers in several parts of the world (Cornelius, 2011).

Teaching has been shown to be among the top six most stressful professions (Johnson, *et al.*, 2005). In a study of 574 secondary school teachers, Punch and Tuettmann (1990) found twice as much levels of stress compared with the general population. Stress among teachers is associated with a wide range of adverse outcomes including physical health complaints, mental disorders, relationship difficulties and reduced productivity (Punch and Tuettmann, 1990). Even more concerning is the potentially long-term negative impact on the children taught by stressed teachers (Delp, 1963). Thus understanding the mental health of trainee teachers is not only important for the trainees but it has additional important implications for the well-being of the pupils they will go on to teach as teachers (Ani, *et al.*, 2011).

On account of perceived impact of stress on various dimensions of teachers, a need is being felt to study the level of stress among teacher-trainees and impact of socio-demographic characteristics of trainees on their level of stress.

Statement of the Problem

The problem of the present study may be stated as follows:

"Study on Stress among Teacher-trainees of B.Ed. Level"

The key words inherent in the study as stated above has been analyzed and operationally defined in following section—

Stress

Stress began as an ambiguous, general, and abstract construct, but as research evolved, the stress conceptualization became more specific. There are essentially three theoretical perspectives on the mechanisms of stress: (1) stimulus-oriented theory, (2) response-oriented theory, and (3) interactionist theory. The first theory, stimulus-oriented theory, focuses on an actual event as a stimulus and does not reflect individual interpretation or perception of the event. Response-oriented theory reflects on how the person responds to the environment. Stress in interactionist stress theory, has been viewed as the result of an interaction between the person and the event (Meena, 2013). Stress is the reaction that people have to excessive pressure or other types of demand placed on them. It arises when they worry that they cannot cope. The pressures of working life can lead to stress if they are excessive or long-term. Examples of long-term or chronic stress are the fear, frustration and anger that may be produced by an unhappy relationship with one's boss or with a difficult customer, and the unhappiness of an unsuitable job. Up to a certain point an increase in pressure will improve performance and the quality of life (Selye, 1950). Auerbach and Grambling (1998) regard stress as an unpleasant state of emotional and physiological arousal that individuals experience in situations that they perceive as dangerous or threatening to their well-being.

Assessment of the level of stress in an individual can be operationalized as self-perceived changes in bodily mechanisms affecting adversely the quality of health, mental and social well-being. This operational definition of stress has been adopted in present study for the selection of 'Stress Scale' for use among teacher-trainees at B.Ed. level.

Teacher-trainees

Teacher-trainees pursuing B.Ed. course from various institutions of Kumaun University, Nainital were selected for the present study.

Need and Significance of the Study

Teaching is a social activity that poses enormous demands on a teacher to fulfil roles, responsibilities/behavioural patterns decided for him/her, besides fulfilling his/her own desires and feelings and these all lead towards a stressful life. Stress is reported to being an important factor that influences the personality of teachers (Brown, *et al.,* 2002). The regular teacher-training programme provides for trainees' professional and personal upliftment. At the college level students are expected to do work on their own and also they have to face cut throat competition in the field. It increases the stress on them. Stress up to the moderate level is inevitable and leads to motivation but prolonged occupational stress in teaching has been found to result in both physiological and psychological ailments, which ultimately have deleterious effects on teacher's professional efficiency (Kyriacou and Pratt, 1989). The overall efficiency and performance of teacher-trainees mainly depends upon their psychological state of mind, as stress affects the physical and psychological well-being of an individual, it definitely has bearing on the efficiency and performance of teacher-trainees.

In order to be an effective teacher, teacher-trainees must possess sound psychological health, enthusiasm and satisfaction in their work. It has been observed that teacher-trainees' behaviour reflected more symptoms of stress in regular classroom teaching-learning situations as well as outside the classrooms in form of frequent strikes after the introduction of new teacher education curriculum in accordance to NCTE-2014. Although all teacher-trainees are not vulnerable to stress but certain demographic factors might result into developing stress among these prospective teachers. So there is a necessity to study the demographic variables related to stress among teacher-trainees of Kumaun University, Nainital. A thorough investigation of interaction between these variables can highlight the ways to raise the coping skills and decrease in stress levels among prospective teachers. It is a necessity to empower dwelling teachers with the knowledge, understanding and skills to cope with stressors by adopting their own appropriate and effective stress management techniques.

Aims and Objectives of the Study

As already stated, the present study broadly aimed to investigate the level of stress among teacher-trainees at B.Ed. level of Kumaun University, Nainital. This broad aim was however, subdivided into following objectives:

- To study the level of stress among teacher-trainees at B.Ed. level.
- To study the level of stress among teacher-trainees across sub-groups identified on the basis of their personal and socio-demographic characteristics.

i. To study groups of teacher-trainees identified on the basis of gender on the level of stress.
ii. To study groups of teacher-trainees identified on the basis of nature of residence on the level of stress.
iii. To study income-wise groups of teacher-trainees on their level of stress.
iv. To study marital status-wise groups of teacher-trainees on their level of stress.
v. To study groups of teacher-trainees identified on the basis of medium of study on the level of stress.

Delimitations of the Study

In reference to limited time and resources, the present study has been delimited in the following aspects:

- Only B.Ed. level teacher-trainees of Kumaun University, Nainital has been taken into consideration.
- The researcher had included only gender, income group, marital status, nature of residence and medium of study as independent variables to study their role in the development of stress.

Review of Related Studies

Research in the area of stress has evolved a large volume of literature which is helpful in recognizing that it has significant influence on the personal and professional characteristics of an individual and can result in developing some undesirable behaviours. The researcher, in the present review, has attempted to highlight few trends in research on stress and understand interaction of stress on various socio-psychological and socio-demographic variables, in order to facilitate development of suitable hypotheses for present study. These selected aspects are focused in following sections.

Studies on Stress

The studies on stress have attempted to understand stress and related phenomena through adopting survey-oriented correlational approach. Such studies also throw light on the processes associated with development of stress and its consequences for the individual. In following sections such studies have been reviewed to derive understanding for present study. The present section of review embodies the studies undertaken to search for the causes of stress in certain background characteristics, such as sex, age, marital status, income group, birth-order, nature of permanent residence, type of school and social group membership.

Bisht (1980) studied the academic stress and institutional stress of students in reference to three main effective variables, *viz.* Need for academic achievement, School climate and Academic achievement. The findings of the study revealed that all the three variables were positively and significantly correlated. Agarwal (1985) conducted a study on stress among University Students and found that the stress scores were higher in the case of males compared to females, rural student scores were higher as compared to urban students, students living in hostels, hired rooms or lodges reported higher stress as compared to those staying in their homes.

Misra, *et al.* (2000) argue that undergraduate students experience higher stress at predictable times each semester because of the academic commitments, financial pressures, and lack of time management skills. Radcliff and Lester (2003) revealed that the most stressful situations for students were the excessive class workload, the socialization pressure, the lack of guidance, and periods of transition. In a study investigating relationship between life-stress and achievement, researchers found that life-stress predicted a decrease in exam performance from the first to the second year (Andrews and Wilding, 2005).

Dusselier, *et al.* (2005) indicated that females perceived more stress than males and that personal behaviours and relationship conflicts contributed to stress. Vondras, *et al.* (2005) examined everyday stress effects on the episodic memory test performance among young, middle-aged, and older adults living in the community. It was revealed through the study that young and middle-aged adults who showed high everyday stress on a perceived stress scale demonstrated memory impairments similar to that of adults who were 40 or above age group. This indicated that stress might impair memory and result in an inability to recall information and, thus, lower academic success. Kaur (2008) in her study on occupational stress in relation to teacher effectiveness among secondary school teachers found that female teachers are under the level of occupational stress than their male counterparts. Brougham, *et al.* (2009) conducted a study on a stress, sex differences, and coping strategies among college students. Results found that college women reported a higher overall level of stress and greater use of emotion-focused coping strategies than college men.

Cornelius (2011), while studying psychological distress among trainee-teachers in Nigeria found that 35 per cent of trainee-teachers were psychologically distressed. Study also reported that trainees in their third year of study were most psychologically distressed and increased frequency of attending religious activities was associated with less psychological distress. Menaga and Chandrasekaran (2014) found that there is a significant difference in the academic stress of higher secondary students in relation to their gender. Singh (2014) found significant difference between the students, perception of academic stress among male and female students. Krishan (2014) found a significant difference in academic stress of male and female students and rural and urban institutions' students. Jayanthi, Thirunavukarasu and Rajamanickam (2014) found self-expectations and perceived pressure are the main causes for academic stress.

A high level of stress was obtained among male teacher-trainees and low users of ICT in a recent study conducted by Kamboj (2015). The study also suggested use of ICT for reducing academic stress among teacher-trainees. In an another study on stress among B.Ed. teacher-trainees, Kumar (2015) found significant differences in level of stress on the basis of academic stream and family types however, no significant interaction between stress and gender of teacher-trainees was found in the study. In a sample of 400 B.Ed. students, Soureche (2015) obtained significant differences in level of stress among teacher-trainees on the basis of gender, dwelling place, marital status and family type.

Discussion and Conclusions that emerged through Present Review of Research

The researcher has tried to include some of the available studies on stress that have significance for present study. This effort helped in identifying certain trends in the area of research on stress among teacher-trainees. These trends of findings may guide further researches in this area and a conceptual framework for present study could be derived from the related studies. The following conclusions seem to emerge through present review:

1. Dearth of research in the area of stress among teacher-trainees after the introduction of two-year B.Ed. curriculum.
2. Stress has significant interaction with socio-demographic characteristics of an individual.
3. Stress has negative consequences on the health and work-efficiency.
4. Need to study the interaction between stress and some important socio-demographic characteristics of teacher-trainees of Kumaun University in the light of new B.Ed. curriculum.

The present investigation is a significant attempt to study levels of stress and interaction between stress and socio-demographic and academic characteristics of teacher-trainees as no research work, similar to the present study among teacher-trainees of Kumaun University, Nainital is available.

Hypotheses of the Present Study

It is well indicated in the review of related research that certain directional hypotheses can be made with reference to the interaction between stress and socio-demographic characteristics of respondents. However, in the context of specific objectives of present study and to facilitate appropriate statistical testing, following hypotheses, framed in null form, were proposed to be tested:

1. There is no significant difference in the level of stress among teacher-trainees on the basis of gender.
2. There is no significant difference in the level of stress among teacher-trainees on the basis of nature of residence.
3. There is no significant difference in the level of stress among teacher-trainees on the basis of income.
4. There is no significant difference in the level of stress among teacher-trainees on the basis of marital status.
5. There is no significant difference in the level of stress among teacher-trainees on the basis of medium of study.

Research Design

The primary aim of present study was to ascertain the level of stress among B.Ed. teacher-trainees, with a subsidiary objective of conducting a survey for analyzing and comparing this among different population subgroups identified on the basis of various personal and socio-demographic characteristics. Significant aspects of research methodology adopted to fulfil these aims and objectives are described in the following sections.

The Survey Method

Survey research method was adopted to assess level of stress among B.Ed. level teacher-trainees, classified on the basis of their personal, socio-demographic and educational characteristics. The details of methodological aspects like population, sampling technique, description of sample, tools for data collection, and analysis of data are presented in the following subsections.

Population of the Study

Teacher-trainees of different B.Ed. training institutions affiliated to Kumaun University, Nainital, functioning as a state university of Uttarakhand, were envisaged to be the population of present study. The B.Ed. training institutions affiliated to Kumaun University, Nainital work under four different administrative setups—(i) the campus of the university, (ii) government colleges, (iii) government colleges, running B.Ed. course in self-financed mode, and (iv) self-financed institutions managed by private sector. In this manner, population of present study was located in four categories of B.Ed. training institutions.

Sampling Method

In view of the fact that population of study was spread over four categories of B.Ed. training institutions, B.Ed. training institutions identified through university list were categorized into government and private institutions. The investigator then selected four institutions from each category in random manner to finally select eight institutions from which the sample was to be drawn. Category-wise list of B.Ed. training institutions selected in this manner is given in Table 19. 1.

Table 19.1: Category-wise List of B.Ed. Training Institutions Selected for the Purpose of Data Collection

S. No.	*Type of Institution*	*Name of the Institution*
1.	Government Institutions	I. Faculty of Education, Kumaun University, S.S.J. Campus, Almora II. M.B. Government P.G. College, Haldwani III. Radhey Hari Government P.G. College, Kashipur IV. H.N.B. Government P.G. College, Khatima
2.	Private Institutions	I. Sarswati Institute of Management and Technology, Rudrapur II. Presentation College of Teacher Education, Kathgodam III. Devbhoomi College of Education, Banbasa IV. L.B.S.S. College of Education, Jaspur

Within each of the selected B.Ed. training institution, twenty-five teacher-trainees present on the day of data collection, were finally selected in a random manner to constitute a sample of two hundred teacher-trainees. Thus, sampling method adopted for present study was multistage random sampling method. However, only one hundred and seventy one trainees could be included in the final sample due to reasons such as incomplete filled-in questionnaires, questionnaires responded in a set pattern without actually reading the questions, questionnaire responded through marking two answer categories on the same question and questionnaire filled-in illegibly— factors that are beyond the control of researcher. Table 19.2 and Table 19.3 present selection of teacher-trainees from government and private institutions respectively.

Table 19.2: Selection of Sample from Government Institutions

Government Institutions	*Number of Trainees Selected*
Faculty of Education, S.S.J. Campus, Almora	22
M.B. Government P.G. College, Haldwani	22
Radhey Hari Government P.G. College, Kashipur	21
H.N.B. Government P.G. College, Khatima	21
Total	**86**

Table 19.3: Selection of Sample from Private Institutions

Private Institutions	*Number of Trainees Selected*
Sarswati Institute of Management and Technology, Rudrapur	21
Presentation College of Teacher Education, Kathgodam	22
Devbhoomi College of Education, Banbasa	21
L.B.S.S. College of Education, Jaspur	21
Total	85

The main characteristics of sample thus selected from government and private institutions are presented hereinafter.

Main Characteristics of Sample Selected for the Study

The sample selected in above manner was analyzed with reference to type of institution, gender, nature of permanent residence, marital status, and medium of study. Family income was also viewed as significant variable in analyzing the sample characteristics. Table 19.4, and related data in Table 19.1, represents the distribution of respondents in accordance to the type of institution in which they were pursuing course.

Table 19.4: Distribution of Respondents in Accordance to the Type of Institution

S. No.	*Type of Institution*	*Number of Respondents (Percentage)*
1.	Government Institutions	86 (50.29)
2.	Private Institutions	85 (49.71)
	Total	171 (100)

It may be observed from Table 19.4 and Fig. 19.1, that the sample was selected from two main categories of institutions. Of the total 171 respondents selected in the sample, 49.71 per cent were receiving training in institutions run by the management bodies, while about 50.29 per cent of the respondents were under training in government institutions.

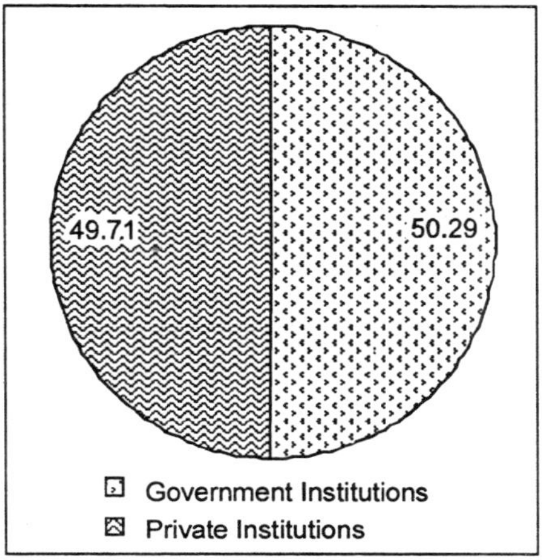

Fig. 19.1: Percentages of Respondents from different Institutions.

Distribution of respondents in accordance to the nature of their permanent residence is shown in Table 19.6 and Fig. 19.2.

Table 19.5: Distribution of Respondents in accordance to the nature of their Permanent Residence

S. No.	*Nature of residence*	*Frequency (percentage)*
1.	Rural	81 (47.37)
2.	Urban	90 (52.63)
Total		**171 (100)**

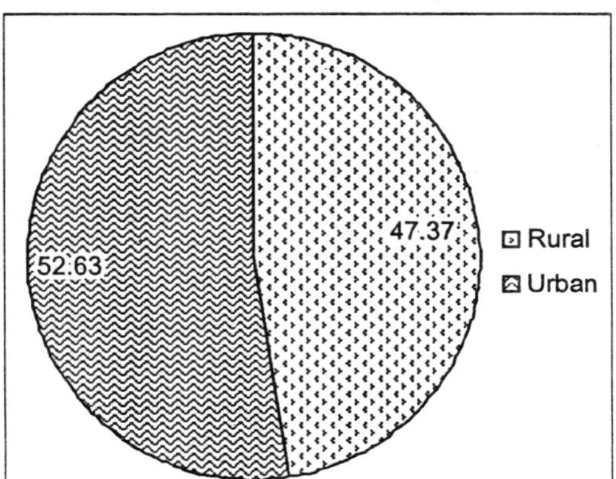

Fig. 19.2: Distribution of Respondents in accordance to the nature of Permanent Residence.

It may be observed from Table 19.5, and Fig. 19.2, that about 52.63 per cent respondents of the study belonged to urban areas and about 47.37 per cent respondents belonged to rural areas. Table numbers 19.6, 19.7, 19.8 and related Figs. 19.3, 19.4 and 19.5 represents gender, marital status and medium of study-wise composition of the sample.

Table 19.6: Gender-wise distribution of Respondents selected in the Sample

S. No.	*Gender*	*Frequency (percentage)*
1.	Male	31 (18.13)
2.	Female	140 (81.87)
	Total	171 (100)

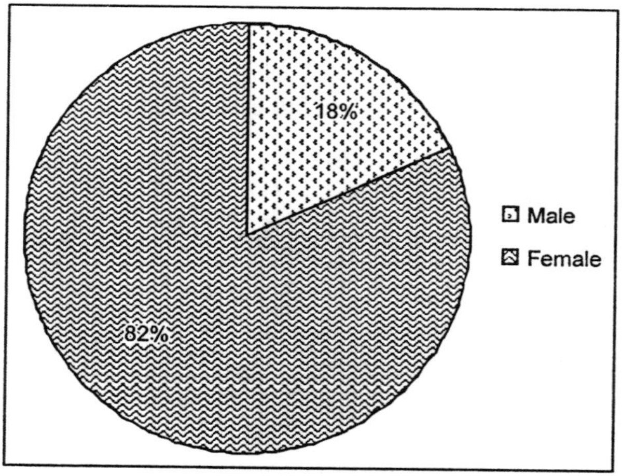

Fig. 19.3: Gender-wise distribution of Respondents.

Table 19.7: Marital group-wise distribution of Respondents selected in the Sample

S. No.	*Marital group*	*Frequency (percentage)*
1.	Unmarried	122 (71.35)
2.	Married	49 (28.65)
	Total	**171 (100)**

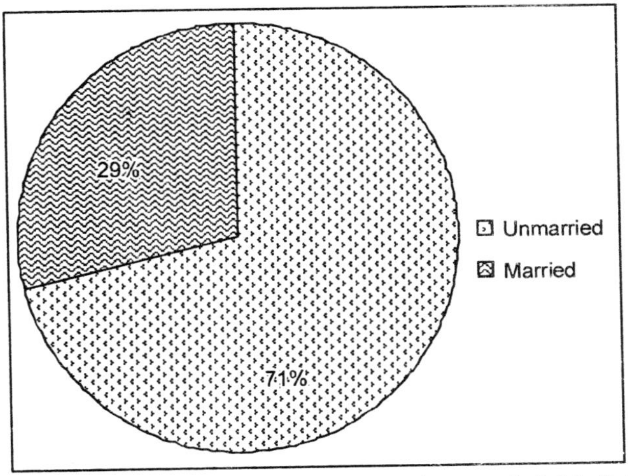

Fig. 19.4: Distribution of Respondents in accordance to their Marital Status.

An observation of Table 19.6 reveals that the majority of respondents, i.e. about 82 per cent, were females, while male respondents were represented by about 18 per cent (See also, Fig. 19.3). It may be observed from Table 19.7 and Fig. 19.4, that majority of respondents (about 71%) were unmarried and about 29 per cent of them reported to be married.

Table 19.8 represents medium of study group-wise distribution of respondents and the related data is also shown in Fig. 19.5.

Table 19.8: Medium of study group-wise distribution of Respondents selected in the Sample

S. No.	*Medium of Study Group*	*Frequency (percentage)*
1.	Hindi	139 (81.29)
2.	English	32 (18.71)
	Total	171 (100)

It may be observed from Table 19.8 and Fig. 19.5 that 81 per cent of respondents belonged to Hindi medium, whereas respondents belonging to English medium were about 19 per cent.

Table 19.9 and Fig. 19.6 present income group-wise distribution of respondents of present study.

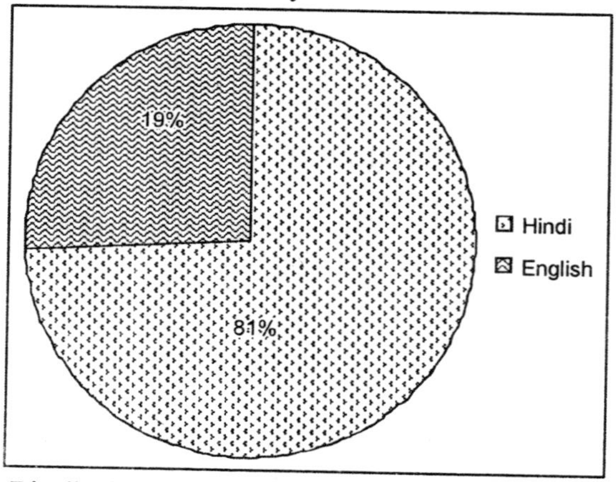

Fig. 19.5: Distribution of Respondents according to their Medium of Study.

Table 19.9: Income group-wise distribution of Respondents of the Study

S. No.	*Income group*	*Frequency (percentage)*
1.	Above Rs. 25001 High income	58 (33.92)
2.	Up to Rs. 25000 Low income	113 (66.08)
	Total	**171 (100)**

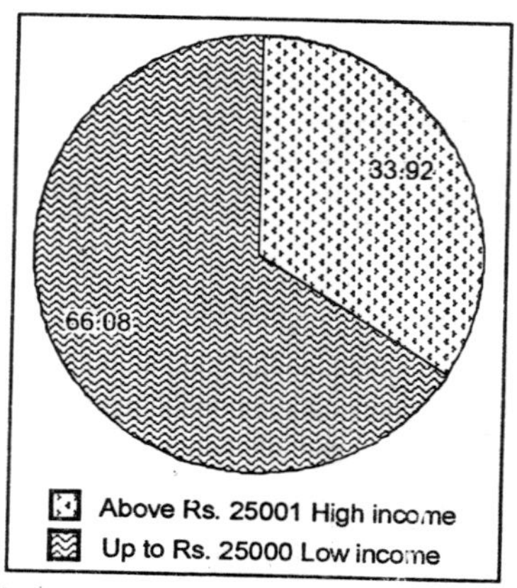

Fig. 19.6: Distribution of Respondents in different Income groups.

An observation of Table 19.9 and Fig. 19.6 revealed that majority of respondents (66.08%) belonged to the families with an income of about Rs. 25000 or below per month. Respondents belonging to the families with income level above Rs. 25001 were reported to be 33.92 per cent in the study.

Research Tools for Data Collection

Following research tools were employed for data collection of present study:

- Personal Information Schedule.
- 'Stress Scale' developed by Lakshmi and Narain (2015).

Description of above research tools is given in following subsections:

Personal Information Schedule

Following aims and objectives of present study, it was required to collect a number of personal, socio-demographic and academic information from each respondent included in the study. Therefore, a Personal Information Schedule was prepared by the researcher herself. The information requested in the schedule were mainly related to gender, marital status, name of B.Ed. institution, nature of permanent residence, medium of study and monthly income of the family. The qualitative information on these variables was obtained by asking respondents to either actually write the information or mark their response by selecting one of the categories provided in relation to specific questions. Questions were framed to elicit information on these variables. The questions included in the schedule were framed in simple language.

Stress Scale (SS)

A forty item, Stress Scale, developed by Lakshmi and Narain (2015), was used to compare level of stress among the subjects of the study. The scale provides a list of 40 statements, each having two alternatives, one indicating stress and the other showing absence of stress, the former to be assigned a score of one and the later a score of zero. The tool was standardized on 300 students (age range 12 to 24 years). The scale can be administered in group as well as individual condition. The usual time-limit is 10-15 minutes, though a few minutes more may be allowed where necessary. The numerical scores in the range of 0-40 are obtained according to the manual and the scoring procedure is described in Table 19.10.

Table 19.10: Scoring Procedure for Stress Scale

Serial wise Item no.	*Correct response*	*Score provided*
1, 2, 3, 4, 5, 6, 7, 8, 9, 10, 11, 12, 13, 14, 15, 16, 17, 18, 19, 20, 22, 23, 24, 25, 26, 27, 28, 29, 30, 31, 32, 33, 34, 36, 37, 38, 39, 40	If box 'Yes' has been ticked	'1' mark for each correct response
21, 35	If box 'No' has been ticked	As above
Total no. of item = 40		

A score of 22 and above indicate high level of stress. Moderate level of stress is indicated by scores between 12 to 21, while a score of 11 or below refer to low level of stress. Test-Retest reliability of the scale was measured to be 0.82. The criterion validity of the tool was established by comparing scores against two scales *viz.*, Singh's Personal Stress Source Inventory (2004) and with Stress dimension of Anxiety, Depression and Stress Scale by Bhatnagar *et al.* (2011) and the resulting validity coefficient was found to be 0.72 and 0.83 respectively (see Appendix-2).

Data Collection

The procedure of selection, development and printing of research tools needed for study, were followed by random selection of institutions for data collection. The investigator visited selected eight institutions and with the permission of concerned Heads, met teacher-trainees of these institutions, who were explained the nature and purpose of questionnaires to be filled in by them. They were also instructed to answer various questions on the basis of their own feelings and not to consult their fellow trainees.

Trainees were also asked to seek explanation of any word they felt difficult in understanding. The investigator promptly explained meaning of the word and/or sentence in simpler manner and through giving suitable examples in some instances, whenever request for explanation was made by subjects. The data were, thus, collected in a group situation, with a provision of providing individual help whenever required. The Personal Information Schedule was provided to trainees at first, for writing information demanded about themselves and their families. They were then supplied with Stress Scale, which required them to report the felt state of mind indicated by different items of the scale. In general, respondents completed two research tools in 20 to 25 minutes. On the basis of procedures followed in data collection, it could be stated that investigator was able to collect data from respondents in a reliable and valid manner.

Method of Data Analysis

Data obtained were analyzed by making use of descriptive and inferential statistical methods. Under descriptive approach, frequency distribution, percentage analysis as well as calculation of mean and median values was undertaken to describe nature of distribution of different variables. However, t-test was carried out to find interaction between selected independent and dependent variable within inferential approach. Gender, income group, nature of permanent residence, marital status and medium of study of trainees were taken as independent variables in the analysis to find out their interaction with level of stress among teacher-trainees. Results obtained through this data analysis are presented and discussed in data analysis and interpretation.

Data Analysis and Interpretation

As par to the aims and objectives of present research, data obtained for the present study were analyzed along with following dimensions:

Comparison of level of stress in population subgroups classified on the basis of following characteristics:

1. Gender
2. Nature of residence
3. Income
4. Marital status
5. Medium of study.

The above mentioned aspect of data analysis was associated with the following objectives of the study:

1. Identification of interaction of gender with level of stress among teacher-trainees at B.Ed. level.
2. Identification of interaction of nature of residence with level of stress among teacher-trainees at B.Ed. level.
3. Identification of interaction of income with level of stress among teacher-trainees at B.Ed. level.
4. Identification of interaction of marital status with level of stress among teacher-trainees at B.Ed. level.
5. Identification of interaction of medium of study with level of stress among teacher-trainees at B.Ed. level.

Various hypotheses proposed to be tested through this study were organized along with above mentioned objectives. Test of these hypotheses was undertaken through employing t-test, taking independent and dependent variables in accordance to the requirement of particular hypotheses. Data analysis carried out in view of above considerations is elaborated in following sections.

Comparison of Level of Stress among Various Subgroups of Teacher-trainees

Table 19.1 shows the distribution of level of stress found among teacher-trainees selected in the sample.

It may be observed from Table 19.11 that stress scores obtained by teacher-trainees ranged from a minimum of 1.00 to a maximum of 30.00. Mean value of this distribution was 12.77, with a standard deviation of 5.87. The values of mean, median and mode of this distribution were found to be more or less equal. Hence, it can be said that stress scores obtained by the respondents tended to be more or less normal, though skewness value (0.47) of distribution indicated it to be slightly positively skewed, with a peakedness value of 0.01. Twenty five per cent of the trainees obtained a score of 8.00 and below, while the uppermost quartile was represented by trainees obtaining a score of 17.00 and above.

Table 19.11: Distribution of Level of Stress among Teacher-trainees

Stress score (class-interval)	*Frequency*	*Per cent frequency*	*Statistical indices*
26-30	4	2.4	Mean = 12.77
21-25	16	9.4	Median = 13.00
16-20	30	17.6	Mode = 12.00 SD = 5.87
11-15	58	33.9	Skewness = 0.47
6-10	42	24.5	Kurtosis = 0.01
1-5	21	12.3	Q1 = 8.00 Q3 = 17.00
Total	171	100	Minimum value = 1.00 Maximum value = 30.00

Gender of Teacher-trainees and Level of Stress

In the sample of present study majority of the respondents were females (81.87%), while male respondents were represented by 18.13 per cent. As the role of gender has considerable influence in shaping socio-cultural experiences in Indian society, it was considered significant to analyze the interaction of gender with level of stress among teacher-trainees.

Table 19.12 presents the comparison of stress scores of male and female trainees. The means on stress scores of respondents have also been shown in Fig. 19.7.

Table 19.12: Comparison of Level of Stress among Teacher-trainees on the basis of Gender

Group	*Number*	*Mean*	*Standard Deviation*	*t-value*	*Significance at 0.05 level*
Male	31	12.22	6.70	0.58	Not–Significant
Female	140	12.90	5.69		

It may be observed from Table 19.12 and Fig. 19.7 that the mean value on stress associated with female trainees was found to be higher (m=12.9), in comparison to the male trainees (m=12.22) indicating that in the sample studied, it were the female trainees, who showed a higher level of stress. However, when the data were subjected to t-test analysis (Table 19.12), the differences between groups came out to be statistically non-significant at 0.05 level of significance.

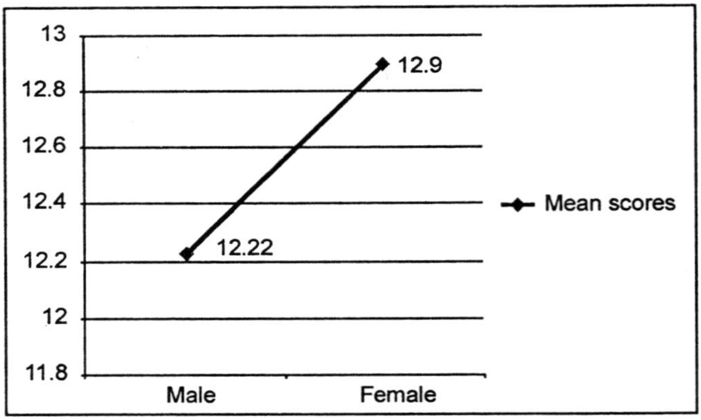

Fig. 19.7: Mean scores obtained by Male and Female Teacher-trainees.

This particular finding revealed that gender does not play a significant role in shaping level of stress among teacher-trainees. In this context, findings obtained by Dusselier, *et al.* (2005) is pertinent which indicated that females perceived more stress than males. Kaur (2008) in her study on occupational stress among secondary school teachers also found that female teachers are under the level of occupational stress than their male counterparts. College women reported a higher overall level of stress and greater use of emotion-focused coping strategies than college men in the study conducted by Brougham, *et al.* (2009) on stress, sex differences, and coping strategies among college students.

Contrary to this trend of findings, Agarwal (1985) revealed that the stress scores were higher in the case of males as compared to females in a study focused on University students. A high level of stress was obtained among male teacher-trainees and low users of ICT in a recent study conducted by Kamboj (2015). In this connection, Soureche (2015) obtained significant differences in level of stress among teacher-trainees on the basis of gender.

Nature of Permanent Residence and Trainee's Level of Stress

Analysis of nature of permanent residence as a factor in developing stress among teacher-trainees has the implicit assumption that characteristics of surrounding not only interacts with the physical health but also has a considerable influence on the psychological well-being. Rural and urban categories of residence are, thus, expected to have a potential in influencing development of stress among grooming teachers. Comparison of level of stress among teacher-trainees belonging to urban and rural areas is presented in Table 19.13, present results of t-test analysis carried out in this context. The mean values on stress level of teacher-trainees belonging to different residence are also shown in Fig. 19.8.

Table 19.13: Comparison of Stress among Teacher-trainees on the basis of Nature of Residence

Group	*Number*	*Mean*	*Standard Deviation*	*t-value*	*Significance at 0.05 level*
Rural	81	14.04	6.10	2.71	Significant
Urban	90	11.64	5.44		

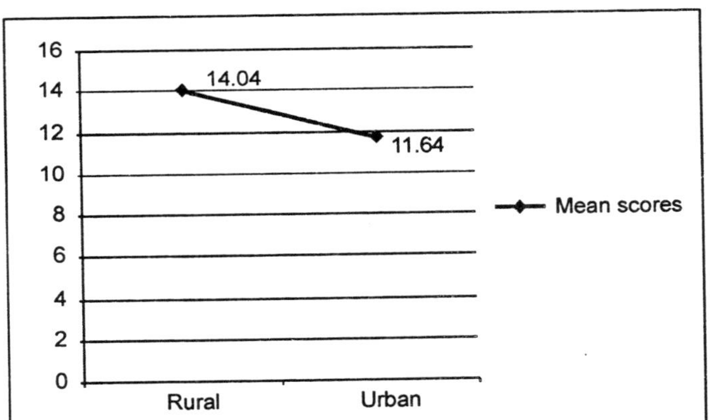

Fig. 19.8: Mean scores obtained by Rural and Urban trainees.

It may be observed from Table 19.13 that the higher mean on stress score (m=14.04) was associated with trainees of rural background. Mean value on stress of trainees belonging to urban areas were, being represented by score of 11.64.

Results of t-test analysis shown in Table 19.13, also indicate presence of statistically significant difference among the groups. This result was congruent with results of Agarwal (1985), who revealed significant relationship between nature of residence and stress level of University Students and found that the stress scores were higher in the case of rural students as compared to urban students. Soureche (2015), also obtained significant differences in level of stress among teacher-trainees on the basis of dwelling place. It may be stated that nature of residence does interact with stress level and has influence on the psychological well-being of trainees.

Income Group and Level of Stress

Stress level may be expected to get influenced considerably by income of parents or family to which a trainee belongs. Families varying in this context are likely to affect need fulfilment among their wards, and thus may develop different levels of stress. Data of present study were analyzed to explore this aspect. Table 19.14 and Fig. 19.9 present results of this analysis.

Table 19.14: Comparison of Level of Stress among Teacher-trainees belonging to Families with different Monthly Income

Group	*Number*	*Mean*	*Standard Deviation*	*t-value*	*Significance at 0.05 level*
High income	58	12.26	5.15	0.83	Not-Significant
Low income	113	13.04	6.21		

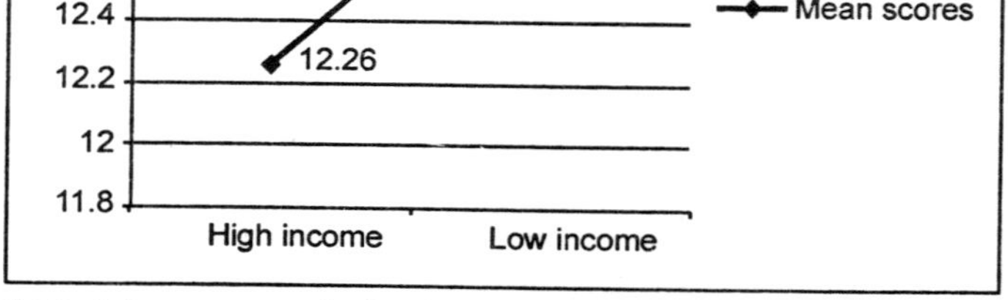

Fig. 19.9: Mean scores obtained by Respondents belonging to Families of different Income groups.

An observation of Table 19.14 reveals that mean value on stress scores attained a higher level in the group which was lower on income

(Fig.19.9). However, results obtained through t-test analysis yielded a non-significant value at 0.05 level of significance. Here, findings revealed that income level of the family does not have a significant influence on level of stress among teacher-trainees. It may be stated that income of family does interact with the fulfilment of general needs but the potential in influencing development of stress among wards decreases after certain age and educational levels. Respondents of present study are more mature as compared to adolescents and they may be expected to be having a better understanding of their needs and income status; thus, relying more on their own abilities, having better sense of responsibilities and thereby being better in managing themselves. Thus, it can be said that at this higher level of education, trainees belonging to families with different income backgrounds do not differ in their level of stress.

Marital Status and Level of Stress

Similar to income and residence, marital status of trainees also has potential of influencing level of stress among teacher-trainees. In this context, comparison of level of stress of married and unmarried trainees was carried out. Table 19.15, Fig.19.4 present result of analysis carried out in the context of marital status of trainees.

Table 19.15: Comparison of Level of Stress among Teacher-trainees on the basis of Marital Status

Group	*Number*	*Mean*	*Standard Deviation*	*t-value*	*Significance at 0.05 level*
Married	49	13.12	5.25	0.49	Not–Significant
Unmarried	122	12.64	6.11		

An observation of Table 19.15 revealed that higher mean on stress score (m=13.12) was associated with married trainees. Unmarried teacher-trainees were found to be less stressed (m=12.64). However, results of t-test analysis shown in Table 19.15 revealed that marital status did not interact with level of stress of trainees. In contrary to this, results of Soureche (2015), revealed significant interaction between stress and marital status of teacher-trainees. It may be stated that marital status does not interact with stress level and has no influence on the psychological well-being of trainees.

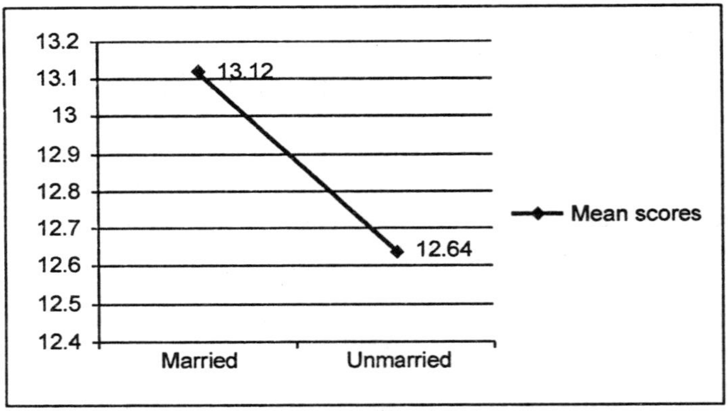

Fig. 19.10: Mean scores obtained by Married and Unmarried Respondents.

Medium of Study and Level of Stress

In the present time no one could deny the fact that language serves as a medium to progress in any field and teaching is not an exemption. Moreover, it promotes teaching effectiveness among trainees. A comparison of level of stress among teacher-trainees on the basis of medium of study was carried out and the result of analysis is presented in Table 19.16., Fig. 19.11.

Table 19.16: Comparison of Level of Stress among Teacher-trainees on the basis of Medium of Study

Group	*Number*	*Mean*	*Standard Deviation*	*t-value*	*Significance at 0.05 level*
Hindi	139	13.13	6.02	1.64	Not-Significant
English	32	11.25	4.96		

It is indicated in Table 19.16. that higher mean on stress scores (m=13.13) were associated with trainees with Hindi medium of study (Fig.19.11) whereas mean score obtained by trainees with English medium was observed to be 11.25. However, results of t-test analysis shown in Table 19.16, revealed non-significant interaction between medium of study and level of stress of trainees. It may be stated that medium of study does not interact with stress level of trainees.

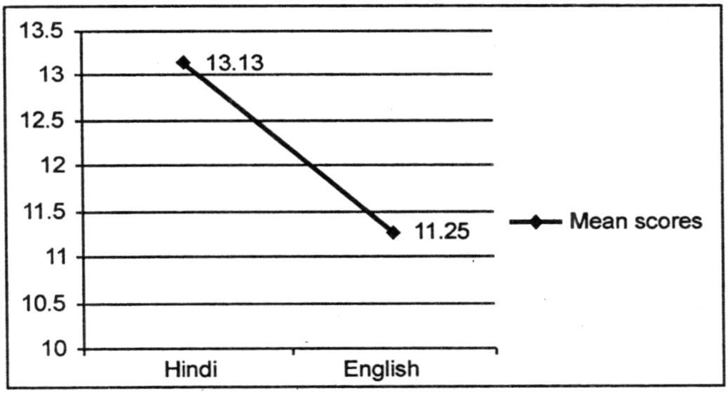

Fig. 19.11: Mean scores obtained by Respondents belonging to different Medium of Study.

Findings, Conclusions and Implications of the Study

The design of the present study was prepared with specific aims and objectives in view. The overall research process of data collection and analysis was guided by these specific aims and objectives. Findings obtained through the analysis of the data can be synthesized into certain broad conclusions. The study also indicated certain implications for practice and further research. These various aspects constitute the content of following sections:

Summary

Present study was designed in view of felt research need of sound physical health and psychological well-being of the teacher trainees which has an impact on their efficiency and overall performance. The study attempted to analyze and compare the level of stress of teacher-trainees across sub-groups identified on the basis of personal and socio-demographic characteristics. A review of related research was undertaken to indicate different populations covered under the research effort initiated by earlier researchers, which pointed out decrease in stress levels among prospective teachers is a necessity to empower dwelling teachers with the knowledge, understanding and skills to cope with stressors and to evolve healthy personality. With the perspective provided by this review of research, following null hypotheses were proposed to be tested.

1. There is no significant difference in the level of stress among teacher-trainees on the basis of gender.
2. There is no significant difference in the level of stress among teacher-trainees on the basis of nature of residence.
3. There is no significant difference in the level of stress among teacher-trainees on the basis of income.
4. There is no significant difference in the level of stress among teacher-trainees on the basis of marital status.
5. There is no significant difference in the level of stress among teacher-trainees on the basis of medium of study.

With reference to the above stated objectives, the overall research work was conducted. Survey research method was adopted for the purpose of data collection and a sample of 171 teacher-trainees of B.Ed. level was selected from eight institutions of Kumaun University, Nainital through a multistage random sampling method. A specifically designed Personal Information Schedule (PIS) was used to collect information on different socio-demographic characteristics of teacher-trainees. Stress Scale, developed by Lakshmi and Narain (2015), was used to assess the level of stress. The data were collected in group situation within the institutions selected in the sample selection process. Analysis of data was guided by the objectives of the study as well as the specific hypotheses proposed to be tested.

Findings of the Study

Findings of the study were directly related to the test of the null hypotheses proposed for the study. Therefore, the findings arrived may be summarized in accordance to the null hypotheses proposed to be tested in following manner-

Hypothesis-1: There is no significant difference in the level of stress among teacher-trainees on the basis of gender.

This hypothesis was tested for the overall group of teacher-trainees. It was found that the null hypothesis was true and there was no significant difference in the level of stress in male and female teacher-trainees. Null hypothesis was thus accepted in terms of interaction between level of stress and gender for the overall group of teacher-trainees.

Hypothesis-2: There is no significant difference in the level of stress among teacher-trainees on the basis of nature of residence.

Test of null hypothesis, specifying no significant difference among the teacher-trainees belonging to urban and rural areas, was rejected for the overall group of trainees through the findings of present study. In general, the study rejected null hypothesis specifying no significant difference in the level of stress among teacher-trainees belonging to urban and rural areas.

Hypothesis-3: There is no significant difference in the level of stress among teacher-trainees on the basis of income.

Test of null hypothesis, specifying no significant difference among teacher-trainees belonging to different income groups, was accepted for the overall group of trainees through the findings of present study. In general, the study accepted null hypothesis specifying no significant difference in the level of stress among teacher-trainees belonging to different income groups.

Hypothesis-4: There is no significant difference in the level of stress among teacher-trainees on the basis of marital status.

This null hypothesis was found to be true for comparisons made across the overall group of teacher-trainees. Null hypothesis-4 was, therefore, accepted for the overall population of teacher-trainees.

Hypothesis-5: There is no significant difference in the level of stress among teacher-trainees on the basis of medium of study.

This null hypothesis was tested in the overall population of teacher-trainees. It was found that there was no significant difference in the level of stress among overall population of teacher-trainees having different medium of study. In general, null hypothesis-5 was accepted for overall population of teacher-trainees.

Conclusions of the Study

In perspective of objectives outlined for the study, findings obtained in the above sections, facilitated derivation of specific conclusions. These conclusions may be stated as follows:

1. On the basis of findings of present study, it may be concluded that gender, family income, marital status and medium of study do not play a significant role in shaping level of stress among teacher-trainees.

2. Nature of residence, however, tends to be particularly important in this respect, as it influences stress level of teacher-trainees in a significant way.

In general, it may be stated that nature of permanent residence is important for teacher-trainees at B.Ed. level because this tend to influence their level of stress. Trainees belonging to rural areas experience more stress which is presumed to effect the overall functioning of teacher-trainees as teachers in classrooms.

Implications of the Study

Significant implications for further research in the area could be derived through the findings and conclusions of present study. Implications of present study for further research in the area and for the improvement of teacher training programme and policy making are indicated in following subsections.

Implications for Further Research in the Area

Significant interaction between nature of residence and stress level explored in present study among teacher-trainees indicates that rural background could affect psychological well-being and facilitate development of stress. The interaction of stress can be analyzed in terms of various socio-demographic as well as personal characteristics of teacher-trainees. Some of these can be age, type of teacher-training institution, academic stream, birth order, educational status, nature of family and family size. The search for factors interacting with stress needs to be directed towards these and similar 'socio-psychological' dimensions of home environment as well as personal characteristics of teacher-trainees. The search for interaction of stress among pre-service and in-service teachers should not remain confined to psychological characteristics of the individuals. Instead, this search should focus attention on variables like quality of teaching-learning, teaching behaviours, teacher-pupil relationship, interpersonal relationship in social spheres and classroom management practices.

The fact that rural teacher-trainees tended to be higher in stress indicates that among rural trainees level of stress tends to be influenced by lack of resources and exposure in a natural way. A search of 'naturally' existing excitatory factors within this group need to be undertaken in a more intensive manner.

The findings of present study have revealed significant interaction between level of stress and nature of permanent residence among teacher-trainees at B.Ed. level. Factors related to trainee's level of intelligence, attitude and interest towards teaching, facilities available for self-development, presence or absence of conducive environment within family etc. may also have a bearing on stress level of trainees. All these factors may interact with the stress in specific ways, and future research in this area needs to consider pertinent mediating variables, while analyzing stress among participants.

In view of above discussion, following research areas ensue directly from the findings and conclusions of present study:

(a) Study of the relationship between stress and classroom behaviours among in-service teachers.
(b) Study of the relationship between stress and teaching effectiveness among in-service teachers.
(c) Study of the relationship between stress and teacher-pupil relationship among in-service teachers.
(d) Study of the relationship between stress and interpersonal relationship among in-service teachers.
(e) Comparative study on the level of stress among in-service teachers at primary and secondary level.
(f) A qualitative study of excitatory factors for stress among pre-service teachers.
(g) A qualitative study of excitatory factors for stress among in-service teachers.

Implications of Present Study for Classroom Practice and Policy Making

Findings of present study indicated the presence of moderate level of stress among trainees at B.Ed. level. The significant interaction between stress and nature of residence of teacher-trainees justify the need of introducing course on stress management and personality development in teacher education curriculum. Besides, organization of activities related to different skills for equipping trainees to cope with stress during teacher training is a need of the hour. The self-enhancement component emphasized in new teacher education curriculum in NCFTE (2010), and (NCTE (2014) documents, seem to be a step in this direction. Teacher education policies, needs to be evolved so that, the stress management among prospective teachers becomes an integral part of teacher-training process.

Limitations of Present Study

The present study was considerably influenced by the following limitations of time and resources:

1. The sample was drawn from the teacher-training institutions affiliated to Kumaun University only.
2. The tools standardized on a more representative sample could be used.
3. The other important socio-psychological variables as causative factors of stress could be included.

These limitations need to be considered before making any generalization from the study. These deficiencies, needs to be removed in future research work.

References

Andrews, B. and J.M. Wilding (2004). "The relation of depression and anxiety to life-stress and achievement in students", *British Journal of Psychology*, 95: 509-521.

Ani, C.; J. Kinanee and B. Ola (2011). "Psychological distress among trainee teachers in Nigeria: Association with religious practice", *European Journal of Educational Studies*. *3*(1):163-172.

Auerbach, S.M. and S.E. Grambling (1998). "*Stress Management*", Psychological Foundations. Upper Saddle River, N.J. Prentice Hall.

Bisht, A.R. (1980). "An investigation into interactive effect of school climate and need for academic achievement on the academic stress of students. Deptt. of Education, Almora Constituent College", In *Third Survey of Research in Education (1978-1983)*, Ed., M.B. Buch (1987). New Delhi: National Council for Educational Research and Training, Shri Aurobindo Marg, (1978-1983), 333-334.

Bisht, A.R. (1980). "A study of stress in relation to school climate and academic achievement (Age group 13-17)", Deptt. of Education, Almora Constituent College. In *Third Survey of Research in Education (1978-1983)*, Ed., M.B. Buch (1987). New Delhi: National Council for Educational Research and Training, Sri Aurobindo Marg (1978-1983), 333.

Brougham, R.R.; C.M. Zail; C.M. Mendoza and J.R. Miller (2009). "Stress, Sex Differences and Coping Strategies among College Students." *Curr Psychol*. 85-97.

Brown, *et al*. (2002). "Gender-related causes of stress in trainee teachers on teaching practice in the school of education", University of Manchester, UK. *International Journal of Research and Method in Education, 25*(2):175-186.

Caplan, R.D.; S. Cobb; J.R.P. French; R. Van Harrison and S.R. Pinneau, (1975). *Job Demands and Worker Health*, Cincinnati, OH: National Institute for Occupational Safety and Health.

Chaplain, R.P. (2008). "Stress and psychological distress among trainee secondary teachers in England", *Educational Psychology*, 28:195-209.

Cooper, C.L.; S. Clarke and A.M. Rowbottom (1999). "Occupational stress, job satisfaction and well-being in anaesthetists", *Stress Medicine*, 15:115-26.

Cornelius, A., *et al.* (2011). "Psychological distress among trainee teachers in Nigeria: Association with religious practice", *European Journal of Educational Studies, 3*(1): 163-172.

Delp, H. (1963). "Mental health of teachers: Still a problem?", *Journal of Teacher Education*, 14:142-149

Dusselier, L., *et al.* (2005). "Personal health, academic and environmental predictors of stress for residence hall students", *Journal of American College Health*, 54:15-24.

Gunnell, *et al.* (2009). "Part and parcel of teaching? Secondary school staff's views on supporting student emotional health and well-being", *British Educational Research Journal* (1): 1-17.

Jayanthi, P.; M. Thirunavukarasu and R.K. Rajamanickam (2014). "Academic stress and depression among adolescents: A cross-sectional study", *Indian Pediatrics*, 52: 217-219.

Johnson, S. and C. Cooper (2003). "The construct validity of the ASSET stress measure", *Stress and Health*, 19: 181-5.

Johnson, S., *et al.* (2005). "The experience of work related stress across occupations", *Journal of Managerial Psychology, 20*(2):178-187.

Kahn, W.A. (1993). "Caring for the caregivers: Patterns of organizational care giving", *Administrative Science Quarterly, 38*(4):539-64.

Kamboj, P.K. (2015). "Study of academic stress among teacher trainees after introduction of two year B.Ed. programme", *International Journal of Innovative Research and Studies, 4*(9):140-147.

Kaur, Satvinderpal (2008). "Occupational stress in relation to teacher effectiveness among secondary school teachers", *Edu Tracks, 7*(10):27-29.

Krishan, L. (2014). "Academic stress among adolescent in relation to intelligence and demographic factors", *American International Journal of Research in Humanities Arts and Social Sciences, 5*(1):123-129.

Kumar, S. (2015). "A study on stress among B.Ed. teacher trainees", *Asian Journal of Multidisciplinary Studies, 3*(3):78-81.

Lakshmi, V. and S. Narain (2015). "Stress scale", *Catalogue*, National Psychological Corporation, Agra.

Lehrer, P. (2007). "Principles and practice of stress management: Advances in the field", *Biofeedback, 35*(3): 82-84.

Lok, C. and G.D. Bishop (1999). "Emotion control, stress and health", *Psychology and Health*, 14:813-827.

Manthei, R., Alison Gilmore and Bryan Tuck Vivienne Adair. (1996). "Teacher stress in intermediate schools", *Educational Research*, *38*(1):3-19.

Meena, N.K. (2013). "Stress and its Effect on Educational Achievement of Student", Unpublished Doctoral Dissertation. Dept. of Education, University of Rajasthan, Jaipur.

Menaga, S. and V. Chandrasekaran (2014). "A study on academic stress of higher secondary school students", *Scholarly Research Journal for Interdisciplinary Studies*, (XIV):1973-1981.

Misra, R.; M. McKean; S. West and T. Russo (2000). "Academic stress of college students: Comparison of student and faculty perceptions", *College Student Journal*, *34*(2):236-245.

Murray-Harvey R., *et al.*, (2000). "Under stress: The concerns and coping strategies of teacher education students", *European Journal of Teacher Education*, 23:19-35.

Punch, K.F. and E. Tuettmann (1990). "Correlates of psychological distress among secondary teachers", *British Educational Research Journal*, 16: 369-382.

Radcliff, C. and H. Lester (2003). "Undergraduate medical education: Perceived stress during undergraduate medical training: Qualitative study", *Medical Education*, *37*(1):32-38.

Selye, H. (1950). "Stress and the general adaptation syndrome", *Br. Med. J.*, 1:1383-92.

Singh, B.P. (2014). "A study of the students' perception of academic stress", *Scholarly Research Journal for Interdisciplinary Studies*, *I*(XIII):1751-1758.

Soureche, R. (2015). "A study of stress level among B.Ed. students", *International Journal of Teacher Educational Research*, *4*(5-7):15-20.

Travers, C.J. and C.L. Cooper (1993). "Mental health, job satisfaction and occupational stress among UK teachers", *Work and Stress*, *7*(3):203-19.

Vijayalakshmi, G. (2004). "Stress among women lecturers working in colleges in relation to some variables", *Edu Tracks*, *4* (3): 36-40.

Vondras, D.D. *et al.* (2005). "Differential effects of everyday stress on the episodic memory test performances of young, mid-life and older adults", *Ageing and Mental Health*, 9:60-70.

Young, K.M. and C.L. Cooper (1999). "Change in stress outcomes following an industrial dispute in the ambulance service: A longitudinal study", *Health Services Management Review*, 12:51-62.

20
Occupational Stress, Well-being and Positive Psychology
As Preventive Stress Management Intervention

Marami Goswami

Introduction

Stress is a fact of modern life that seems to be on the rise. In this context, the 21st century is called the "century of stress". From little child to old person everyone has stress. Stress means, an imbalance. It can be considered as an adaptive response to an external situation. Stress is our physical, mental and emotional response to the various demands, changes and events of our life. In general, stress can be defined as the reaction of individuals to the demands (stressors) imposed on them. Dr. Hans Selye, a leading authority on the concept of stress, described stress as the rate of wear and tear caused by life, which results in physical, psychological and behavioural deviations, a state characterized by high levels of excitement and distress often by feelings of not coping.

Occupational stress, workplace-stress, job stress etc. derive from the wider phenomenon of stress. Working life is one of the important parts of our daily life that causes a great deal of stress. Stress caused by work or occupation of the person is called work stress. This occupational stress is the inability to cope with pressures in a job (Rees, 1997). From the point of view job/work, this problem of occupational stress causes considerable stress to contemporary employees. This stress derives from the interaction between the worker and the working conditions (Quick *et al.*, 1997). It can be defined as a model of emotional, cognitive, behavioural and physiological reactions to the negative and harmful aspects of the content of the work, the organization of work and the working environment.

Stress at work is a relatively new phenomenon of modern lifestyles. In today's world of work one cannot imagine life without stress both for employees and for the employer. The nature of work has gone through drastic changes over the last century and is still changing at a whirlwind speed. They have touched almost all professions. Work-related stress and health at work have become issues of great concern over the past decade, both nationally and internationally. Given the value of work in society, the amount of time spent at work and the current changes that are affecting the nature of work, it is natural that work stress appears to be increasing (Szynamski, 1999). Because of the competitive nature of the work environment, most people in the world are spending their time working for work.

Occupational stress is defined as the harmful physical and emotional responses that occur when the job requirements do not match the worker's skills, resources or needs. This stress can be explained as the physiological and emotional responses that arise when workers feel an imbalance between their job demands and their skills and/or resources to meet these demands. It occurs when the work requirements do not match the capacity or resources of the worker. Workers' responses to stressors can be positive or negative depending on the type of demands placed on them, the amount of control they exert on the situation, the amount of support they receive, and also on the individual's personal response. Work stress derives from worker interaction with the working conditions. Luthans (1988) defines work stress as "an adaptive response to an external situation that results in physical, psychological and behavioural deviations for the participants of the organization".

Occupational stress is a more serious problem in the modern world all over the world encompassing any job. This entails considerable costs for individual employees and the organization. In today's society, the world of work differs greatly from the work environment of 30 years ago. Longer working hours, frequent changes in culture and structure, and loss of lifetime career paths etc. generally, lead to a greater presence and levels of stress at work. The changing nature of work has placed unprecedented demands on employees and has fueled concerns about the effect. It affects the well-being, productivity, effectiveness, personal health and quality of an individual's work.

People with a higher percentage of job stress may not be satisfied with their job and therefore they will not feel happy working in the organization. They may feel frustrated or "burned out".

Occupational stress has also important impact on society as a whole. It is unlikely that a person subjected to constant stress at work will work effectively in his or her roles as a husband, wife, neighbours and a member of the community. Occupational stress is clearly not the "cause of all the ills of society" but has an important and real impact on individual organizations and societies as well.

Sometimes job stress is confused with challenge. It is often linked or equated with challenge, but the two are very different. Challenge energizes us psychologically and physically. Challenge motivates us to learn new skills and master given tasks. By meeting a challenge, we feel a great sense of accomplishment. We feel relaxed and satisfied. The challenge acts as an important element for a healthy and productive work. Thus, it is beneficial for the work environment. The importance of challenge in our work lives is emphasized when people glorify the stress and claim that a little bit of stress is good for employees. But the situation is different when the challenge turns into job demands that are hard or cannot be met. At this point relaxation turns into exhaustion, and a sense of satisfaction into feelings of stress.

Approaches of Occupational Stress

Occupational stress can be approached from four different perspectives as follows:

(1) **Medical:** The medical approach to occupational stress is focused on the contribution of stress in the workplace to the health and illness of employees.

(2) **Clinical/Counselling:** The clinical/counselling approach emphasized the impact of the stressful working condition on mental health outcomes. For example, anxiety, depression. This approach tends to focus on developing methods to alleviate stress-related symptoms.

(3) **Engineering psychology:** The engineering psychology approach to occupational stress focused on sources of stress originating from the physical work environment. This

approach focuses on the interface between the employee and the physical environment.

(4) **Organizational psychology:** The organizational psychology approach tends to focus heavily on cognitive appraisal or the process by which employees perceive the work environment and decide whether it is stressful. It tends to focus on sources of stress that emanate from interaction with others.

Causes of Occupational Stress

The causes of occupational stress are many and different for each individual. Differences in individual characteristics such as personality and coping skills predict the professional stress of an individual. In other words, what is stressful for one person may not be a problem for someone else. In examining the causes of occupational stress, three groups of demands command our attention—occupational and work, home-base or family, and individual generated or imposed internally.

Many studies on stress at work have shown that there are a variety of organizational factors that are active in causing stress (Sutherland & Cooper, 2000). McGrath exposed that there are six possible causes of stressors in an organizational context that includes task based stress; role based stress, stress based on role, stress intrinsic to behaviour, stress deriving from the physical environment, stress deriving from the social environment and stress within the personal system. Cary Cooper has developed a concise but complete list of six sources of work stress. These are Job conditions, Role stress, Interpersonal factors, Career development, Organizational structure, and Home work Interface. Likewise Colligan, Thomas W., Colligan MSW and Higgins M. (2006) maintain that a variety of factors contribute to stress at work such as negative workload, isolation, lack of autonomy, extended working hours, toxic work environment, difficult relationships between colleagues and managements, harassment, managerial bullying and lack of opportunities or motivation to advance in one's skill level. These authors have pointed out that there are a total of five categories of causes that show that stress can occur in particular when a conflict arises from the job demands of the employer and the employee himself.

- The first category is unique factors for the job. It refers to the employee's ability to cope with the specific hours worked, the expected level of productive rate, the physical environment, as well as the expectation of management from the employee.
- The second category, the role in the organization is related to the hierarchical positioning of an employee within his organization. The senior management has the right to monitor the general functioning of the organization which causes potential distress as the employee requires performing simultaneous tasks.
- The third category is *career development*. Security of employee, his promotion etc., are all sources of stress because technology and economic domination are constantly evolving, which requires a constant development of the employee's career. Career development is another area that has stress impact and a lack of safety.
- Interpersonal relationship is the fourth category of workplace stress. These relationships have developed or are developing and can be problematic or positive.
- Finally, the fifth category is the organizational climate or structure. In this category important variables like communication, management style, and participation among groups of employees are to be considered. Therefore, the resulting total influence of the high participation rate, collaborative planning and equally dispersed responsibilities has proven to provide a positive effect on stress reduction, improvement of work performance, job satisfaction and reduction of psychosomatic disorders.

Thus, by reviewing different research works we can point out some most visible common causes of occupational stress which include—

(a) **Role overload:** Taking extra duties in job is stressful. The number of dissimilar roles an individual has to complete can lead to extreme demands on the individual's time and may create doubt about the ability to do these roles adequately (Driscoll & Cooper, 2002). Seyle believes that a positive level of stimulation is necessary for performance but when the stimulation exceeds the ability to satisfy the demand posed to the employee, one experiences a feeling of exhaustion.

(b) **Role ambiguity:** Role ambiguity refers to the degree to which employees have no clarity about their role or task. It can be considered vagueness of the role. This ambiguity/ vagueness about work roles or being unsure about duties can lead to stress.

(c) **Role conflict:** One of the most sought after dimensions of role stress are role conflict. Role conflict occurs when an employee experiences mismatched stress or incompatible goals in the vicinity of tasks linked with their job that can persuade a negative emotional response due to the apparent inability to be effective on the job. Furthermore, having to perform tasks that are not perceived as part of one's job role can potentially lead to stress related to role conflict (Cooper & Sutherland, 2000).

d) **Increased workload:** Increased workload is a potential cause of occupational stress. The extremely long hours of work and the intense pressure to perform at the highest levels for the same salary can leave the employees physically and emotionally drained. Unhealthy and unreasonable pressures on the employee can be a tremendous source of stress and suffering. Likewise, excessive travel and too much time away from family also contribute to an employee's stressors.

(e) **Job insecurity:** Feeling insecure about job performance is a major source of stress for many people. Organized workplaces are going through metamorphic changes under intense economic transformations and consequent pressures. Reorganizations, takeovers, mergers, downsizing and other changes have become major stressors for employees working in different sectors of work.

(f) **Lack of control:** The feeling of having no control over work or work duties among employees is the main cause of stress at work. People who feel they have no control over work are more likely to get contact with stress-related illnesses.

(g) **Management style:** Tension on the job often comes from management style. Lack of workers' participation in management decisions, poor organizational communication, lack of employee-friendly policies, insensitivity to employees' family needs may largely contribute to occupational stress among employees.

(h) **Lack of support:** Negative relationships and lack of support from colleagues may cause stress for employees. According to Sutherland and Cooper (2000), the quality of interpersonal relationships at work is an important factor in an organization. Friendly relations among members of an organization are less likely to create unbridled competition. Furthermore, the relationship can be potentially stressful when the leadership style is demanding and recognition and praise for the effort are valuable to the subordinate association of the boss.

(i) **Workplace culture:** Adapting to the workplace culture can be extremely stressful. Making one that adapts to various aspects of workplace culture, such as communication patterns, hierarchy, dress code, work space and, above all, working and behavioural patterns of the boss and co-workers can be stressful. In many cases, office policies or gossip can be important stressors. Sometimes, the mismatch of cultures in the workplace can lead to subtle conflicts with colleagues or even with superiors.

(j) **Technology:** The expansion of technology, computers, the Internet, etc. has led to higher expectations in terms of productivity, speed and efficiency, increasing the pressure on the individual worker to constantly operate at the highest levels of performance. There is also the constant pressure to keep up with technological innovations and improvisations, forcing employees to learn new technical skills. Likewise, workers who work with heavy machinery are constantly under stress to remain vigilant. In this case both the worker and his family live under constant mental stress.

(k) **Personal or family problems:** Employees who face personal or family problems tend to worries and anxieties to the workplace. When one is in a depressed mood, his unfocused attention or lack of motivation affects his ability to carry out job responsibilities.

(l) **Qualitative excess to work**: Qualitative excess as a source of stress is linked to low levels of self-esteem since individual slack the necessary ability to do a new job. On the contrary, the qualitative underload is harmful because the individual does not have the possibility to use acquired skills and abilities, giving rise to feelings of impotence to demonstrate talents (Sutherland & Cooper, 2000).

(m) **Poor working conditions:** Unpleasant or dangerous physical conditions such as crowding, noise or ergonomic problems can cause stress. Working conditions of work have been linked to mental health. It was found that poor psychological health was directly related to unpleasant working conditions.

(n) **Work-related stress and women:** Women can suffer from mental and physical harassment at work, apart from common work stress. Sexual harassment at the workplace has been an important and constant source of concern for women in the working sectors. Together with these subtle discriminations in the workplace, family pressure and societal demands contribute to a woman's stressors.

To sum up, stress is a highly subjective experience. Many factors lead to the experience of stress which includes individual biography and previous experiences, demands and requirements of work performance, family situation and others.

Preventive Stress Management and Positive Psychology Interventions

Occupational stress is considered as one of the most serious occupational health problems. But considering stress more positively leads to higher productivity and better performance, while negative stress leads to many problems in organization and work. Work stress is a situation in which the skills, knowledge and skills of employees do not meet organizational requirements. The ability to manage stress in the workplace cannot only improve your physical and emotional health, it can also make the difference between success and failure on the job. The ability to manage stress at work cannot only improve physical and emotional health, but it can also make the difference between success and failure at work. The concept of stress management was used to denote various activities aimed at mediating the impact of stress inoccupation.

Occupational stress is not an acute or toxic condition that can be cured through treatment. Rather, it is a chronic condition that requires an understanding of the epidemiology or life history of the problem before exploring alternatives of protection, prevention and intervention. As a chronic issue, eradication of occupational stress can never be the goal. Protection and prevention are at the heart of a health response to occupational stress. Therefore, the concepts of preventive management of public health lend themselves well to regulating occupational stress, bringing out the positive aspects and minimizing the suffering caused by anxiety. The differing viewpoints suggest different ways to prevent stress at work.

Defense against adverse outcomes of occupational stress begins at the organizational level. Organizational protection and prevention are particularly important because they involve stress and risk factors at the workplace, with the aim of changing the environment. There is an emerging priority on organizational responsibility in relation to stress and health at work. Adkins defined job health as a challenge to leadership and developed an approach to promote it. From her pioneering work, the organizational health centre has arrived as a complete, multidisciplinary and multi-component system designed to implement key elements of public health, preventive medicine and health protection. An organizational health centre has three distinctive characteristics:

1. Collaboration among all organizational functions concerned with people's well-being;
2. Surveillance systems for early warning of distress and dysfunction;
3. The complete continuum of protection and prevention interventions to benefit everyone in the organization.

It is worth mentioning that regardless of how much organizational protection leaders of the organizations provide, occupational stress will have different impacts throughout a working population. Therefore, organizational protection and work environment prevention come first in managing occupational stress but must be supplemented because of individual differences. Stress manifests itself in the thoughts, emotions and movements of individual human beings. These literature and research on occupational stress suggest that stress is primarily seen as an individual or personal problem. Therefore, proactive stress management programmers focus on what people can do to manage their stressful work activities and events. The studies of stress acknowledge stress as a double-sided quality. It is both personal and social. It is caused or "given" by social relations. It is expressed as a highly subjective experience. It comes from "above" but experienced "from within". Therefore, there is an additional need for the individual management of preventive stress. Individuals can use different personal tools to reduce stress and tension in the workplace.

Despite the best organizational programmes for the work environment, individual differences call for supplementary individual skills. The greatest benefits as from the best methods that are appropriate for a specific person and her/his circumstances. Preventive stress management for individuals offers such skills through three sets of interventions that aim at countering the sources of stress (primary prevention), alter the responsibility to inevitable stress (secondary prevention), and help alleviate any suffering that may arise (tertiary prevention).

- Primary prevention is stressor directed and aims to help the individual manage personal perceptions of stress, elevate her/his personal work environment, and maintain work-life balance. While a number of techniques can help achieve the best results, two of the primary prevention tools are appropriate ratio of positivity and good social support. Fredrickson suggests that individuals flourish when their positive feelings outweigh their negative feelings. Social support is a valid primary prevention intervention for occupational stress.
- Secondary prevention is response directed and aims to help the individual regulate energy, emotions, and physical form induced by stress. Physical fitness programmes have become widely available to employees as a means to prevent distress. The relaxation response continues to be a stress antidote.
- Tertiary prevention is symptom directed and draws on treatment therapies and counselling interventions to restore health and functionality. While a number of psychological and medical treatment interventions can help individuals suffering from occupational stress, emphasizing emotional health in the workplace should be a priority for organizations and occupations.

Individuals today are on a quest for happiness, meaningfulness, and inner peace, yet many find this pursuit challenging due to stress at work and home. Occupational stress can detrimentally affect the body and mind of employees. An area of research germane to occupational stress is the burgeoning field of workplace health and well-being and positive psychology. Addressing organizational protection, prevention, and individual well-being raises the overall public health of the work environment. Therefore, we can see a move from stress prevention to enhancing well-being by introducing positive psychology to broaden the Preventive Stress Management framework.

Sauter, Murphy, and Hurrell began developing a prevention agenda by incorporating enhancement of well-being and positive psychology with the known theory of preventive stress management to address what some called a stress epidemic. The most serious stress malfunction always affects personal well-being. The term well-being is defined as "peoples' positive evaluations of their lives, (which) includes positive emotion, engagement, satisfaction, and meaning". Well-being is in fact a complex construct with two distinct approaches: the hedonic and the eudaimonic. The hedonic view, also called subjective well-being, focuses on happiness. This approach studies subjective well-being (how and why people experience life in a positive way). Researchers using the hedonic perspective seek to understand the conditions and processes for attaining pleasure and avoiding pain. The eudimonistic approach (i.e., psychological well-being), on the other hand, focuses on meaning and self-self-realization and conceptualizes well-being as a person's ability to function fully.

As psychological well-being this approach focuses on personal development, coping effort, and the desire to achieve relevant goals. The eudaimonic tradition integrates not only psychological aspects, but also takes into consideration the individual and social dimension. It is thus understood that the hedonic tradition, as an indicator of quality of life, is based on the characteristics of the environment and degree of satisfaction experienced by people. In contrast, the eudaimonic tradition is understood as an approach that focuses on the development of skills and personal growth as indicators of positive functioning. By promotion of well-being "we can make people healthier by making them happier". Happiness cannot cures illness but it serves as a protective factor against getting ill. Happy people make better life choices and are more prone to avoid distress.

Psychology as a scientific discipline has traditionally focused on studying constructs such as depression, anxiety, self-esteem, and others. However, in recent years there has been a considerable effort in psychology to deal with issues such as happiness, meaning in life and the strengths. Seligman has defined this field of psychology as positive psychology. This "positive psychology," movement has brought together many social and behavioural scientists, who have studied various aspects and benefits of human strengths. Positive psychology is defined as the scientific study of positive experiences, positive individual traits, institutions that facilitate their development and programmes that help improve the quality of life of people and prevent or reduce the incidence of psychopathology. It is called "the science of happiness". It studies how to develop positive emotions, life satisfaction, and identify interventions to promote mental health and quality of life. It focuses on issues related to well-being and happiness. This perspective of psychology should act to promote the well-being or health of individuals and communities, thus making it necessary to explore the variables that may contribute to well-being in the different areas in which they develop. Positive psychology shifts the narrative from the need to fix to a mind-set that is based on positive qualities that capture the entire spectrum of human experience. At the individual level, positive psychology examines positive traits such as courage, perseverance, spirituality, wisdom, and forgiveness; the group level highlights civic virtues, social support, tolerance, and other factors that attract people to engage in more responsible initiatives and acts of citizenship. Positive psychology includes the processes that lead to flourishing and optimal functioning as well as the study of positive emotions and character traits and their enabling factors, which can be useful for the prevention and management of stress. Some examples of PPIs are writing gratitude letters, thinking optimistically, reimagining positive experiences, and socializing.

The introduction of positivity to the literature on stress is not a new idea. Positive Psychology Interventions (PPIs) stem from research that focuses on teaching individuals how to increase positive thinking and behaviours through brief, self-administered exercises. Positive psychology interventions used in conjunction with the theory of preventive stress management is a promising way to enhance well-being of employees and reduce occupational stress. Positive Psychology Interventions (PPIs) can be administered at the primary, secondary, and tertiary levels of preventive stress management. Furthermore, these interventions can work at both the individual and organizational levels.

- At the primary prevention level, PPIs focused on building strong, supportive social networks can be instrumental in coping with stress. Social support is a valid primary prevention intervention for occupational stress. Cohen and Wills found that social support buffers stress, which contributes to greater well-being. Mentoring, building meaningful family relationships, and creating cohesive networks with colleagues are some of the interventions available to combat stressors in the workplace. At the organizational level, goal-setting interventions, including career path planning and heightened role clarity, help organizations reduce stress as primary intervention.

- Secondary prevention PPIs include life coaching and awareness training, as well as education and development programmes that reinforce the character strengths. Berg and Karlsen argue that coaching intervention plans, including positive visualization and self-talk, provide employees the means to cope with work pressures. The organizational policies that promote team building and a strong relationship between supervisor and employee have also been shown to protect employees from the negative effects of stress.
- At the tertiary prevention level, interventions are designed to heal. PPIs here may include therapy, medical assistance, and meditation. For organizations, PPIs include development interventions and wellness programmes as a means of remedying the negative consequences of stress and tension.

Increasing well-being through the use of PPI positively influences the mental and physical health outcomes of employees. These interventions are relatively inexpensive options to combat stress occupational stress. These measures provide individuals with the personal resources they need to become productive and healthy employees.

Conclusion

Stress is inevitable in the work environment. Occupational stress can have far-reaching consequences. The ability to manage stress in the workplace cannot only improve physical and emotional health, but it can also make the difference between success and failure in the workplace. The better the management of our own stress, the more positively we will affect those around us and the less stress of other people will have negative consequences on us. Learning how to deal with and manage stress is essential for optimizing our work performance, staying safe in the workplace and maintaining our physical and mental health. Occupational stress is an inevitable element, even if sometimes necessary, of the working environment, but it must not result in organizational dysfunctions or medical, psychological or behavioural discomfort. While many of the methods of preventing job stress need to be developed and supported by the organization, there are things that workers can do to help manage work-related stress better. In this regard positive psychological skills for occupational stress can have positive effects on well-being of employees.

References

Adkins, J.A. (1999). "Promoting organizational health: The evolving practice of occupational health psychology", *Prof. Psychol. Res. Pract.*, *30*:129-137.

Avey, J.B.; Luthans, F.; Jensen, S.M. (2009). "Psychological capital: A positive resource for combating employee stress and turnover", *Hum. Resour. Manag.*, 48:677-693. [CrossRef]

Bharathi; T. Gupta, K.S. (2009). "Job stress and productivity: A conceptual framework", *International Journal of Emerging Research in Management & Technology", 6*(8):393-399.

Cockburn, A. (1996). "Primary teachers' knowledge and acquisition of stress relieving strategies", *British Journal of Educational Psychology*, 63:399-410.

Colligan, Thomas W.; Colligan MSW and Higgins M. (2006). "Workplace stress: Etiology and consequences", *Journal of Workplace Behavioural Health, 21*(2): 89-97.

Cooper, C.L. and Marshall, J. (1978). *Understanding Executive Stress,* London: Macmillan.

Cooper, C.L. (1998). *Theories of Organizational Stress*, Oxford University Press: Oxford, UK.

Diener, E. and Seligman, M.E.P. (2004). "Beyond money: Toward an economy of well-being", *Psychol. Sci. Public Interest*, 5:1-31. [CrossRef]

Elkin, A.J. and Rosch, P.J. (1990). "Promoting mental health at the workplace: The prevention side of stress management", *Occup Med State Art Rev.*, *5*(4):739-754.

Fredrickson, B. (2009). *Positivity: Groundbreaking Research Reveals How to Embrace the Hidden Strength of Positive Emotions, Overcome Negativity and Thrive*, Crown Publishers: New York, NY, USA.

Lazarus, R.S. (1966). *Psychological stress and the coping process*. New York, Toronto, London: McGraw-Hill Book Co.

Lazarus, R.S. (1971). "The concepts of stress and disease", In L. Levi (ed.) *Society, Stress and Disease*, Vol. 1, London: OUP.

Luthans, F. (1995). *Organizational Behaviour,* N.Y., McGraw Hill.

Manduku, J.; Koech Z.; Chepkirui, P. (2016). "Stress management strategies and their effects on teachers' commitment in primary Schools in Sabatia district", Vihiga County, Kenya, *Education Research Journal, 6*(1): 1-12.

McGrath, J.E. (1976). "Stress and behaviour in organizations", In M.D. Dunnette. (Ed.) *Handbook of Industrial and Organizational Psychology*, Palto. C.A.

Papathanasiou, I.V.; Tsaras, K.; Neroliatsiou, A. and Roupa, A. (2015). "Stress: Concepts, theoretical models and nursing interventions", *American Journal of Nursing Science*, *4*(2-1): 45-50.

Quick, J.C.; Quick, J.D.; Nelson, D.L. and Hurrell, J.J. (1997). *Preventive Stress Management in Organizations*, Washington, DC.: American Psychological Association.

Quick, J.C.; Murphy, L.R. and Hurrell, J.J., Jr. (Eds.). (1992). *Stress and Well-Being at Work: Assessments and Interventions for Occupational Mental Health*, Washington, DC: American Psychological Association.

Quick, J.C. and Cooper, C.L. (2003). *Stress and Strain*, 2nd ed.; Health Press: Oxford, UK, p. 75.

Rajpreet Kaur and Kiranjit Kaur (2018). "Coping with job stress: A conceptual evaluation framework for coping measures of stress", *International Journal of Research in Humanities, Arts and Literature, 6*(2): 1-14.

Sauter, S.L.; Murphy, L.R. and Hurrell, J.J. (1990). "Prevention of work-related psychological disorders: A national strategy proposed by the National Institute for Occupational Safety and Health (NIOSH)", *Am. Psychol.*, 45:1146-1158.

Sauter, S.; Murphy, L.R. and Hurrell, J.J. Jr. (1990). "A national strategy for the prevention of work related psychological disorders", *Am Psychologist*, 45:1146-1158.

Seligman, M.E.P. and Pawelski, J.O. (2003). "Positive Psychology: FAQs", *Psychol. Inq.*, 14:159-55.

Selye, Hans. (1974). *Stress without Distress*. Philadelphia, PA: J.B. Lippincott Company, p. 171

Schwarzer, R. (2009). *Stress and coping resources: Theory and review*. Berlin, Freie University. Retrieved from http://web.fu-berlin.de/gesund/publicat/ehps_cd/health/stress.htm

Singh Narban J.I.; Singh Narban, B.P. and Singh, J.A. (2016). *Conceptual Study on Occupational Stress (Job Stress/Work Stress) and its Impacts, Vol.2 Issue-1, IJARIIE-ISSN (O)-2395-4396.*

Sutherland, V.J. and Cooper, C.L. (2000). *Strategic Stress Management,* London.

W. Colligan, T. and M. Higgins (2010). *Workplace Stress: Etiology and Consequences*. PER1 Pakistan.

Zaheer, A.; Islam, J.U. and Darakhshan, N. (2016). "Occupational stress and work life balance: A study of female faculties of central universities in Delhi", *India Journal of Human Resource Management*, *4*(1): 1-5.

21
Religion as a Resilience Tool to Manage Stress among Teenagers
An Islamic Approach

Afa Dul Mujiaba

Generally, stress is a common factor that influences every human being throughout their life time. The way people handle it depends on the stress retention level and the way they manage the stress. Hence, to experience and having stress is considered normal to every human. However in some cases stress become too pressurizing, uncontrollable and damaging. To deal with stress and its adverse effects, there are various proven ways practiced by professionals involved in stress treatment as such; meditation, sleep, exercise, socialization, biofeedback, psychotherapy tranquilizers etc. However in certain condition it does work on some people and not to the other. And the process cycle is repeated again until the patient feel better or otherwise the counsellor will suggest a different technique and strategy. In general, most people will turn back to their own religion for the final option in finding answer or solution to their miserable or constrained life. Knowing that there is a superpower 'God' that can help human being in all occasions and repent after wrongdoers make a relief to human and as a source of great comfort to all human beings. It is universally understood that there is a power of God above human power by all religions in this world. This has been mentioned by Hill & Butter (1995) and Pargament (1997) that religious beliefs can affect the degree of stress people experience and the ability to cope with that stress. While Cashwell and Young (2011) are of the opinion that both religious values and beliefs can positively affect a person's general wellness and can serve as a key role in providing support as individual face existential crises. According to Peres, Moreira-Almeida, Nasello, & Koenig (2007) religion can provide answers to the wisdom behind the difficult situations and past tragic events, which can alleviate stress symptoms. Kneier, Rosenbaum, & Rosenbaum (2006) also stated that people with spiritual beliefs can benefit from their faiths and prayers in different ways; such as having a strong sense of peace, exercising their inner strengths and capabilities to cope with challenges, and improving their psychological status and quality of life.

Islamic Approach and Youth

Islam pays a special attention to stress and its effects on one's life. Also, it mentions that adolescents are an important factor in building healthy societies. Practically, Islam employs the power of the three principles; Mind, Consciousness, and Thoughts, through encouraging people to empower their inner strengths to have a comfortable life, not wait for external circumstances to change. Islam recognizes spiritual forces as an influential tool that can impact both mental and physical wellness; Muslims usually use and value their belief as a remedy for the psychological problems by changing their insides (Laher and Khan, 2011). The Islamic approach to face life's adversities include different strategies to alleviate the burden of life, which may push some people, especially youths, to hurt themselves so much so they commit suicide. Sedgeman (2005) stated people who understand the foundation of their thoughts' nature and healthy state of mind can enjoy the privileges of inner wisdom, calmness, and wellness. Therefore, by following the Islamic employment of the Principles, youth would be able to achieve innate health.

The first technique is to improve people's perception of life's events through having a clear consciousness, which in turn leads to positive thoughts that result in positive attitudes. Islam states that whatever happens to a Muslim carries good ultimate outcome, prophet Muhammad peace be upon him (PBUH) says: "How wonderful the statuses of a believer are, for there is a good in every affair of his, and this is not the case with anyone else except in the case of a believer for if he has an occasion to feel delight, he thanks (God), thus there is a good for him in it, and if he gets into trouble and shows resignation (and endures it patiently), there is a good for him in it" (Bin al-Hajjaj, & Siddiqi, 1981, 1779). This assurance can help adolescents to receive all events with a quiet mind and healthy consciousness. As a result, they would be able to build a constructive experience that can help them fill their thinking with optimistic feelings, regardless of the external incidents. Moreover, the *Quran* instructs Muslims to not grieve devastatingly over unpleasant events that are because everything that happens has already been predestined before the creation of the universe. Allah says: "No disaster strikes upon the earth or among yourselves except that it is in a register before We bring it into being-indeed that, for Allah, is easy — In order that you not despair over what has eluded you and not exult [in pride] over what He has given you. And Allah does not like everyone self-deluded and boastful "(*Saheeh International*, 1997, 553). As Banks (1998) mentioned, that satisfaction and gratitude can have positive impacts on the souls and minds and can assist people to be contented and wise. Second, be optimistic, do and say good things to people: "Do not worship except Allah; and to parents do good and to relatives, orphans, and the needy. And speak to people good words and establish prayer and give charity" (*Sahih International*, 1997). This will encourage adolescents to feed themselves with good the three Principles, where he encourages people to have a quiet Mind, positive Consciousness, and healthy Thoughts. For instance, he promotes Muslims to say only the good things and do not criticize, and if someone were obligated to comment on something not good, he/she should use the gentlest terms (Areefi, 2008). Also, he calls people to avert from trouble: "Do not torture yourself and do not gather dust upon you", and if there is a speech of hatred or vulgar language do not accompany those people (Areefi, 2008). I believe this approach can purify adolescents' insides and clean their feelings by discarding those illusionary negative thoughts, which turns any potential distressing experience into a positive one. Moreover, he instructs to not commit suicide because Allah is very merciful, and he is only testing them in this life, so enjoy your days with what you have available, and you will always be happy (Areefi, 2008). Allah says in *Quran* "do not kill yourselves or one another; Indeed, Allah is to you ever Merciful" (*Saheeh International*, 1997). Another important advice was that a Muslim should appreciate the valuable things in his/her life before he thinks how disadvantageous he/she is, surely that could make him/her pleased (Areefi, 2008). These concepts have been mentioned by Sedgeman (2005), where she stated that people who live their daily lives in a quiet state of mind despite their current external circumstances, past adversities, or being worried about the future can have a pleasing life and better health. He also promotes people to respond positively and with a smile to everyone, Muhammad (PBUH) says your smile and good word are a charity. Moreover, do not get preoccupied with what people say and should not burden yourself with what you are not able to do. Forgiveness and emotional balance are crucial attributes that can guarantee both internal and external peace (Areefi, 2008). These last mentioned characteristics were also stated by Banks as an important asset for tranquillity, he said that "Love and understanding harmonize the mind of humanity to its true inner nature" (Banks, 1998). Fifth, Dr. Ayaid Al-Qarni wrote another book "Do not be Sad" where he collected so many Quranic and prophethood recommendations that aim to make people not get sad or frustrated. The core issue of most of these advices is Health Realization, which arises from a real understanding of human psychological functioning and provides a model for practical applications of this concept. He advocates people to be thankful, forget the past, do not bother yourself with the future, keep busy with a fruitful work, live your life as it is, learn how to stay happy, and avoid anxious thoughts (Al-Qarni, 2005). These advices have been mentioned by Kelly (2004) where he stated that the best technique for young people to resolve "specific adaptive problems" is to avoid painful thoughts and gain the wisdom and healthy thinking. Also, Al-Qarni (2005) endorses Muslims to not give up on the mercy of Allah, inputs through the words and actions that would help others, and can in turn lead to healthy feelings, which can evolve a serene state of mind and fruitful thoughts. Also, Muhammad (PBUH) says; "There is no divination but the best type is the good omen. It was said to Allah's Messenger: What is good omen? Thereupon he said: "A good word which one of you hears" (Bin al-Hajjaj, & Siddiqi, 1981). This concept of getting used to saying good and optimistic words is also promoted by Taylor *et al.* (2000) and Banks (1998), who discussed the positive impacts of optimism and hopefulness on psychological well-being in general and after traumatic incidents. Therefore, the adolescents could use this principle to help themselves and each other to overcome stressful events in their lives. Third, do not feel failure. Islam promotes those people who start a journey to have a clear mind that can connect them with the ultimate power, Allah, that leads to release their inner strengths. Muhammad (PBUH) says: "the strong believer is better and more beloved to Allah than a weak believer, although there is good in both. Strive to attain that, which benefits you, seek help from Allah and do not lose heart. And if anything befalls you, do not say: 'If only I had done this and that, such and such would have happened.' Instead say, 'It is the decree of Allah and He does whatever He wills'; for (the\ word) 'if' surely opens the door for Satan's work" (Bin al-Hajjaj, & Siddiqi, 1981). These encouraging words help youths, who usually need to choose certain things over others or work to achieve their dreams, to have a quiet mind, get rid of any potential ill thoughts, and therefore can access their inner wisdom. As a result, youth may not get frustrated, and do not regret any choice they take. All of these assurances can bring peace, comfort, quietness, and release the inner strengths that can help adolescents enjoy, rather endure, their lives. Healthy feelings can develop good ways of thinking by eliminating deceptive thoughts, which can result in productive feelings and a peaceful mind (Sedgeman, 2005). Fourth, Dr. Muhammad Areefi, one of the most famous scholar in the Muslim world, wrote a book under the title of "Enjoy Your Life" in about 600 hundred pages where he used the Quranic versus and the prophets' statements that encourage people to live a better life. In this Chapter, Author will summarize some of those conclusions. I think the main foundation of these recommendations is who can turn any bitter situation into a good one, and not be frightened by difficult events. People should not let disasters shook them, have a permanent hope, have true faith in God Who will help them be a better person, and pay attention to their inside (Al-Qarni, 2005). These recommendations can have positive impact on youths to develop healthy feelings and improve the quality of their thinking through having a serene mind, which can create healthy experience from inside to handle the external circumstances. Al-Qarni (2005) insists on that Allah Who took care of people in the past, and he will do the same in the future, do not complain too much, and have security of souls and calm mentality. When those inner sources, secured soul and quiet mind, are determined and released, they can alter the worldview of those young people, then can pursue their lives in a healthy perspective. Furthermore, as advices fit the best to youths, having positive attitude is the cornerstone of living well, do not get angry, and do not hate people, and keep praying and look for refuge with Allah that will give you— tranquility and peace. In *Quran* Allah says "Allah sent down His calmness, tranquility, and peace, upon His Messenger and upon the believers" (*Saheeh*

International, 1997). This approach has been adopted by Sedgeman (2005) who stated that when people recognize and access their own innate power sources can develop a calm mind by using healthy feelings to evolve positive thinking and be able to manage all difficulties. Al-Qarni (2005) says "Happiness is a divine gift that does not distinguish between the rich and the poor." These words are very similar in meaning to Banks' statement (1989) "Thought is a divine gift, which serves you immediately after you are born."

Summing Up

Trust and faith towards religion indeed play a vital role in contributing most meaningful life to all people. Religious values and beliefs provide deep sense of purpose and meaning in life. Where both values and beliefs offer hopes and solutions during the period of adversity and suffering simultaneously provides solution perspectives whenever people are overwhelmed by their life's problem. It is undeniably an accomplishment to all sorts of problems and pressure faced by human being. It creates a sense of belonging among the believer, caring and strengthening the brotherhood relationship among each other. Definitely Muslims believe that religion is a fundamental source in resolving conflict, in development and unity of the *ummah* as a whole. Undeniably, current practices demonstrate that there are various effective approaches in handling stress situation particularly on financial and workplace stress within the modern counselling process. It includes numerous therapy models practiced in resulting successful therapeutic outcomes. However, Muslim therapeutic model which give emphasis to religiosity approaches based on Islamic principles purely adopt the holy *Quran* and the Sunnah as main guidance. In fact, by exploring the *Quran*, the *Seerah (historical)* of the Prophet and his traditions, as well as the biographies of the Prophet's companions, will provide detailed instructions and teachings on implementing Islamic counselling process in the daily life. In essence, stress affects everyone and must be managed effectively to reduce its chronic and deleterious effects to the whole life system. A preponderance of research data indicates that stress management offers diverse interventions that promote healthy lifestyle changes. Ultimately, successful stress management involves willingness to change one's appraisal systems and mobilize resources and inner strengths that promote health and a sense of holistic well-being.

The Quranic verses and Hadith provides evidences on how to manage stress based on Islamic principles. The hasty and restless nature of human being could be cope with the recitation of Quranic verses, prayer, patient, helping and supporting each other, and practice *Dhikr* (remembrance Allah), without doubt would able to give solution in managing stress. This will certainly be a great support in establishing a person who practice 'a just balance' throughout the life and avoid 'extravagant/extreme' since those two habitudes are the causes to the stressful and pressurize life. In these circumstances, Islam is compatible with the nature of human beings. Therefore, every command and prohibition of God is for the good and happiness of human life in this world and hereafter. For the survival of goodness in self, family, society and country thus the culture of advice, enjoin to goodness and forbid evil must be inculcated and implemented. Even though Muslim has to encounter stress as part of tribulation in life hence by being patient means willing with the certainty prearranged by Allah and with prayer human being always seeking the protection and guidance from Allah in whatever difficulties and situation. In all consciences, the total submission should only be to God Allah s.w.t. For that reason, most importantly, a Muslim must have trust in Allah s.w.t. and regards all trials come from Allah s.w.t. in order to get rewarded in the world hereafter. It is clearly stated in *Surah At-Taghabun*, Verse (11)-means "No disaster strikes except by permission of Allah. And whoever believes in Allah; He will guide his heart. And Allah is knowing of all things".

References

Abdulraouf Y. Lamoshi (2015). "Religion as a resilience tool to manage stress in adolescents: Islamic approach", *Golbal Journal of human-social science: H Interdisciplinary*, (3):5-7.

Al-Qarni, A. (2005). *Don't be sad.* International Islamic Publishing House: Riyadh, Saudi Arabia: (2nd ed., Vol. 1, 28-466).

Areefi, M. (2008). *Enjoy Your Life*. Riyadh, Saudi Arabia: Darussalam. (1st ed., 50-570).

Banks, S. (1998). *The Missing Link: Reflections on Philosophy and Spirit.* Manitoba, Canada: International Human Relations Consultants Inc. (1st ed., 117-131).

Bin al-Hajjaj, M.A., and Siddiqi, A.H. (1981). *Sahih Muslim.* (1st ed.). Ashraf. Cuyahoga Falls, OH US.

Csikszentmihalyi, M. (1999). "If we are so rich, why aren't we happy?", *American Psychologist*, 54:821-827.

Kelley, T.M. (2004). "Positive psychology and adolescent mental health: false promise or true breakthrough?", *Adolescence*, *39*(154):257-278.

Kneier, A.; Rosenbaum, E. and Rosenbaum, I. (2006). *Coping with cancer: 10 steps towards emotional well-being.* Retrieved from http://www.cancerlynx.com/10steps.html

Laher, S. and Khan, S. (2011). Exploring the Influence of Islam on the Perceptions of Mental Illness of Volunteers in a Johannesburg Community-based Organisation. *Psychology and Developing Societies*, *23*(1):63-84.

Osteen, J. and Osteen, V. (2008). *God's Promises for a New beginning.* (p. 12). Houston, TX, USA.

Peres, J.F.; Moreira-Almeida, A.; Nasello, A.G. and Koenig, H.G. (2007). "Spirituality and resilience in trauma victims", *Journal of Religion and Health*, *46*(3):343-350.

Saheeh International (1997). *The Qur'an: Arabic Text with Corresponding English Meanings*, Riyadh: Abulqasim Publishing House.

Sedgeman, J.A. (2005). "Health Realization/Innate Health: Can a quiet mind and a positive feeling state be accessible over the lifespan without stress-relief techniques?", *Medical Science Monitor: International Medical Journal of Experimental and Clinical Research*, *11*(12), HY47.

Van Dyke, C.J.; Glenwick, D.S.; Cecero, J.J. and Kim, S.K. (2009). "The relationship of religious coping and spirituality to adjustment and psychological distress in urban early adolescents", *Mental Health, Religion and Culture*, *12*(4):369-383.

Zarrett, N. and Eccles, J. (2006). "The passage to adulthood: Challenges of late adolescence", *New Directions for Youth Development*, Vol. (III): 13-28.

Index